THE WAY AHEAD

Note from Oxfam America

The publishers of *The Way Ahead* will donate the royalties from this book to Oxfam America, Inc. The monies will be utilized internationally for development programs. However, Oxfam America Inc. has not endorsed or sponsored this publication in any manner, and is not responsible for the contents thereof. The positions set forth in this publication should not be deemed to be those of Oxfam America Inc. or to reflect any of its policies or practices.

THE WAY AHEAD

A Visionary Perspective
for the
New Millennium

Foreword by Richard Gere

EDITED BY
EDDIE AND DEBBIE SHAPIRO

E L E M E N T
Shaftesbury, Dorset ● Rockport, Massachusetts
Brisbane, Queensland

© Eddie and Debbie Shapiro 1992

Published in Great Britain in 1992 by
Element Books Limited
Longmead, Shaftesbury, Dorset

Published in the USA in 1992 by
Element, Inc
42 Broadway, Rockport, MA 01966

Published in Australia by
Element Books Ltd for
Jacaranda Wiley Ltd
33 Park Road, Milton, Brisbane, 4064

Cover design by Max Fairbrother
Designed by Roger Lightfoot
Typeset by Falcon Typographic Art Ltd, Fife, Scotland
Printed and bound in the USA by Edwards Bros, Inc.

British Library Cataloguing in Publication
data available

Library of Congress Cataloging in Publication
data available

ISBN 1–85230–317–4

Contents

PART TWO: *Self, Family, and Society*

PART THREE: *Dimensions of Healing*

Acknowledgements

There are many exceptional people who were involved in the making of this book. Our most special thanks go to Susan Mears, our editor at Element Books, for starting the ball rolling and for her vision and commitment – at all hours of the day and night! A deep thank you to John Hammock at Oxfam America for sharing the vision. Thanks also to Michael Mann, David Alexander, Del Riddle, Fiona McIntosh, Jenny Carradice, Alun Williams, Maureen Kimbrey, Valerie Finlay, and all those people at Element Books who worked so hard on this project. Also Debra Richman at National Book Network.

Our sincere gratitude to Dane at Yoko Ono's, Jeff Baker at Paul and Linda McCartney's, Howard Cohen at Mickey Hart's, Mona Friedman at Richard Gere's, Karen Fertita and Diane at John Bradshaw's, Ellie Deegan at Helen Caldicott's, Robert Thurman, Lex Hixon, Paul at the 'Brain-Mind Bulletin', Shardananda at Yogaville, Alex at The Bear Tribe, Arnold Kotler at Parallex Press, Bill and Barbara Howell at Father Thomas Keating's, Bob Rosenthall at Allen Ginsberg's, Kathy Flynn for Jeremy Rifkin, and Martin Palmer for HRH Prince Philip.

Our kind thanks to Elaine Brooks, Kathy Adams and Tim Lobstein, Anne and Richard Bancroft, Ed and Ann Byrne, Ken Wilber, Sheila Hixon, Mary and Andy Dinsmoor, Nancy Larson, Ruth and Ken Leiner, Mort Shapiro, Rhoda and Howard Weber, Rama Vernon and Max Lefser, Liz and Dennis Southwood, Julie and Dee, Nancy Stetson, Barbara and Bob Ankers, Mary and Ian Wilson, Swamis Nishchalananda and Sivadhara, Jonathan and Karen Goldman, Carol Kramer, Jack and Norma Groverland, Marcus and Marion Hampton, David Yoder, Deanna DiBella, Alex and Virginia, Norm Hirsch, Peter Goldfarb, Vickie Dodd and Eric Neurath, Demaris and Jym MacRitchie, Johanna Alpert, Beth Sosnick, Otto and Mickey Lobstein, Sumi Komo, Colin Egan, Michele Wand, Nancy and Gregory Ford Kohne, Doreen and David Osborne, Joni and Theo, George Nieto, Fiona Frederichs,

Linda and J. P. Scratz, Richie Shapiro, Sandy Cole, Bruno Bossio, Scott and Nancy, Steve and Stacey Glazer, and the late Stephen Homsey.

Foreword

RICHARD GERE

Richard Gere, actor who has starred in *Final Analysis, Pretty Woman,* and *An Officer and a Gentleman* among others. Founding Chairman of Tibet House, New York, dedicated to the preservation of Tibet's cultural and religious heritage. An International human rights activist, he has twice testified before the Congressional Human Rights Caucus concerning El Salvador and Tibet. Writer of the foreword for *Ocean of Wisdom* by HH The Dalai Lama.

As we enter the precarious new century and millenium we, as custodians of this planet, find ourselves at the unpleasant end of a botched experiment. True happiness still eludes us and now our very survival depends on our ability and determination to utterly change our ways – politically, economically, spiritually.

Through ignorance, greed and hatred we have tortured the earth and each other, leaving us desolate and unhappy. The seductive promise of industry and competition have led to the obsessive exploitation of the physical universe and our fellow beings, only serving to further numb our hearts and isolate us one from another. Our garden home Earth has been fouled and its bounty squandered by our short-sighted selfishness. But while the gods gave us the freedom to make horrendous mistakes they also gave us the capacity to amend them. In our truest selves we are, after all, beings of Silence and Light.

The breakdown of the established social and political order over the last few years presents, ironically, an extraordinary opportunity to actualize the radical changes we all know must take place. If the cycles of conditioned violence and counter-violence can be avoided (or transformed) we may be entering a Golden Age of responsibility and love for all beings. We may re-enter the Garden of Peace and Bliss.

Herein lies writ a call to action by some of our most prominent and compassionate voices – from an astonishing poem by Yoko Ono to a moving plea for universal responsibility from His Holiness the Dalai Lama. From Václav Havel to Allen Ginsberg to Thich Nhat Hanh, taken all in all they constitute a vision of how we might proceed into our adulthood as a race – through love and wisdom.

Introduction

What is the way ahead? Each of us must ask ourselves this question and discover what it means in our lives. For each one of us *is* the way ahead. Let us see through the superficial differences that bind us, for we are caretakers not only of ourselves, but also of each other, and of this extraordinary world around us. Someone once asked us, 'Have you ever experienced other dimensions?' We replied, 'Have you ever experienced this one?' For surely we need to fully enter into this beautiful place and make it our sanctuary? We can do it, and the joy it will bring is insurmountable. Let us not give in to the ignorance and prejudice that breeds pain and suffering but see through the darkness to the light within us all.

Those who have contributed to this book are only a few, but each of us has a role to play – not just one but every single one. As His Holiness the Dalai Lama said to us, 'We are all equal.' No one is unimportant or insignificant, no head is higher than another. Through our thoughts, attitudes and actions, by having an open heart and a generous mind – in this way we can make changes. We can move into the new millennium as true human beings and world citizens, so that the walls of separation come down and we see unity in the diversity! For are we not all part of the same creation?

The Way Ahead is a collection of writings from some of the world's most inspired thinkers and activists, all contributing to the vision of a more compassionate humanity. As you read what each contributor has written you may see how their words convey this simple message. The book is arranged according to subject, yet each piece is universal in nature. Part One gives us a visionary overview – a look at the whole which is made up of so many diverse pieces. In Part Two this vision is applied more directly to ourselves and the changes we need to make which will radiate out from ourselves to our family and thus to society. Though we may think globally, we need to act locally!

Part Three explores different aspects of the healing journey, from the essence of healing itself – love – to the application of this in our daily lives. Part Four looks at the world around us – politically, environmentally, and in business – and at how we can work with these areas both within ourselves and actively in the world. Part Five brings us to the spiritual journey, an integral part of the change that is needed in order for the way ahead to become a living reality.

With each contributor who became a part of this book so the project grew. It became a coming together of many people with the one purpose of serving all in the quest for happiness, wholeness, and deeper understanding, both personally and globally. Oxfam America was chosen as the recipient of the author royalties to help them continue the valuable work they are doing in fostering education, self-help, and relief in many of the countries most in need.

May this book be a simple offering to benefit all beings; may it be a contribution towards world peace and a one-world family.

Eddie and Debbie Shapiro

About Oxfam America

JOHN HAMMOCK

John Hammock PhD, Executive Director of Oxfam America. Has had first-hand experience of many of the world's disasters, served as Visiting Professor at the University of Costa Rica and Universidad del Valle, Columbia. He has written extensively on international relations and developmental issues. He says: 'Hopefully, in the next millennium, we'll get it right if we can realize that it is necessary to deal with the issue of poverty, because all societies – both rich and poor – are unstable and insupportable without resolving this issue.'

Oxfam America is a non-profit, international agency that funds self-help development and disaster-relief projects in poor countries in Africa, Asia, Latin America, and the Caribbean. It also produces and distributes educational materials for people in the United States on issues of hunger and development.

Overseas, our grants support local groups working to increase their food production or economic self-reliance. In the United States, we conduct educational campaigns and speak out about public policies that affect our grassroots development work abroad.

The name 'Oxfam' comes from the Oxford Committee for Famine Relief, founded in England in 1942. Oxfam, now in its fiftieth year, has earned a global reputation for innovative yet realistic aid to some of the poorest people in the world.

Oxfam America, with US offices in Boston and San Francisco, was established in 1970, and is one of seven autonomous Oxfams around the world (in the United Kingdom-Ireland, Canada, Quebec, Australia, Belgium, Hong Kong, and the United States).

In our work overseas, we are likewise committed to a grass-roots approach. Oxfam America looks for small-scale projects where a few dollars go a long way – projects that set an example or create changes reaching beyond the project itself. Our funds go directly to project partners overseas; we work with them to assess local needs, develop programs, and monitor the results.

Although we concentrate on funding self-help projects in developing countries such as Bolivia, Mozambique, and the Philippines, we also provide aid when disaster strikes – during the floods in Bangladesh, for example. Oxfam America is a nonprofit, nonsectarian organization. Unlike many international aid agencies, Oxfam America neither seeks nor accepts US government funds.

All the good intentions and careful planning of Oxfam America mean nothing unless they lead to real improvement in the lives of poor people.

People like Asiya, a Bangladeshi woman, who has persevered despite long odds, teach us the value of development aid.

When the flood waters came in September 1988 Asiya had no choice but to leave her home. Flood waters poured over the foundation of her house in Aladipur in southern Bangladesh, and washed it and her family's few belongings away. They had to flee for shelter, having lost all but their lives.

Now Asiya tells her family's story with pride, without a trace of fear or anguish. She tells it sitting on the steps of a new house she has built, with the support of her women neighbours and a community development organization called Uttaran ('upliftment').

After the floods, Asiya and her family took shelter in a neighboring house that survived the disaster. After discussions within the local women's organization, which Uttaran staff helped to organize, the group decided that she and four other women would get priority for new housing, designed by Uttaran and funded with a grant from Oxfam America. The simple design – costing less than $200 per unit – is intended to be 'disaster-proof': concrete pillars at the corners, a raised foundation higher than even abnormal flood levels, and a tile roof secure enough to withstand the high winds associated with coastal cyclones. Uttaran staff assisted the women in obtaining the building materials, and the five women, with assistance from their families, built each other's houses. The process took more than a year, but resulted in five new houses and an evident sense of pride and accomplishment.

The housing component is but one aspect of Oxfam America's support of Uttaran. Their program also includes small-scale community loan programs – entirely managed by women – for projects such as goat-rearing and vegetable production. Oxfam currently supports the development of community fish ponds and a duck-raising project, in addition to an expansion of the housing program.

But Uttaran believes in more than just community-based economic projects. They help build self-esteem and a sense of pride and power among poor women in Aladipur and other small villages in southern Bangladesh. Woman after woman interviewed individually and in group meetings attested to the dignity they have achieved through Uttaran's organizing process. The names of the village women's groups speak for themselves! First Step, Commitment, Extraordinary, Demand for Freedom, Build up the World, Towards the Light, Advance! Clearly Uttaran staff have initiated a process which defines what Oxfam America intends by the word 'empowerment', a process that has poor women defining and creating their own path towards dignity and economic progress.

People like Asiya (and organizations like Uttaran) have shown, time and again, the power of the human spirit. So often it takes what seems to be so little – a few building materials, a training course, a reliable well – to make a huge difference in people's lives. Oxfam America's program is based on that simple truth.

Other project partners of ours are working, for example, in:

Guatemala, assisting landless urban families as they organize for housing;

Cambodia, establishing fish hatcheries and irrigating rice fields;

Sudan, providing boats, nets and transport to market for war-displaced fisherfolk and their families;

Dominica, diversifying agriculture and supporting the development of local markets;

Namibia, mounting a nationwide literacy campaign;

Ecuador, developing indigenous women leaders;

El Salvador, strengthening a rural health and nutrition program;

Ethiopia, introducing an improved plow that doubles crop yields;

Vietnam, supplying basic equipment to village-level health clinics;

Mozambique, improving the water supply for the war-displaced;

India, assisting women artisans in marketing their work.

PART ONE

A Visionary Overview

Pat A. Paulson

PURPOSE STATEMENT

Pat A. Paulson, teacher and Life Purpose Consultant. Co-author of *Living on Purpose*, *A Matter of Choice*, and *Little Bits*. She says: 'Knowing that individual actions and activity affect the collective, this book is a statement of profound possibility that avails itself through personal commitment.'

With each glimpse of a
personal journey,
a quest,
a calling,
a vision,
following destiny
or a purpose,
comes the question:
what is The Way Ahead?

This book is a personal invitation
to reflect upon this question
and to acknowledge the responsibility
that participation in living demands.

The wisdom contained within this book
is intended to give meaning
to the journey of a lifetime,
to validate the quest,
to give credibility to the calling,
to maintain the vision,
to encourage destiny
and to engage purpose.

With vibrant implication,
The Way Ahead
gives voice to the promise of yesterday,
it gives credence to the depth of today,
and it gives dimension to the design of tomorrow.

Knowing that individual
actions and activity
affect the collective,
this book is a statement
of profound possibility
that avails itself
through personal commitment.

Accepting that the future is born
of the substance of today
and thrives upon the energy of yesterday,
this book lives to reignite,
with vivid recollection,
the passion of Spiritual Values
that live within.

The purpose of this book
is to honor the community of people
who dare to stretch themselves
beyond their known capacity,
who follow their silent wisdom,
and to those who are secretly discovering
the Self
that yearns to make a difference.

Jean Houston

I SEE A CHANGE

Jean Houston PhD, psychologist, scientist, philosopher, and teacher, Director of The Foundation for Mind Research in New York. Author of, among others, *Mind Games, Life Force, The Possible Human, The Search for the Beloved, Godseed*, and *A Feminine Myth of Creation*. She says: 'The change comes slowly. A sleeping giant, it wakes in the hearts and minds of millions . . . The idea of freedom is expanding because the idea of what it is to be a human being is expanding . . . I see a change and you are part of it.'

I see a change. It is vested in the greatest rise in expectations the world has ever seen. It is so far-reaching in its implications that one might call it evolution consciously entering into time, the evolutionary potential asserting itself. It needed a certain critical mass, a certain merging of complexity, crisis, and consciousness to awaken. Now it is happening.

The change comes slowly. A sleeping giant, it wakes in the hearts and minds of millions. Four hundred thousand years of being humans-in-search-of-subsistence, ten thousand years of being humans-in-search-of-meaning, and two centuries of modern economic and social revolution have prepared the way for the deepest quickening in human and cultural evolution. The events of recent centuries were the social and political churnings of the change. They were the manifestations of the deep seismic seizures happening and rehappening in the depths of ourselves. And what is happening constellates around the ideas of human freedom and human possibilities. The idea of freedom is expanding because the idea of what it is to be a human being is expanding.

The traditional views of freedom and the possible human have served as moral beacons, drawing forth the highest aspirations and noblest actions of those who sighted them. The uncompromising light brought oppression into high relief and sparked the courage needed to confront the squalor of social evils. But now the beacons must be tuned to even greater brilliance. The old gleamings are no longer adequate to the time, and to follow them is to fall among the shadows that confound, leading us to shores both dangerous and archaic. Perhaps this is why so much of current social and political thought is lacking in confidence and why so many governmental and organizational decisions are ridden with perilous banality. Short-term solutions to complex problems blight both landscape and inscape with a crazy-quilt patch-work of Band-Aids. Each of our so-called 'successes' generates ten new problems and becomes, in the collapsed space/time of the global village, a world-eroding failure. Our national and international policies are mostly the results of sophisticated cause–effect, stimulus–response patterns appropriate to much simpler societies, which themselves were grounded in the cultural trance of tribe or village. The society-wide slavery seen in Orwell's *1984* or Huxley's *Brave New World* are but the logical projections of what could happen to complex societies that insist on maintaining atavistic psychologies. These atavisms persist because of the lack of a thrilling and appropriate notion of freedom, one that joins the new vistas of the nature of human possibilities to the consideration of social and educational programs that would nurture these possibilities. Better that we extend that notion now and hope that by extending the horizon of human possibilities other domains will similarly improve.

Never before has the responsibility of the human being for the planetary process been greater. Never before have we gained power of such magnitude over the primordial issues of life and death. The density and intimacy of the global village, along with the staggering consequences of our new knowledge and technologies, make us directors of a world that, up to now, has mostly directed us. This is a responsibility for which we have been ill-prepared and for which the usual formulas and stop-gap solutions will not work.

We find ourselves in a time in which extremely limited consciousness has the powers once accorded to the gods. Extremely limited consciousness can launch a nuclear holocaust with the single push of a button. Extremely limited consciousness can and does intervene directly in the genetic code, interferes with the complex patterns of life in the sea, and pours its wastes into the protective ozone layers that encircle the earth. Extremely limited consciousness is about to create a whole new energy base linking together computers, electronics, new materials from outer space, biofacture, and genetic engineering, which in turn will release a flood of innovation and external power unlike anything seen before in human history. In short, extremely limited consciousness is accruing to itself the powers of Second Genesis. And this with an ethic that is more Faustian than godlike.

We must therefore begin to do what has never been done before. We must assume the *Imago Dei* and humbly but tenaciously educate ourselves for sacred stewardship, acquiring the inner capacities to match our outer powers. We must seek and find those physical, mental, and spiritual resources that will enable us to partner the planet.

But how can we bring on the *Change*? How can we possibly undertake so giant a task when failure of nerve is rife throughout the planet, when we are everywhere experiencing a breakdown of all the old ways of knowing, doing, being? We don't even know what to tell children any more: how can we dare so great a venture? For we are clearly at the end of one age and not quite at the beginning of the new one. We are the people who are treading air over the abyss, the people of the parentheses.

But as anyone who has ever worked on a farm or in a garden knows, breakdown is always the signal for breakthrough. After the harvest, during winter's parentheses of life, the sere and decaying stalks of the previous year's vegetation collapse to provide the nutrients for the spring breakthrough of the reseeded earth. So too with ourselves. I am reminded of a recent conversation I had while running after a seventy-eight-year-old retired nurse in Helsinki as she bounded up the stairs to open a conference on human possibilities: 'So many people are losing heart, but not me! I have lived through four wars, have seen unbelievable suffering and misery, and you know what? I am full of hope for the human race. We are tied to each other in ways not possible before. We must now begin to live and grow together to become what we can be. I have dedicated the rest of my life to helping make this possible. I have no money and few have ever heard of me outside of Finland, but no matter. The time is ripe, ripe, ripe, and I know that what I do will make a difference.'

This remarkable woman is a member of a new breed of heroes, one that we might call the *people of the breakthrough*, men and women who find the present parentheses an extraordinary opportunity for seeding and nurturing both personal and social transformation. I find them everywhere – in citizen's volunteer associations, in store-front self-help agencies, in teachers who stay after school to help the child whom society forgets, in physicians who are attempting to treat the whole person. Young and old and in between, and from all walks of life, they demonstrate some remarkable similarities in both commitment and belief.

For the most part, they feel that as of now the future is wide open, and that what we do truly makes a difference as to whether humanity fails or flourishes. They have little interest in protecting their own turf, and therefore freely network and exchange ideas, information, and resources. If meaning eludes them, they act *as if* it were there and keep on working until it shows up. Nor are they afraid of the bouts of despair that occasionally attend the quest for the Pattern that Connects, knowing full well that this suffering is integral to the coming of wisdom.

Most important of all, they do their homework, by which I mean that they have a healthy and spirited appreciation of the complexity and capacities of their own being, and regularly spend time in discovering, refining, and applying the latent potentials of their own body-minds. There is little of narcissism here, as daily they rid themselves of unneeded rancor and deliberately pursue ways both mental and physical of deepening into the Depths of which they are a part. In this they become in some sense citizens of a larger universe, who take time to prepare themselves so that they can listen to the rhythms of awakening that may be pulsing from a deeper, more coherent Order of Reality.

They rarely make the papers or show up on the media, *because* they do not care for the credit, *because* most of their activities are ones of quiet and creative persistence and not of the order of catastrophe or the grandstand play, *because* their news is good news. They are the most important people in the world today, these *people of the breakthrough*, and it is for them that I write these words.

I see a change. And you are part of it.

Joan and Myrin Borysenko

MAKING THE OUTSIDE LIKE THE INSIDE

Joan and Myrin Borysenko, both PhDs. Joan is a clinical psychologist, co-founder of the Mind/Body Clinic at the New England Deaconess Hospital, Harvard Medical School. Author of bestsellers *Minding the Body, Mending the Mind* and *Guilt is the Teacher, Love is the Lesson*. Myrin is a pioneer in the field of mind/body research. They say: 'Do we want peace on earth? Then we must simultaneously seek peace within. Social activism that is based on anger and judgmentalness reflects the very isolation and fear that has been characteristic of the last millennium.'

Resting on a small blue-green marble, rocking in the vast womb of space, we hardly hear the great whooshing, the ebb and the flow, the systole and diastole of the cosmic heartbeat – the play of opposites out of which life is born. Heraclitus observed that in time, everything turns into its opposite:

> out of life comes death, out of the young the old, and out of the old the young, out of waking sleep and out of sleep waking, the stream of creation and dissolution never stops.

It seems that only as the great cosmic tide turns do we feel its pull and sense that we have just rested momentarily on the brink, only to be pulled back again into an opposing flow whose energy gives rise to change – to newness.

The earth is ailing from the pollution of an exploitative technology on the one hand, and the groaning weight of world poverty and over-population on the other. We are at the end of a cycle of contraction and separation that is unique in the known history of the planet. At the end of previous cycles where various lifeforms have disappeared, plagues have arisen, natural cataclysms have wrought large-scale disaster or the climate has changed, humankind had no recourse but to wait out the changes. In this instance, we ourselves are at the root of many of the disasters we face. We are also capable of staving them off.

For the first time in history, problems in one area are appreciated as global rather than local. The nuclear disaster in Chernobyl affected plants, animals, water, and people around the globe. The fall of the Berlin wall unleashed political forces that likewise affected the global community. The terrible genocide and rape of natural resources that the Chinese perpetrated on the Tibetans in the 1950s was likewise felt around the world – but in an unexpectedly positive sense. Buddhist ideals of compassion and *ahimsa* (non-violence), relatively unappreciated in the West, have been modeled by the Dalai Lama and the Tibetan community in exile, providing a new model of dealing with aggression and a new hope for world peace.

At all levels – in spite of and perhaps because of the growing desolation and fragmentation – there is an increasing realization of the fragility, sanctity, and interconnectedness of life. This realization, I believe, will be the hallmark of the coming millennium and the hope for a more peaceful, compassionate world order. Inherent in the realization of interconnectedness is a moving away from the polarity of either/or, toward an understanding of both/and.

If we reject any aspect of the old order to form a new order, we run the risk of wasting our energy by living in opposition to rather than in union with. The seeds of this understanding are present in psychology and its recent emphasis on healing the inner child lest we grow up in rebellion to – in opposition to – parents, and thereby perpetuate our wounds. The seeds of this understanding are likewise present in the theological movement known as creation-centered spirituality where the divisive argument about 'patriarchy' and 'matriarchy' – God the Father or God the Mother – dissolves in the celebration of a cosmology that honors the whole.

The more usual separation of politics-as-outer-life and spirituality-as-inner-life is brought into stark relief by the thirteenth-century Islamic mystic and poet Jelaluddin Rumi who wrote these startlingly contemporary lines.

> Outside, the freezing desert night.
> This other night inside grows warm, kindling.
> Let the landscape be covered with thorny crust.
> We have a soft garden in here.
> The continents blasted,
> cities and little towns, everything
> becomes a scorched, blackened ball.
>
> The news we hear is full of grief for that future,
> but the real news inside here
> is there's no news at all.*

No news at all. The stream of creation and dissolution never stops. And there's the rub. Here's the challenge. There is both an inner life – a soft garden – and an outer life – the scorched and blackened cities. In times past spiritual growth was mostly an inner concern, an ideal for the time of life when one's outer work was done, when life as a householder and a community member could be put aside. At that time a person could afford to become inner directed and contemplative, to ask the age-old questions: Who am I? What is the purpose of life? What is sacred? What is lasting?

But the pulse of the universe has quickened. The systole and diastole of life, the ebb and flow of events and conscious-ness, has quickened. There are growing signs that in the next millennium the inner and outer life must become one. Do we want peace on earth? Then we must simultaneously seek peace within. Social activism that is based on anger and judgmentalness reflects the very isolation and fear that

---

* *Open Secret, Versions of Rumi*, translated by John Moyne and Coleman Barks, Threshold Books, 1984.

has been characteristic of the last millennium. That fearful, separatist energy fueled the crusades, the burning of several million women as witches, the burning of several million Jews during the holocaust and the recent episodes of genocide in Tibet, Iraq, Central and South America.

The new millennium is ushering in the seeds of a cosmology in which the inner life and the outer life are reflective of one another and in balance. Witnessing a beautiful sunset, feeding the homeless, sitting with a person who is dying, working for a political cause out of compassion rather than anger – are these not spiritual experiences through which we reconnect with a larger whole and transcend our isolation?

This next millennium is a time when the old wisdom is coming to new light. We are challenged to make the outside like the inside – to act with integrity, literally with wholeness – so that what we bring forth on this planet is a reflection of what we have brought forth within ourselves.

The quality of our thinking affects the world around us in direct and indirect ways. The esoteric core of the world's great religions, the 'perennial philosophy,' states that we need to love ourselves before we can love our neighbors. Self-acceptance precedes acceptance of others. Appreciation of the dignity of other people and of the earth is predicated upon perceiving our own dignity. This psychospiritual healing puts us in touch with our own true nature – that core of peace, safety, serenity, wisdom, interconnectedness, fountainhead of generativity and global healing.

We have come to a point in our history where we are called to self-healing as part of the planetary healing. The inner and outer lives can no longer be separate. What, then, does it mean to be politically active? Perhaps it means to be related. To be connected. To be picked up once more by the incoming tide and to recognize the unity and interconnectedness of all things. To ask the questions: If I put this detergent in the washing machine how will it affect the environment? If I drink these three martinis how will it affect my family life? If I eat these hamburgers what does it mean to the cow, to the rainforest, to people in third-world countries? If I vote in this election how will it affect the town meeting, the city, the state, the country, the world? If I choose to watch this television program how will it affect my state of mind? How will that affect the world around me? If I take this job, how will I participate in creating the future?

Peace Pilgrim was a much-loved woman who criss-crossed the United States over 25,000 miles on foot between 1953 and 1981 on a mission of inner and outer peace and global understanding. Her power was not in talking about peace, it was in being peace – embodying peace. She was politically active at the extreme, having renounced her entire personal life in the service of world peace at the most grassroots level – person to person. She left simple counsel: 'There is a criterion by which you can judge whether the thoughts you are thinking and the things you are doing are right for you. The criterion is, *Have they brought you inner peace?*' This is the crux on which the future of world peace hinges in the next millennium.

His Eminence Tai Situpa

A CALL FOR PEACE IN ACTION

His Eminence Tai Situpa, Tibetan Buddhist who fled Tibet when six years old, international teacher and founder of Maitreya Institute. Author of *Way to Go, Tilopa*, and *Relative World, Ultimate Mind*. His monastery in India – Sherab Ling – houses over a hundred monks and many refugee children. He says: 'Do not make the mistake of thinking you are a powerless individual in a vast world. Know that you are armed with three great powers. You have the power of the body (the source of all action), the power of speech (the source of all expression) and the power of the mind (the source of all thought). Use them wisely and with great compassion.'

In the world today where deepening poverty exists side-by-side with horrific waste, where chronic boredom leads to drug abuse and crime, where the pollution of oceans and destruction of rain forests seem like insoluble problems, there is a vital need to act and find some remedies now!

Already there is a spark of hope as more and more people of every country stand up against injustices and awake from their lethargy to protect the world's valuable resources and call for peace. But peace is not simply an avoidance of war. True peace, real peace in action, has its roots in the well-being of the individual. How can we honestly, unhypocritically, march for peace and betterment when we do nothing about our own development as well?

We thus have a double-edged mission not only to create an enormous call for peace, harmony, prosperity, and above all justice; but also to work constantly, sincerely, and responsibly to improve our own minds, to become beacons of inspiration to people around us and in the world. Those who have self-respect, confidence and faith in themselves and their path, those who know they are doing the best that they can in a positive and caring way, they shine gloriously and inspire all of us.

One of the most important aspects to cultivate is compassion. Compassion is the wish that all beings be free from suffering and its causes. This does not mean some kind of emotional piety. Getting drawn into touchy sentiments is of little help, if at all. For instance, tears or anger will not help a beggar to eat! However, a beggar can open the eyes of compassion to action, as happened to the wonderful and noble Mother Teresa.

Compassion should be a spontaneous concern carefully tendered. So how do we generate it? By looking at the causes of suffering, the effect such suffering has, and investigating the ways of removing suffering. By truly studying the means of developing a 'good heart', a heart and mind dedicated to the well-being of everyone, and by going over it again and again until it becomes second nature to us. Then everything we do becomes an expression of our heartfelt commitment to the happiness of all beings. And by all beings I mean everyone, impartially, without exceptions, limits, or conditions.

One method for training the mind addresses the problem of negative situations. Basically there are two types of negativity: that which comes from the world in general, and that which arises from the interaction between beings. We can chose to relate to it in a destructive way thus giving fuel for further negativity in the future; or we can relate to it with a positive attitude by staying aware and observing what is happening, and thus turning the situation into food for our development and growth.

For example, if someone becomes hostile to us and we retaliate, then the whole situation becomes worse. If instead we respond to it as an opportunity to learn patience, then the situation becomes a teacher to us and is transformed. This does not mean we have to become submissive, always bowing and scraping to the world. Wisdom has to be applied with responsibility. There will always be events in the world that are inevitable, that we cannot change or improve. But we can act wisely and even reduce the damage.

A constant, sincere, personal involvement in the question of compassion will bear fruit – to act in everyday life with compassion as a source of inspiration will create a purity of mind and a strength that will give clear vision. Thus universal compassion can be generated. Such compassion is the selflessness of seeing that the normal beliefs of self and ego are relative illusions influenced by conditions. When there is a fusion of universal compassion and the wisdom of selflessness, then there will automatically be unlimited spontaneous activity to help all beings without exception.

It is necessary for us all to be concerned about the real issues in the world today and to put dedicated effort into finding solutions. My heart says that if we can send people to the moon, if we can build weapons that can destroy the world, then surely we can find solutions to the present earth challenges.

Mankind's future must be striven for with a sincere passion and persistence. Do not make the mistake of thinking you are a powerless individual in a vast world. Know that you are armed with three great powers. You have the power of the body (the source of all action), the power of speech (the source of all expression), and the power of the mind (the source of all thought). Use them wisely and with great compassion.

I contribute to this book as a Buddhist, using Buddhist ideals that were taught to me by my teachers, just as they were learnt from previous teachers. This does not mean that what I say will have relevance only to Buddhists. Rather, I hope that these words will contribute to all people's inspiration in trying to make this world a happy, peaceful, content, and more meaningful place that respects all life.

Eddie and Debbie Shapiro

A SHIFT IN CONSCIOUSNESS

Eddie and Debbie Shapiro, international teachers and seminar leaders.
Authors of *Out of Your Mind, the Only Place to Be!*, and editors of *The Way
Ahead*. Eddie is author of *Inner Conscious Relaxation*; Debbie is author of
The Bodymind Workbook, and co-author of *The Metamorphic Technique*
and *The Healer's Hand Book*. They say: '. . . we find that we are creating a
planet where environmentally we cannot survive, and yet we are reluctant to
change. The environment is dying while we hold on to our fear of the
future. Is there not a paradox here? That perhaps our fear of death . . . is
actually holding us back from changing, yet the transition is essential if human
life is to continue.'

If we take a moment to be objective we may find that our
experience of the world is based on our inner feelings and desires
– that the external is a reflection of the internal. Similarly we find
that the internal is affected by the external – world events and
changes have a deep impact on our inner state of being. We
can then see how all things are intimately related and bound
to each other, that there is no real difference between our own
experiences and those in the world around us. For instance, is
our own inner conflicts, confusion and prejudice any different

from the conflict, chaos and fighting that occurs between nations? Is the the way we treat our bodies any different from the way we are treating the environment? We are, surely, not just the victims of events who have to suffer accordingly; we actually play a significant role in creating the world we live in.

However, we do tend to be victims of our own self-centeredness. Rather than seeing a connectedness and relationship between all things, we usually view the world as if we were an independent and separate center, where everyone and everything revolves only in reference to us. This is because we believe ourselves to be solid and fixed: the conviction that we are real is so powerful that we regard our feelings and experiences very seriously. We become consumed in preserving this separate existence by obsessively needing to fulfil our desires, promoting our image and imposing our opinions.

Yet every so often, beneath this self-created fixed image, we find the ominous suspicion that there is actually something very unsolid and insubstantial after all! Many of us have such moments of awareness, a sneaking suspicion that all is not as we think it is, that in one way or another life cannot be so easily explained. In fact, there is an innate knowledge, intimate to our very beingness, that knows we are in reality groundless and impermanent, only here temporarily. However, this knowledge, rather than inspiring us to seek out its true meaning, usually creates a fearful and desperate need in us to hold on even tighter so that insubstantiality is avoided and our continuing existence is therefore safe.

We are thus caught in an interesting dilemma! Intuitively we know that there is a deeper reality that speaks of freedom and contentment; yet to enter into this is scary, ungrounded in our normal world. There is no safe, well-trod path to follow with clear guidelines on how to overcome fear, to leave behind the known and enter into the unknown – this is new territory. So when confronted with this situation we tend not to become explorers of the unknown, but we choose instead to create an enormous array of paraphernalia – all the content in our lives – to build a seemingly solid structure. Once built, we rarely move out of this structure, like mice in a cage going round and round. We have a more complicated cage perhaps, but it is just as fixed and our activities just as repetitive.

For few of us are free thinkers. Generally we are conditioned to believe in labels such as profession, country, or religion – I'm American, I'm English, I'm Russian, I'm white and you are black, I'm Protestant and you are Catholic. These labels are like credentials through which we identify ourselves; they form the content, that which gives meaning to our lives. We find our identity through our job or our spouse's job, our children, our illnesses and hardships, our successes, beauty, or possessions; through labels such as housewife, businessman, athlete, abuser, victim of abuse, recovering alcoholic, healer, minister, millionaire, politician, and so on. The label stays as long as it serves us, for without content there is no identity. Content gives us solidity, something to hold on to.

Thus we set up a fixed reality through which we relate, while the truth beneath it all is often lost, obscured, or becomes incidental. We identify so strongly with the content that we forget about compassion, caring, generosity, and forgiveness. Living in the myth of accumulation we believe that content is essence and put desire before truth and understanding.

The unknown is the big problem. For the unknown contains the one thing that constantly disputes our efforts to be solid, and that is death. At some point we are going to die, to be leaving this physical realm, and we will certainly not be taking any of the content with us. Yet we go on accumulating things and people and opinions, growing in our attachment to them. By holding on to the familiar and that which has already been experienced, the past then becomes like a bag of antiques that we carry around. For past events may have been painful and difficult, traumatic or life-changing, but we got through them safely and are here to tell the story; death did not trip us up on the way. So the past is safe and constantly referred to – we dip into our bags whenever we are in need of reassurance. The future implies being different from how we are now, of being without that which supports us, and few of us are willing to let go of our carefully constructed support systems.

However, we may not voice our concerns as an actual fear of death, for that would be simultaneously acknowledging that death exists! We express them rather as a fear of movement, of dealing with the unpredictable and therefore disconcerting and threatening aspects of life. This fear then becomes a sense of discomfort and inadequacy, of not being able to cope, of being overwhelmed by the problems of the world, or by anything that appears threatening.

Thus we find that we are creating a planet where environmentally we cannot survive, and yet we are reluctant to change. The environment is dying while we hold on to our fear of the future. Is there not a paradox here? That our fear of death (and therefore of the future) is actually holding us back from changing, yet the transition is essential if human life is to continue.

When we really consider this we confront the reality of impermanence. For there is nothing in the world that is permanent – all things will eventually go, whether it be our own lives, our relationships, health, or our possessions, let alone the trees, animals, and the world around us. Recognizing this fact and integrating its implications is actually very liberating – it can free us from the confines of having to control or hold on. We can let go and allow all things their rightful place in the universe.

But letting go of that to which we are attached is intricately connected with our ability to let go of our solidity, and this is where we stumble. It is far easier to let go of something we are not very attached to, than it is to let go of that which supports us. And so we suffer. The inability to accept the truth of transiency creates a longing for permanence, which can never be.

The shift in consciousness that is needed is therefore a shift away from this experience of ourselves as separate and independent towards one of recognizing our essential unity and interdependence with all things. For there is nothing that is free from this dependency. As Anne Bancroft says in *The Spiritual Journey*:

> Dependent co-arising is a vision of reality as dynamic relativity, a process of inter-existence and interdependence in which the doer and the deed, the person and the environment, are mutually causative.

We all, therefore, reflect and are connected to each other, as well as to all other things – each plays its own unique part, being both a cause and an effect. To believe that we are separate and independent is a delusion. There is no America, no England, no Protestant or Catholic. The only real separation that exists between these is in our own minds. Yet it is such limitations that cause so much pain, both to individuals and to the world as a whole.

Realizing unity is realizing essence. The content in our lives is not the essence, for content is limited and impermanent, while essence always was and always will be free. Essence does not identify with name and form, with differences and labels. It is unidentified, at one with all things. This is the recognition that if everything is in a constant state of movement and there is nothing fixed or identifiable, then there is simply unfoldment. To be at peace with this is true freedom.

We can acknowledge our differences without being attached to them, we can honor the essence in all beings without needing to impose ourselves. For the diversity is there to enjoy, not to compare or to make inferior or superior. We become fearless by going beyond the limitations. Such acceptance furthers the development of awareness and compassion. As Thomas Merton says in *The New Man*:

> Compassion is a keen awareness of the interdependence of all living things which are all involved in one another and are all a part of one another.

Compassion is the objective expression of unconditional love, where we are motivated to act through the depth of our empathy and understanding. Compassion is beyond thoughts of 'I' or 'me'. It enables complete forgiveness to take place both of ourselves and of others, for we realize that pain and suffering are simply due to the ignorance of our basic unity. And we can forgive ignorance. Compassion is seeing and reveling in the divinity in all beings.

Let us now make that shift in consciousness by recognizing our essential oneness with all life! Let us honor each other and the very miracle of existence! The awakened mind – enlightenment – is our natural state, it is inherently our real Self; it is ordinary. All the fear, prejudice, guilt, anger, and neurosis in which we immerse ourselves is extra-ordinary. Can we not drop the 'extra' and become 'ordinary' – become fully alive, fearless, compassionate, and loving human beings?

Marilyn Ferguson

TOWARDS THE LIGHT

Marilyn Ferguson, author of the international bestseller, *The Aquarian Conspiracy*, publisher of the 'Brain/ Mind Bulletin', a clearing house for consciousness research worldwide. Her next book is *The New Common Sense: Secrets of the Visionary Life*. She reminds us to: 'Ask, ask, and then, of course, listen.'

Contemporary mystical experiences from many individuals and many parts of the world have centered in recent years on a collective and intensifying vision, the sense of an impending transition in the human story: an evolution of consciousness as significant as any step in the long chain of our biological evolution.

The consensual vision, whatever its variations, sees this transformation of consciousness as the moment anticipated by older prophecies in all the traditions of direct knowing – the death of one world and the birth of a new, an apocalypse, the 'end of days' period in the Kabbalah, the awakening of increasing numbers of human beings to their godlike potential. 'The seed of God is in us,' Meister Eckhart said. 'Pear seeds grow into pear trees, nut seeds into nut trees, and God seeds into God.'

Always, the vision of evolution is toward the light. Light is the oldest and most pervasive metaphor in spiritual experience. We speak of enlightenment, the city of light, the Light of the World, children of light, the 'white light experience.'

'Light . . . light,' wrote T.S. Eliot,' visible reminder of invisible light.' To Honoré de Balzac, it seemed that humankind was on the eve of a great struggle; the forces are there, he insisted. 'I feel in myself a life so luminous that it might enlighten a world, and yet I am shut up in a sort of mineral.' Arthur Young offers in speculative scientific terms an idea as old as myth and Plato: We represent a 'fall' into matter from light, and the lightward ascent has begun again. Lawrence Ferlinghetti wrote a poem about 'Olbers' paradox,' the observation of a learned astronomer that there were relatively few stars nearby; the farther away he looked, the more there were:

> So that from this we can deduce
> that in the infinite distances
> there must be a place
> there must be a place
> where all is light
> and that the light from that high place
> where all is light
> simply hasn't got here yet . . .

'Let the light penetrate the darkness until the darkness shines and there is no longer any division between the two,' says a Hasidic passage. Before a soul enters the world, it is conducted through all the worlds and shown the first light so that it may forever yearn to attain it. The *tsadik* in the Hasidic tradition, like the Bodhisattva of Buddhism, has allowed the light to enter him and shine out in the world again.

To the third-century mystic Plotinus, it was 'the clear light which is Itself.' The Sufi dervish dancer does the 'turn' with upraised right hand, symbolically bringing light to the Earth. The shaman achieves a state of perfect balance so that he might see a blinding light.

The dream of light and liberation is poetically expressed in an apocryphal contemporary *Aquarian Gospel of Jesus Christ*. For too long, it says, our temples have been the tombs of the hidden things of time. Our temples, crypts and caves are dark. We have been unable to see the patterns:

In light there are no secret things . . . There is no lonely pilgrim on the way to light. Men only gain the heights by helping others gain the heights . . .

We know that the light is coming over the hills. God speed the light.

YOUR RIGHT MIND

To feed your right mind:
    Moonlight.
    Douse the lights, douse even the candle
    Speak to her gently; she's been shunned
        so long, she runs away.
    Suggest, don't expect
    Invite
    Wait

Let being fill up the space
    of doing
So that what you're doing
    is being.

Let the message emerge
    from the sea of understanding
        like a mermaid singing her seduction.
Think fishes, flying through dark waters.
Think night, moonlit seas, and
    no moonlight at all.
    Think water. Think depths, dampness.
      Think subtle. Think subtler.
    Think feelings.

Your wis-dame, your wisdom,
    is an archivist. She knows what happened.
    Just ask.
    She isn't afraid, she's been here before.

Another kind of clarity, silvery, not stark,
    emerges.
    Your wis-dame is your oldest ally,
    your mother-wit.

Without her you are less than half yourself;
    with her you are whole and ready.
Like a dolphin she is beside you
    when you are goalless
and seeking only to satisfy your higher yearning.

Be attracted, addicted to life
    and life's deeper demands.
Love, don't curse, the blind alleys
    the red lights and lost luggage.
Without guessing there's no game.
Not 'no pain no gain'
    but 'no love no gain.'

Your mother-wit,
your wise dame
The sage speaks in patterns and pictures,
a scatter tongue. Catch as you can
    her butterfly dust

But if you treasure her treasures
    be loyal.
For eons she has been wooed in the dark
    and spurned in the sun.
If she was with you then
    she's with you now.

Ask
Ask
and then, of course,
                    listen.

Anne Bancroft

THE TRANSLUCENT OPTION

Anne Bancroft, teacher, and author
of many books, including *Religions
of the East, Zen, Direct Pointing to
Reality, The Luminous Vision, Origins
of the Sacred, Twentieth Century
Mystics and Sages, Weavers of
Wisdom*, and *The Spiritual Journey*.
She says: 'The way ahead . . . is one
where existential fear and doubt are
laid to rest and a new relationship
with the whole energizes the person
towards the good of all. That this must
become the common way is essential.
Humanity is adrift because the whole
is no longer seen, only the parts.'

We are conditioned to live our everyday lives in a world that
is fragile and in great peril – the list of its ills seems infinite.
However, it does not help to blame any particular time in
history for the situation we are in. We were dazzled by
modern science in the eighteenth century and saw a future
full of marvellous discoveries such as electricity and steam.
Every problem could be answered by using scientific methods
– a habit of thinking that still dominates us today. All that
cleverness was admired so much, but nobody noticed that the
inner world of imagination and intuition was being forgotten
and neglected in the process. It is not until the last half of
this century that we have begun to wake up and to reach out,
before it's too late, to the sublime reality behind the world of
appearances, to listen to the deep heart within as well as to the
clever inventive mind.

For we are now discovering that life has no true meaning or even any real sense unless it is a process of creation and development, a journey to clarity, to self-transcendence. Our personality is transformed if we make that journey; and the newness of transformation revitalizes not only ourselves but also the world about us.

Everywhere we see lost and bewildered people behind the masks they wear for social interchange. Masks, alas, because the spiritual nature of the world – the mysterious miracle of its being – is not visible when you believe that gaining and having are all that matters and feel impelled to present your personality accordingly. Such materiality denies all growth; it brings about a host of social evils – crime, wars, starvation, poverty. We are so clever we can invent a computer or a missile to intercept another missile. But because we are so ignorant we miss the real meaning of our lives.

A change of priorities is essential to the life of this planet – a form of mutation. Perhaps the mutation has already begun with the coming of the New Age and the rediscovery of the spirit within. Perhaps it will be energized by the threat of the warming of the planet and the necessary green revolution. Whatever its beginnings we need to work at self-transformation while at the same time we must put right injustices in the world, feed the starving, and restore the forests. The inner and the outer must begin to act in harmony together.

We can't do any of this by simply laying down laws, by standing outside the problem. We have to get right in. This means developing a whole range of under-used qualities such as intuition, openness, and acceptance of change. These are our tools for gaining insight and perception and beginning to practise a selfless way of life.

As we feel ourselves part of an interrelated whole, the divisions between religions can fade. More people can then feel faith, perhaps for the first time, in the true Reality that imbues all creation with its presence. If we can only trust it, this has the power to heal the wounded planet. Once felt, even for a moment, such Reality seems to change the universe. All things become invested with intensity of being. The solid-seeming world grows translucent. Our concepts drop

away and we catch a glimpse of another level of being where
values are of a different order.

Everything we have learnt – all our small discoveries within
and without – are surely only a fraction of what there is to be
found. Thoreau once said, 'We are still being born, and have
as yet but a dim vision.' The Buddha said, 'Behold I show
you sorrow; and the ending of sorrow.' He believed that the
sorrow we cause ourselves and others through greed, fear, and
delusion can come to an end. He urged us to wake up and to
become aware of the other dimensions that await us.

The way ahead is towards the realization of the spiritual
path. If we are to have a future at all we have to accept that
a deepening and stretching of consciousness must now be
undertaken. Those who are mutating, who are working within
the new consciousness, must work all the harder to serve those
who either cannot or will not awaken to it. The old concepts
of religion need to go. 'Your God is too small,' said Nietsche.
Religious thinking should now explore other worlds, the stars
and planets of the mind as well as of the cosmos. For if we want
to create a new self we have to explore everything that we are
as well as all that is. 'To overcome the blind drift to automatic
living, mankind must deliberately resume the long effort that
originally turned hominids into men,' said Lewis Mumford.

And it need not be so difficult to welcome the spirit. Many
people long to find its presence but cannot start. The language
of mysticism and the New Age is sometimes no help –
'expanded consciousness' and 'no self' can merely mystify and
baffle without arousing response. But by learning to keep the
mind so open that every experience evokes a feeling of being
in touch with the Mystery enables the way to become clear.

We live in a translucent, numinous world if only we have
the eyes to see it. The new consciousness that is awakened by
the act of simply seeing with a receptive and open mind is the
breakthrough action which will lead us into the way ahead.
Such a consciousness will manifest a new stage in the evolution
of man. The difference between this new cosmic consciousness
and ordinary selfconsciousness can seem to be as great as the
difference between human consciousness and animal.

In the timeless moment of such awareness we enter a
different sphere of being, one in which the contradictions

of our lives are transcended. It is then we know the Mystery exists, we experience another dimension and feel it embrace us. There is an ultimate certainty which enriches our lives. We realize our relationship to the whole, and that realization becomes the rock on which we can build our lives.

A new spirituality – the translucent option – will see the colours and shapes of the world as miracles, as shimmering enchantment. And such a way of sacramental seeing is greatly helped, strangely enough, by the science of our day. The movements of electrons have been likened by physicists to those of a dancer responding to a score. The score, the music, is the common pool of information that guides each of the dancers as he takes his steps, each of the electrons as it responds to the others. The way we see existence has always been conditioned by what the scientists tell us of the world. Now it seems to be made of dancing steps and we can learn to follow the dance, to accept that there is consciousness in the very atoms that make up the universe. Such an understanding brings about a shift in our whole relationship with the material world. We can realize that we are living in a universe pervaded by consciousness – a dancing universe.

What does such a dance mean, in human terms, for us? I believe it means the recognition of delight, of finding a world of wonder within the known world, of becoming aware of the enchanted essence that lies within appearances.

Delight springs up when we see the ordinary as transparent, translucent, revealing the Mystery to us if we are ready to enter the colourful, immediate world of here and now with all our being; and are ready at the same time to surrender ourselves totally to the Mystery which lies beyond space and time.

A spirituality of delight is one in which we will often say 'Ah!' A Zen master once said: 'Have you noticed how the pebbles of the road are polished and pure after the rain? And the flowers? No words can describe them. One can only murmur an "Ah!" of admiration. We should understand the "Ah!" of things.'

'We need nothing but open eyes to be ravished like the Cherubims,' says Traherne. To be ravished in this way is to be no longer closed in by our separate selves but to be open to the new. It means being ready for this exact moment now, available to all that will happen in it.

The translucent option is the sacramental way of feeling ourselves to be part of something infinitely wonderful and mysterious – a dance of the universe which can only be known by entering into it. It is not the mechanistic goal-orientated world of the past, but is where people live like artists creating their lives in harmony with what the world offers.

The way ahead, then, is one where existential fear and doubt are laid to rest and a new relationship with the whole energizes the person towards the good of all. That this must become the common way is essential. Humanity is adrift because the whole is no longer seen, only the parts. These make little sense on their own and people come to believe they live in a senseless and meaningless world, where nothing really matters.

Now is the time when consciousness of infinite Reality must pervade everybody's lives. It will bring interrelationship, interconnectedness and new reverence for the planet. The infinite dimension exists. To find it and to live by it is the way ahead.

Soozi Holbeche

WHAT IS HAPPENING TO US?

Soozi Holbeche, international teacher, healer and counsellor. Author of *The Power of Gems and Crystals* and *The Power of Your Dreams*. She says: 'Instead of wringing our hands at the apparent rise of disorder and conflict in the world, I believe we should rejoice that all the ills are coming to the surface so that we can see what is confronting us. Without pain, discomfort, a lump or a rash, we remain unaware of disease.'

Listen as you walk upon the earth. Listen to all the beings coming to life, coming into their own, growing into their new expressive selves. It is the time of manifesting the dreams that were brought to us during the time of the North, the winter. As you look around you will see that it is a time of love. A time to watch all creatures doing their dance of life.

Painted Arrow

Economists, scientists, environmentalists, astrologers, psychics and visionaries all over the world predict that the 1990s will be the most dramatic decade in history. Warnings of ecological disaster, the world turning on its axis, economic collapse, geographical upheaval, nuclear war, extraordinary genetic and technological discoveries have radically changed both life and our attitude to it.

As if to confirm these predictions, we have already seen

changing weather-patterns, earthquakes, hurricanes, holes in the ozone layer, and many animals brought to the point of extinction, while thousands of people die daily from disease, accident, and needless starvation.

Alongside such doom, gloom, and despondency, we are told the end of the twentieth century heralds a new and glorious era of peace, love, and understanding. The words of Painted Arrow above imply a worldwide transformation of consciousness, and we can see a reflection of this with the plans for a United Europe, the collapse of the Berlin Wall, the end of the domination of orthodox communism in the USSR, and peace negotiations between many world leaders.

The world is going through a huge metamorphosis. The planetary being on which we live, the earth, is literally giving birth to a new age and form. Caught in the limbo between the death of the old and the birth of the new, experiencing the pains of both, many of us are finding it hard to cope. The growing dichotomy between the good and the bad is becoming more visible and confusing. A polarization is taking place, both in the individual and universally. Life is not easy. This in-between state stimulates feelings of deep loneliness, and pushes us to question every facet of life we have previously taken for granted.

The patriarchal domination of the world is coming to an end. Men and women are becoming more androgynous, which means that the relationship between men and women is changing to one of empathy and companionship, rather than that of master and slave. As a result, the stereotyped male-female roles of the past are no longer valid. Many men today embody a stronger feminine energy and are more ready to show their feelings than they were in earlier generations, while many women assert and express themselves in a way previously considered to be exclusively masculine. This causes a great deal of confusion and upset, especially in matters of sexuality.

In the legend of Psyche and Aphrodite, Psyche was born when a dewdrop fell from heaven to earth. Psyche therefore symbolizes the fragile, vulnerable side of a woman's nature. By contrast, Aphrodite was born as a result of the seeds of Uranus being scattered on the oceans of the world. She arose from the depths, and symbolizes the deep, primeval power of ancient femaleness. She is the wise, nurturing woman, the priestess who can also become the witch-bitch if scorned or ignored.

I see a warring all over the world today between the Psyche and Aphrodite sides of a woman's nature, as well as in the inner woman in each man. Aphrodite in each of us, male and female, is clamouring to be heard. She tugs at our entrails and says: 'Get up! Show yourself! Do something!' The woman feels impelled from within to stand up and flex her muscles a little. Suddenly her inner Psyche pops up and says in a trembling voice: 'I *can't*! I don't know how!' and the woman sinks back, feeling frustrated and unable to help herself – often taking out her frustration on those she loves the most. In a man, Aphrodite pushes him to respond from feeling, emotion and intuition, rather than logic. Often when he does, he frightens himself: he might lose control. His family, as well as his own inner Psyche, put him off by saying: 'Whatever's come over you? You've never behaved like this before!' And he closes down again.

Not until the Psyche-Aphrodite battle works itself out in men and women, when we stop using each other as supportive props and become whole within ourselves, sometimes receptive, sometimes assertive, will we be able to talk to each other as fellow human beings, instead of trying to fulfil pre-ordained male and female roles.

Just as men and women are now expanding their roles, the widespread availability of computers and advanced technology means that new generations are evolving who will never work in quite the same way as man did in the past. Ultimately this will dissolve the barrier between the left and right brain, so that we will balance analytical thought with imagination and intuition, thus becoming far more spontaneous and creative. In the interim, however, unemployment is likely to be a major problem. Without work, what happens to our self-worth and identity, our sense of being an integral part of society?

In ancient China this crucial time between cultures – the ending of one civilization and the beginning of another – was known as Wei Chi. Wei Chi implies radical change, the midpoint between life and death, the moment of crisis or danger in the delivery room when a woman is in labour but the baby has not yet emerged. Wei Chi also means a major initiation, a moment of choice and of opportunity to change. Wei Chi stimulates excitement and a sense of our own power, while stirring up fear and panic: 'I can, I will, I want to!' versus 'I cannot, I'll make a mistake, I'll fail!'

Our choice is between standing still and clinging to the apparent safety of the past, or taking the risk of leaping forward into the unknown. In my work as a healer, I have found this dilemma often symbolized by the number of people who currently develop sore throats, mouth, neck and chest problems. A part of us says: 'I really want to find out what I came here to do.' We stand at a crossroads waiting for the hand of God to drop a sign out of the sky to make everything clear. At the same time, another part of us panics and says: 'But if I find out what I'm supposed to do, maybe I'll have to do it!' The unconscious fear that this may mean our having to leave job, home, family and so on grabs us by the throat, which is where we give birth to a new identity, and we become symbolically paralyzed, which in turn leads to our contracting chest or throat infections.

One of our greatest fears as human beings is our fear of change, of losing hold of the familiar. Our terror of the unknown in the form of death may indeed prevent us from living fully and enjoying life. This fear is like that of a child who climbs so high in a tree that he is afraid to move further up or down. His loving father stands underneath with outstretched arms, saying: 'Jump! I'll catch you!' The child knows that he cannot stay where he is forever, but he clings to the security of the branch underfoot, afraid to let go in case his father fails to catch him, and he falls. Many of us are like that child. The tree is the safety and familiarity of the past. We know we cannot stay there forever, but we are afraid to let go, to jump and move on.

Encounters with danger and change are part of life. From them we can emerge stronger and, as from a near-death experience, with a new awareness of life. These encounters usually accompany major initiations, or shifts from one level of consciousness to another. Our current point of Wei Chi is bringing us to the brink of an initiation so great that it is as if we were stepping from water to land for the first time. We are part of an emerging new form of life, and it is imperative for the earth's future that we all jump out of our tree and participate fully in this new form of life.

The 1990s are pushing us to make a quantum leap in consciousness, to clear ourselves of the fears that bind and blind us from recognizing that we are multi-dimensional beings who came here as midwives, custodians, god-parents and caretakers for the new planetary consciousness now emerging.

If, as I and many others believe, life is a school and we are the students in it, is it not possible that we are being moved from the lessons of kindergarten, first grade and high school, to college, university, and even to taking our final exam – our Master's degree?

The 1990s are under the influence of Pluto, a planet discovered in 1930. Pluto rules the unconscious; it pushes forward transformation and evolution by bringing to the surface all that we have repressed, denied, or just do not want to see. Plutonian energy brings us to the point of crucifixion, stirs us to face our shadow, our ego, our past. It urges us to live our own truth and to let go of whatever is obsolete and outgrown. It triggers identity crises, discomfort, and disruption, maybe through loss of job, relationships, money, or home. The decade when Pluto was discovered ushered in an era of chaos. It was the mid-point between two world wars. The economy crashed worldwide. Plans for nuclear weapons were being developed. Racism, violence and world crime increased. Pluto represents a downward spiral of spirit into matter, into the underworld, confrontation with fear, despair, loss and death. Pluto is the great initiator that clears the way for new beginnings, by liberating us from the past.

Instead of wringing our hands at the apparent rise of disorder and conflict in the world, I believe we should rejoice that all the ills are coming to the surface so that we can see what is confronting us. Without pain, discomfort, a lump or a rash, we remain unaware of disease. When we experience its symptoms we can do something about them. As an illustration, when we make soup stock we simmer bones in water over heat, and gradually a froth or scum comes to the surface. Before the heat was applied, the water looked clear. Now, when we scoop away the surface froth, we find clear liquid underneath. In the same way we can be brought face to face with hidden aspects of ourselves so that we recognize and do something about them. Often the very fact that they are no longer hidden changes their effect on our lives. When a pattern of behaviour is buried in our unconscious it has power over us. When it is brought into our consciousness we have power over it – the ability to change it.

The influence of Pluto, the transition point of Wei Chi, may bring us to the dark night of the soul, ripping away the very fabric and foundation of the persona we have developed from childhood. The phrase 'dark night of the soul' comes from the writings of the sixteenth-century Spanish mystic St John of the Cross. Today it implies the crisis when the things that used to work for us no longer do so. If we rely solely on rational thought and external props, this crisis brings us to a standstill, and forces us either to scream for help to something beyond ourselves, or to look within and delve deeply into our unconscious. The shock of being at these crossroads helps our evolution by stimulating our re-evaluation of past, present and future, of our relationship to everyone and everything around us. A near-death experience does exactly the same thing. For many people, it provides the opportunity to change their entire attitude to life.

We are all suffering – the literal meaning of the word is to 'undergo' – an identity crisis, a planetary near-death experience, stimulated by the earth herself. By manifesting symptoms of disease, she forces us to look at our relationship with all of life. In the process we must heal what is called the 'Fisher King wound', which continues to plague many people round the world. This allegory comes from the centuries-old story of Parsifal and the quest for the Holy Grail. Today it symbolizes the state of being in which we have access to virtually all the world's riches and technological knowledge, yet our life simply does not work. We are dysfunctional and unfulfilled, unable to express our joy or spontaneity. We do not celebrate life. The Fisher King wound is symbolized by people who at best do not express their full potential, and at worst become addicted to alcohol, drugs, gambling, excitement, and escape.

The original story starts with the arrival in a wood of a

twelve-year-old boy – the Fisher King. He finds the embers of a fire still glowing hot, and the remains of a fish on the spit above it. He picks up the spit to taste the fish but it is so hot that he drops it. The spit pierces his thigh and from that moment he cannot walk. The story says he can only be healed by a naïve and innocent fool – Parsifal. Meanwhile the land he rules is also afflicted – the crops will not grow and the sun does not shine.

The Fisher King wound pierces us so deeply that we close off emotionally and hold back from expressing all that we are. It can come as a result of a powerful emotional experience which we are too young to comprehend, such as rape, incest, rejection, death or a sudden change of environment. The story is especially relevant for anyone who during childhood, above all at pre-teen age, experienced something so traumatic that at some level they switched off. Part of my own Fisher King wound was caused by the nuns at my convent school forcing me to stand in front of five hundred girls at morning prayers while they declared: 'Your mother is a sinner, because she is divorced, which makes you a sinner too. Now, girls, this is what a sinner looks like.' I did not even know what a sinner was. I only knew I was one, so I played the fool and pretended I did not care, and thus became virtually unteachable.

In some of the old stories the Fisher King was pierced in the groin, not the thigh. He was therefore not only unable to walk, but also unable to 'express himself as a man'. The male drive is what we use to express ourselves in life. It is outgoing, active, creative. We use its power to run, walk, talk, scrub floors, make love, bake a cake, paint a picture or write a book. Female energy is ingoing, receptive. We use it to listen, think, imagine, feel, intuit. Our relationship with our inner man and woman is modelled on the attitude of our mother and father to each other from the moment they met; in other words, the quality of their relationship with each other preconception, at the moment of conception, during our time in the womb, at birth, and during our childhood, as well as their attitude to us, *all* affect our acceptance or rejection of ourselves, and can lead to a chronic lack of self-worth on our part. Many of us have a mother/father wound that triggers a lack of trust in our own male/female energy which incapacitates us in the same way as does the Fisher King wound.

If on some level our mother was 'not there' for us, we will not trust our feelings, imagination or intuition. We will hold back from 'heartfully' relating to others. If our father was 'not there', the energy of the inner man will not be there either. To compensate, we will then become either extremely hard-working, competitive, conscientious perfectionists, or procrastinators and start-stoppers who never get anything done. We need to stop this pattern for future generations by spiritually educating men and women about the importance of the influence of pre-birth, conception, pregnancy and so on for the incoming new soul. We must educate children for the twenty-first century instead of for the 1800s, and recognize that the new children being born today and in the future are highly evolved spiritual beings with a very different purpose from ours for occupying a physical body. We must change the thought system that teaches fear and guilt, often established in children by adults who give love when behaviour and performance 'fit', and withdraw it when they do not. This teaches that love, acceptance or approval are conditional on how we behave or perform, instead of being unconditional for whom we are. Children need to be reminded that the soul is androgynous, without colour, race or creed. A man is born ebony black, for example, because that colour best suits his climate or suited that of his ancestors. A particular form of life is chosen for the lessons it can teach.

When the Parsifal legend says that the Fisher King can be healed by a naïve and innocent fool, it means that no matter how frozen and wounded we are, we can still heal and free ourselves. To do so we must listen to our own inner child, the naïve, innocent, joyous, foolish, spontaneous part of us that can heal and balance us, and ultimately becomes the Christ-child. The story also stresses that the only relief the Fisher King can get from his pain and paralysis comes from fishing alone in his boat. In other words, his outer life disability and problems have pushed him into contact with his inner wisdom, his inner self. By exploring his innermost feelings and by constantly delving into his unconscious, the young king finds peace. So too can we.

In *Modern Man in Search of His Soul* Jung wrote: 'If it were possible to personify the unconscious, we might call it a collective human being combining the characteristics of both sexes, transcending youth and age, birth and death, from having at his command a human experience of one or two million years, almost immortal.' With such a source of wisdom, inspiration, healing and balance within us, how sad it is that most of us struggle blindly through life without making any attempt to get in touch with it, especially when it is made available to us every night through our dreams.

Most of us have no conception of how little we use the wide array of capabilities open to us. The majority of us do not even use ten per cent of our brain. I believe that the average person uses only five or six per cent. By thinking differently, by acting instead of reacting we can tap into limitless creativity, infinite possibilities. In Latin, the word 'disaster' means 'separation from the stars', and it is obvious that much of our life on earth has been disastrous. The shift that is now taking place, the lifting of the earth to a higher level, is reconnecting us to our own divinity, reminding us of our own perfection, and ensuring that we once again take our place among the stars.

Each chakra in the human body – *chakra* in Sanskrit means 'wheel' – is a whirling vortex of energy vibrating at different frequencies. The lowest three chakras vibrate at a lower frequency than do the heart, throat, third eye, and crown chakras. As the heart chakra of the earth expands, as we move into and through the fourth dimension and prepare for the fifth, we experience the vibrational frequency of the planet speeding up, a sense of accelerated change. Until we adjust to it, its effects can cause chronic glandular-fever-type tiredness, insomnia, emotional vulnerability, forgetfulness, vague cramp-like pains in the bones and joints, a sense of life running out of control, of time shrinking and general feelings of craziness. Many of us go to bed tired, yet jolt awake at 2 or 3 am and remain sleepless for the rest of the night. For others, relationships are either falling apart, or not working as they did in the past. For some, friends, lovers and acquaintances are suddenly not around as they used to be. It is a time of making decisions and choices, facing and living one's own truth, taking responsibility for what we know and believe, while not judging others' reality as being good or bad, but merely the experience they feel appropriate for them at the time, while, with discernment, accepting that it may not be so for us. In fact, events are occurring to challenge our belief system, so that we move beyond the structure of beliefs that limit us. Visible and invisible worlds are merging, science and spirit are coming together.

We must become open, flexible, responsive, willing to die and let go of the past, reincarnate into a new life without a physical death. If we move with the accelerated energy of the 1990s life can be full of excitement. If not, we'll experience fear, panic, and the disintegration of life.

To live from the heart is the key.

Perhaps the pains of the changes moving across the face of the earth are no more than the labour contractions of the expectant mother. Maybe the opening of the ozone layer, the earth changes, and the fact that some animals are on the point of extinction, are not only to shake us awake and remind us of our responsibility as co-creators with God, but are also part of this birth, and meant to happen. For example, maybe some animals have fulfilled their time here and need to move on. Maybe the ozone layer is opening a window to other dimensions, and we too are being reminded that we have reached the end of a certain phase of evolution, and must now move forward into a different, more etheric body, a new and lighter consciousness. A death on this plane is a birth into another, and vice versa. Parents delight in a birth. They do not focus on the pains of labour, but plan for the future and the new life emerging. It is a time of joy and celebration.

Let us assume that the great Earth Mother on which we live knows exactly what she is doing; that she is initiating us into another form of life, and that the best way in which we can help is first to put our own lives in order, and second to focus on the positive outcome of the new life emerging instead of the critical period of the birth itself.

I am reminded of the story of the teacher who tears to shreds a map of the world and, thinking it an impossible task, gives it to a recalcitrant student to put together. Within ten minutes the boy is back, the task completed. Astounded, the teacher asks him how he did it. The boy replies: 'When I turned the pieces over, I found a torn-up man. I put him together, and when I looked at the other side the world was whole again.'

Babatunde Olatunji

FOR A BETTER WORLD: THE BEAT OF MY DRUM

Babatunde Olatunji, *the African Master of Drums, whose releases include 'Drums of Passion: The Beat' and 'Drums of Passion: The Invocation'. Founder of the Olatunji Center of African Culture in Harlem, New York, and in Washington DC. Received the 1986 Liberty Award from the New York Mayor. He says: '... rhythm is the soul of life; everything revolves around, in, and through that rhythm.'*

I am the drum, you are the drum, we are the drum.

I left Ajido, a small fishing village where I was born, with a *sakara*, a flat hand-drum made from goat skin stretched over a circular clay body, like the tambourine. I left to start on a journey to the New World by boat and to fulfil my scholarship at Morehouse College in Atlanta, Georgia. On arrival I soon discovered I was on a mission not only to destroy the myths, stereotyping, and ugly image of Africa, but also to bridge the gap that has existed between Africans at home and abroad. With the beat of my small drum I found I could reconcile, connect, and unite myself with my peers. Through that beat I discovered that rhythm is the soul of life; everything revolves around, in and through that rhythm.

With the beat of my drum I began to discover my inner strength and the capacity to understand that I am one with the men and women of all walks of life, of different shades and color, on different levels of consciousness.

With the beat of my drum I accepted the fact that we are all in the Father's mansion yet there are millions who remain in the basement of this mansion, who grope for the step that leads to the first floor and to equality.

With the beat of my drum the veil was lifted off my face and I could see the light and uniqueness of *Oyigiyigi* – God – in the faces and voices of those far and near.

With the beat of my drum I eliminate from my consciousness the fear that paralyzes the soul in all humankind, and I invoke exuberance, joy, the spirit of oneness, togetherness, and transformation as we dance.

With the beat of my drum I envision coming together with a unity of purpose: engaging ourselves in a global circle of drummers, men and women of goodwill engaged in the difficult task of building and rebuilding, of learning why we are here, who we are, whence we came and where we go. Learning from one another about service – the greatest and most divine word. From the rhythmic renditions of the sacred circle of global drummers we become the *Planet Drum* that will beat out rhythms of joy, celebrating and embracing all in reverence for life, reminding all concerned of the purpose for which each and every one is created, repeating over and over again that love is a lifetime process; that peace can only be watertight peace if there is peace among equals; that if the heaven shall fall it shall not fall on one shoulder; that if one is imprisoned, all people's freedom is threatened.

With the beat of my drum the spirit of the Gods will descend upon those who answer the clarion call to the service to free humankind of our inhumanity to each other.

With the beat of my drum I envision with the sounds of exhilarating rhythmic rendition from the *Planet Drum* of which we shall become, the message of life everlasting, lover supreme, which shall be fulfilled and demonstrated through all the people of God, soon to become that One Spirit that rules the universe.

PART TWO

Self, Family, and Society

Yoko Ono

RAINBOW
REVELATION

Yoko Ono, artist, poet, musician. Has paintings and sculptures in galleries and museums worldwide. Grammy Award Winner 1981 for Album of the Year with husband John Lennon for 'Double Fantasy'. Opened Strawberry Fields, a Garden of Peace in Central Park, in memory of John Lennon. She says: 'Bless you for your fear for it is a sign of wisdom. Do not hold yourself in fear. Transform the energy to flexibility and you will be free from what you fear.'

It was after the rain. I was looking out from my window. The buildings on the opposite side of the park were shining with a touch of pink in the evening light. There was a faint rainbow hanging in the park right in front of my eyes. I said to myself. 'Wait a minute, an arch is a segment of a circle and usually it has a support underneath it. Is there a support for a rainbow like the fertile ground that supports the trees? Is there a part of a rainbow we're not seeing? It could even be that a rainbow is a circle!' Then a tiny voice said to me. 'Yes, a rainbow is a circle, and more. You are just shown an inkling of a rainbow. Just like the best of you think and communicate in shorthand, things are shown to you in little bits. And you know why?' I heard myself say 'Why!' with an exclamation point. A perfect silence is what came back. Only the park was still shimmering in its full glow. The little voice started to whisper to me again, this time in what I call long hand. I kept writing it down as it came to me until it was about a hundred pages, and the sun started to rise from the window. This is its first page. I hope it will be of some use to you.

Bless you for your anger for it is a sign of rising energy. Direct not to your family, waste not on your enemy. Transform the energy to versatility and it will bring you prosperity.

Bless you for your sorrow for it is a sign of vulnerability. Share not with your family, direct not to yourself. Transform the energy to sympathy and it will bring you love.

Bless you for your greed for it is a sign of great capacity. Direct not to your family. Direct not to the world. Transform the energy to giving. Give as much as you wish to take, and you will receive satisfaction.

Bless you for your jealousy for it is a sign of empathy. Direct not to your family, direct not to your friends. Transform the energy to admiration and what you admire will become part of your life.

Bless you for your fear for it is a sign of wisdom. Do not hold yourself in fear. Transform the energy to flexibility and you will be free from what you fear.

Bless you for your poverty for it is a sign of great possibility. Do not hold poverty in your mind. Every drop of your generosity will come back in tenfold. Give as though you were a king, and you will receive a king's due.

Bless you for your search of direction for it is a sign of aspiration. Transform the energy to receptivity and the direction will come to you.

Bless you for the times you see evil. Evil is energy mishandled and it feeds on your support. Feed not and it will self-destruct. Shed light and it will cease to be.

Bless you for the times you feel no love. Open your heart to life anyway and in time you will find love in you.

Bless you, bless you, bless you. Bless you for what you are. You are a sea of goodness, sea of love. Count your blessings every day for they are your protection which stands between you and what you wish not. Count your curses and they will be a wall which stands between you and what you wish. The world has all that you need and you have the power to attract what you wish. Wish for health, wish for joy. Remember you are loved. Remember I love you.

His Holiness The Dalai Lama

THE GLOBAL COMMUNITY AND UNIVERSAL RESPONSIBILITY

His Holiness The Dalai Lama, exiled spiritual and temporal leader of Tibet, now leading his government-in-exile from India. Recipient of the 1989 Nobel Peace Prize. Author of many books on Buddhism; international and highly esteemed teacher. He says: 'To meet the challenge of our times, I believe that humanity must develop a greater sense of universal responsibility. Each of us must learn to work not just for our own individual self, family, or nation, but for the benefit of all mankind.'

As the twentieth century draws to a close, we human beings are witnessing our world growing smaller. The world, it seems, is becoming one community, one unit. Political and military alliances have created large multinational groups. Industry and international trade have produced a global economy. Worldwide communications are reducing ancient barriers of language and race. We are also being drawn together by the very serious problems we face: over-population, dwindling natural resources, and an environmental crisis. These threaten the very foundation of existence on this one small planet we share: its air, water, trees, and vast and beautiful number of life forms.

To meet the challenge of our times, I believe that humanity must develop a greater sense of universal responsibility. Each of us must learn to work not just for our own individual self, family, or nation, but for the benefit of all mankind. Universal responsibility is the real key to human survival. It is the best foundation for world peace, the equitable use of natural resources and, through concern for future generations, the proper care of the environment.

For some time I have been thinking about how to increase our sense of responsibility for others as well as the altruistic move from which it derives. I would like to offer my thoughts.

Whether we like it or not, we have all been born on this earth as part of one great human family. Whether we are rich or poor, educated or uneducated, belonging to one nation, religion, ideology or another, basically each of us is just a human being like everyone else. Like others, we desire happiness and do not want to suffer. Furthermore, we all have an equal right to avoid suffering and pursue happiness.

Today's world requires us to accept the oneness of humanity. In the past, isolated communities could afford to think of one another as fundamentally separate. Some could even exist in total isolation. But nowadays, whatever happens in one region of the world will eventually affect, through a chain reaction, peoples and places far away. Therefore, it is essential to treat each major problem, right from its inception, as a global concern. It is no longer possible to emphasize, without destructive repercussions, the national, racial, or ideological barriers which differentiate us. Within the context of our new interdependence, self-interest clearly lies in considering the interest of others.

I view this fact as a source of hope. The necessity for cooperation can only strengthen mankind. It will help us to recognize that the secure foundation upon which to build a new world order is not merely one of more comprehensive political and economic alliances, but that of each individual's belief in a genuine practice of love and compassion. For the future of mankind, for a better, happier, more stable and civilized world, we must all develop a sincere, warm-hearted feeling of brotherhood and sisterhood.

In Tibetan we have a saying: 'Many illnesses can be cured by one medicine: love and compassion.' Love and compassion are the ultimate source of human happiness. Our need for them lies at the very core of our identity. Unfortunately, however, they have for too long been omitted from many spheres of social interaction. Most often confined to family and home, their practice in public life is thought of as impractical, even naïve. This is tragic. In my view, the practice of compassion is not a symptom of unrealistic idealism. Rather, it is the most effective means to pursue one's own interest as well as that of others. To the extent that one is dependent on others, whether on the level of a nation, group or individual, the maintenance of their well-being is naturally in one's own interest as well.

The real source of compromise and cooperation lies in the practice of altruism. A mind committed to compassion is like an ever-full reservoir; a constant resource of energy, determination, and kindness. It is like a seed which, when cultivated, gives rise to many other good qualities, such as forgiveness, tolerance, inner strength, and the confidence to overcome fear and insecurity. It is like an elixir; capable of transmuting many unhappy situations into a beneficial outcome. Therefore, the expression of love and compassion should not be limited to one's friends and family. Nor is compassion just the responsibility of clergy, health care, or social workers. It is the necessary business of every sector of the human community.

When I consider the failure to cooperate in society, I can only believe that it stems from ignorance of our interdependent nature. Thinking of this, I am often moved by the example of small insects, such as bees.

Nature's law dictates that, in order to survive, bees must work together. As a result, they instinctively possess a sense of social responsibility. They have no constitution, no law, no police, no religion or moral training, but because of their nature they labor faithfully together. Occasionally they may fight, but in general, based on cooperation, the whole colony survives. We human beings have a constitution, laws, and a police force. We have religion, remarkable intelligence, and a heart with a great capacity to love. We have many extraordinary qualities, but in actual practice I think we are behind these small insects. In some regards I feel that we are poorer than the bees.

For instance, millions of people live together, all over the world, in large cities. Despite such proximity, many are lonely. Some, lacking even a single human being with whom to share their deepest feelings, live in a perpetual state of agitation. This is very sad. People are not like solitary animals who only associate in order to mate. If that was our character, why would we have to build such large towns and cities to begin with? Unfortunately, though we are social animals compelled to live together, we very much lack a sense of responsibility for our fellow human beings.

The most important field in which to sow the seed of greater altruism is, of course, international relations. In the past few years the world has changed dramatically. I think we would all agree that the collapse of communism in Eastern Europe and the end of the cold war have ushered in a new historical era. Ours has not only been the most painful period in human history – a time when, due to the vast increase in the destructive power of weapons, more people have suffered and died by violence than ever before – but it has also seen a penultimate competition between the fundamental ideologies that have always torn our community: those of force and the exercise of raw power versus the belief in freedom, pluralism, individual rights, and democracy. I believe that the results of this great competition are now clear. Though the good human spirit, the spirit of peace, freedom and democracy, may still face many forms of tyranny and evil, it is perfectly clear that the vast majority of people everywhere want it to triumph. Because of this, the tragedies of our time have not been entirely bad. They have, in fact, been the very means by which the human mind has been opened.

I feel that the peaceful revolutions of the last few years have taught us many great lessons. One is the value of truth. People don't like a person or system that bullies, cheats, and lies. These activities are essentially opposed to the human spirit. Therefore, even though those who practice deception and the use of force may gain considerable success in the short term, eventually they will be overthrown. On the other hand, everyone appreciates the truth. Respect for the truth is really in our blood. Moreover, truth is the best guarantor – the real foundation – of freedom and democracy. It doesn't matter if one is weak or strong, if one's cause has many or only a few adherents, the validity of the truth will still pertain.

A second great lesson from Eastern Europe has been that of peaceful change. In the past, enslaved people have always resorted to violence in their struggle to be free. Now, the peaceful revolutions following in the footsteps of Gandhi and Martin Luther King have given future generations a tremendous example of successful, non-violent change. When, in the future, the need arises to change society, our descendants can look back to this period of time as a paradigm for peaceful struggle; a real success story on an unprecedented scale, involving more than half a dozen nations and hundreds of millions of people. Moreover, these changes have shown that human nature at its most fundamental level not only desires freedom but peace as well.

Each day the news media reports incidents of terrorism, crime, or aggression. I have never been to a country where I did not find newspapers and news broadcasts featuring some tragic story of death or bloodshed. But the fact is that the overwhelming majority of the human race is not engaged in destructive behavior, they are instead engaged in acts of loving, caring, and sharing. Only a small number of the five billion people on this planet actually commit acts of violence.

Ultimately, it is important to explore both one's own motive as well as that of an opponent. There are many varieties of both violence and non-violence. External actions alone cannot differentiate them. If one's motive is negative, while the action one employs is smooth and gentle, then that, in a deeper sense, is very violent. Conversely, if a person has a sincere, positive motive which, due to circumstances requires harsh behavior to implement, he or she is essentially practicing non-violence. No matter what the case may be, a compassionate concern for the benefit of others – not oneself – is the sole justification for the use of force. The practice of genuine non-violence is something like an experiment on this planet. Its pursuit, based on love and understanding, is very sacred. If our experiment succeeds, it can open the way to a far more peaceful world in the twenty-first century.

Of course, the greatest source of violence in our world lies

in the waging of war and the existence of large military establishments. Whether for defensive or offensive purposes, these
vast powerful organizations have no other function than to kill
human beings. We should think carefully about the reality of
war. Most of us have been conditioned to see military action
as something exciting and glamorous – an opportunity for
men to prove their competence and courage. Because armies
are legal, we all feel that war is acceptable. Nobody feels that
war is criminal; no one thinks that acceptance of war is itself
a criminal attitude. In fact, we are brain-washed. War is not
glamorous or attractive. It is monstrous. Its very nature is one
of tragedy and suffering.

I believe that war is like a fire in the human community:
a fire whose fuel consists of live human beings. Actually,
modern warfare is primarily waged with different forms of
fire, but we are so conditioned to see it as thrilling that we
talk about this or that marvelous weapon as a remarkable
piece of technology without thinking that, if it works, its actual
result will be to burn people. When a war starts, it really does
resemble a fire. If the fire grows weak in one area or another,
the commanding general will order an additional division of
men to that sector, to renew it. That, in fact, is putting live
men on the fire. At that time however, nobody thinks about
the suffering of the individual soldiers. None of them wants to
die or be wounded. None of their loved ones want any harm
to come to them. If they are struck down or maimed for life, at
least five to ten other people – all close to them – will suffer
as well. If we were not confused we would all be horrified by
this tragedy.

Frankly, I myself, as a child, was attracted to the military. I
thought the uniforms were quite smart and guns were very
beautiful. But that is exactly how the seduction begins, by
playing a game that one day leads us into trouble. There
are plenty of exciting games to play and costumes to wear
for little children, other than those based on killing human
beings. I know some former soldiers who told me that when
they first shot another person they felt uncomfortable, but as
they continued to kill it became quite normal. In time anything
can be taken for granted in that way.

The quest for peace has been pursued by mankind throughout

history. Is it too optimistic to imagine that achieving peace may finally be within our reach? I do not believe that the quality of hatred in human beings has increased, only our ability to manifest it in vastly destructive weapons. On the other hand, I do believe that the tragic evidence of mass slaughter caused by such weapons in our century has given us the opportunity to control war. To do so it is clear we must disarm.

Of course, the immense dividend reaped from the cessation of arms production would provide a fantastic windfall for global development. Today roughly $1,000 billion is spent annually by the nations of the world on military upkeep. Even India spends roughly Rs.16,850 crores per year. Can you imagine how many hospital beds, schools, and homes that could fund? And, as I have said, the awesome amount of scarce resources governments must allot to their military budgets not only hinders the eradication of poverty, illiteracy and disease, but also requires the sacrifice of precious human intelligence. Our scientists are extremely bright. Why should their brilliance be wasted on such an unfortunate purpose when it could be turned to global development? The great deserts of the world – the Sahara, the Gobi, and the Australian outback – could be cultivated to increase food production and ease overcrowding. Many countries are facing a water crisis. New, less expensive methods of desalinization could be invented so that sea water would be rendered suitable for human consumption. Our planet is blessed with vast natural treasures. If we were only able to use them properly, beginning with the elimination of militarism and war, truly every human being could live a wealthy, well-cared-for life.

Naturally global peace cannot occur all at once. Given varying conditions around the world, the process would have to be incremental. But there is no reason why it cannot start on a regional basis and gradually spread from one continent to the next. As late as the 1950s and 60s people believed that war was an inevitable condition of mankind. The cold war, in particular, reinforced the notion that opposing political systems could only confront, not compete or coincide. This view, it is now clear, has diminished. Today people all over the globe are genuinely concerned about world peace. They are far less interested in propounding ideology and far more committed to coexistence. This is a very positive development.

For centuries many people have believed that human society could only be governed through an authoritarian structure employing rigid discipline. But of course humanity's innate desire is for freedom and democracy. These two forces have competed. Today the victor is clear. The emergence of non-violent 'People Power' movements have indisputably shown that the human race can neither tolerate nor function properly under tyrannical conditions. This recognition represents remarkable progress.

Another hopeful development lies in the growing compatibility between science and religion. Throughout the nineteenth century and for much of our own, many people experienced profound confusion from the conflict between these seemingly opposed world views. Today, the discoveries of physics, biology, and psychology have reached such a sophisticated level that many researchers are beginning to explore the most profound questions concerning the ultimate nature of both the universe and life. These same questions, of course, are of primary interest to religions. In particular, I believe that a new concept of mind and matter is emerging. Eastern civilization has engaged itself more with the mind; Western with matter. Now that the two have met, far more harmony may develop between the material and spiritual views on life.

Hope also lies in the rapid change in our attitude towards the earth. As little as ten or fifteen years ago we thoughtlessly consumed its resources, as if there was no end to them. Now, not only individuals but governments as well, are seeking a new ecological order. I often joke that the moon and stars look beautiful but if any of us tried to live there we would be miserable! Our planet, this blue planet, is the most delightful place for us. Its life is our life; its future, our future. And, though I do not believe that the earth itself is a sentient being, it does act as our mother. And like children we are dependent on her. Now nature herself – our mother – is telling her children to be sensible. In the face of global problems such as the deterioration of the ozone layer, individual organizations and nations are helpless. Unless we all work together no solution can be found. Our mother is teaching us universal responsibility.

I think it is safe to say, based on the lessons we have begun to learn, the next century will be more harmonious, less violent, more friendly. Compassion, the seed of peace, can flourish. I am very hopeful. At the same time, I believe that every individual has a responsibility to help guide our global family in the right direction. Mere good wishes are not sufficient; we must assume responsibility. Large human movements come from individual human initiatives. If we feel that we cannot have much of an effect, the next person may also feel the same way, and a great opportunity will be lost. On the other hand, simply by working to develop our own altruistic motive, each of us can inspire others.

I am sure that millions of honest, sincere people all over the world must already hold the views that I have mentioned here. Unfortunately, nobody listens to them. Although my voice may go unheard as well, I thought that I should try to speak on their behalf. Of course, some people may feel that the Dalai Lama is being presumptuous to write in this way! But since I received the Nobel Peace Prize, I felt I had a responsibility to do so. If I took the prize money and did nothing, it would appear that all the nice words I said in the past were only uttered to get the prize! But, in fact, now that I have received the Nobel Prize, I have to repay it by continuing to state these views that I have always expressed. I, for one, really do believe that individuals can make a difference in society. Because periods of change, such as the present, come so rarely in human history, it is up to each of us to use our time well for the creation of a happier world. For me, actually, the propagation of compassion, and thus peace through it, is part of my daily practice. And as a Buddhist monk I try in my daily practice to develop compassion – not just from a religious but also from a humanitarian point of view. I believe that as long as one is a human being, compassion is essential.

Joanna Macy

HARVESTING THE GIFTS OF OUR ANCESTORS

Joanna Macy PhD, teacher of Buddhism, General Systems Theory and Deep Ecology. Author of *Despair and Personal Power in the Nuclear Age* and *World as Lover, World as Self*, and co-author of *Thinking Like a Mountain: Toward a Council of All Beings*. Founder and Director of the Nuclear Guardianship Project. She says: 'They who loved and tended this Earth, bequeath you the strength and wisdom you will need now to do what must be done so their journey may continue.'

Our culture encloses us in a tiny compartment of time, increasingly cut off from past and future. But we can reclaim our birthright and inhabit broader reaches of time by sensing the companionship of those who have gone before. They are with us. Even as you read this page, your ancestors are present – in your curiosity or in the set of your jaw. When I lead the following visualization exercise in workshops, we stand and move to music – actually walking backward and then forward with eyes closed – but you can also do it standing still. Take at least half an hour.

From this present moment begin to move back in time – through the events and encounters of this day, this week, this month, this year . . . Walk back through the decades into your young adulthood, your adolescence, your childhood . . . Soon you are a baby in your mother's arms, now back in her womb and returning to the climactic point of this life's conception . . . But what lives in you did not begin then. Walk back into your parents, into their lives, then back into the wombs that bore them, back into your grandparents . . . Continue slowly back, into and through the nineteenth century, into ancestors whose names you no longer know but whose gestures and smiles live on in you . . . Keep moving back upstream in this river of life, back through the Industrial Revolution . . . back into simpler, harsher times marked by the seasons, back into the Middle Ages . . . Move back through times of plague and pilgrimage into the lives of ancestors with hands – like yours – that chiseled the stones of great cathedrals, and eyes – like yours – that tracked the movement of the stars . . . Keep going back, to the dawning of the civilizations we know, and enter the early, wandering times . . . the small bands in forest settlements, their feasts and rituals around the sacred fire, and their long marches in the ages of ice.

Back through the millennia you walk with them, to your beginnings in the heartland in Africa. And now, with the very first ones, you stand at the edge of the forest. Pause now, looking over the savannah. The journey of your people lies ahead. Walk forward on it now. Retrace your steps, returning through time. Each ancestor has a gift to bestow . . . Open your arms and hands to receive it, as you walk forward through the centuries.

They who passed on to you the texture of your skin, the shape of your back, the marrow in your bones, also have courage to bequeath, and stubbornness, and laughter. These gifts are yours for the taking.

Garner them as you come forward through the years to this present moment, this brink of time. They who loved and tended this Earth bequeath you the strength and wisdom you will need now to do what must be done so their journey may continue.

LISTENING TO THE BEINGS OF THE FUTURE

Just as the life that pulses in our bodies goes back to the beginnings of the Earth, so too does that heartbeat carry the pulse of those that come after. By the power of our imagination we can sense the future generations breathing with the rhythm of our own breath or feel them hovering like a cloud of witnesses. Sometimes I fancy that if I were to turn my head suddenly, I would glimpse them over my shoulder. They and their claim to life have become that real to me.

Given the power of the life that links us, it is plausible to me that these future generations want to lend us courage for what we do for their sake. As they look back across time to this critical period, when we are inflicting so much on our world that is and will be irremediable, I imagine they wish they could help and be heard. So I listen to them in my mind.

What I imagine hearing them say keeps me going. Sometimes it's just a whisper of 'thanks' when I crawl out of bed an hour early to finish a report, or squeeze in a late-night meeting with environmentalists. I hear them thanking my activist colleagues too, who also get tired and discouraged. Sometimes the comments of the future generations erupt unbidden. More than once I have been tempted to throw in the sponge on the Nuclear Guardianship Project because I lack organizational and technical skills. 'I'm no expert on radioactive wastes,' I mutter. 'It's not my job to store them. It's depressing and I'm tired and I have better things to do with my life.'

Then comes this presence at my shoulder, and I feel an almost physical nudge. 'Come on now. Just do what you can. This "poison fire" is going to be around for so long, help your people contain it while they still can.' And there's an edge of laughter in the words I imagine I hear. 'After all, you're the one who is alive now!'

So at gatherings and workshops we often begin with an evocation of the 'Beings of the Three Times.' We invite their presence at our deliberations. Calling first on beings of the past, we take a moment to speak their names out loud, spontaneously and at random – names of ancestors and teachers who came before us and cherished this Earth. Then we call out the names of those living now, with whom we work and share this time of danger. When we call on the beings of the future, however, there is silence – for we do not know their names.

Still, though they are faceless and nameless, we ask for a sense of their presence, so that we may be faithful to the work that must be done. For it is for their sake, too, that we work to restore our land.

Robert A. F. Thurman

A GLIMPSE OF SHAMBHALA

Robert A. F. Thurman (Tenzin Chotrag), Jey Tsong Khapa Professor of Indo-Tibetan Studies at Columbia University, New York. Author of, among others, *The Central Philosophy of Tibet*, and *Wisdom and Compassion: The Sacred Art of Tibet*. He is presently completing *The Politics of Enlightenment*. He says: 'The twenty-first century could be the time for us finally to find the way to live transcendentally, non-violently . . . democratically compassionately, and globally responsibly. No one can say that it is impossible.'

The *Time Machine Enlightenment Technology (Kalachakra-Buddha Tantra)* spread in India and Tibet toward the end of the first millennium CE, and states its origins as the teaching of the Buddha. The *Time Machine* literature contains a detailed prophecy about the future of the planet. It predicts that some time around now the entire planet comes under the control of a Big Brother, unified under oppressive, militaristic rule. At that time, the land of Shambhala, previously hidden, becomes visible to the rest of the world. Big Brother decides to conquer it but the Shambhala forces emerge with overwhelmingly superior technology and in one short battle remove Big Brother and his coterie of power. This ushers in a golden age on earth, during which individuals all over the globe find the conditions ideal for pursuing personal evolution and enlightenment. Science and technology develop unprecedented understanding and effective methods of improving the quality of life. The earth is restored and regains abundance. All beings are happy, healthy, growing intellectually and spiritually, living life meaningfully.

This prophecy is good for us because, though it has a base in spiritual tradition, it does not confirm the cosmic inferiority complex which, as Buckminster Fuller so perceptively said, many religious teachings tend to foster in human beings. Religious orthodoxies tend to say that the planet can't work, the mind can't work, life is essentially awful, sin-ridden or suffering-driven, and the only salvation is some alternative to life, a heavenly joy for the elect with the rest consigned to oblivion or worse. To counter this kind of doomsday depression, what we need to kindle our optimism is the vision of at least the possibility of a desirable outcome.

Whenever or whether the Shambhala prophecy will come true, if we look at the world today, in spite of appearances, a Big Brother culture of power is unquestionably in charge. Its basic thrust can be summarized in five trends:

1. It denies power to individuals and demands their allegiance, due to much promoted dangers of war, poverty, crime, addiction, disease, and dissension.
2. It devotes the bulk of the earth's resources to the bureaucracy, technology, and promotion of war as the top-priority human occupation.
3. It prevents or restricts individual access to real education to develop learning skills, precise information, and critical understanding, while promoting enforced allegiance to ideologies of ruling establishments.
4. It preserves a situation of scarcity of resources, keeping majority populations insecure through poverty, destitution, and despair. Meanwhile it actually destroys the resource base of the planet itself.
5. The power culture, in an ironic twist, makes it impossible for those on the top to lead meaningful or even enjoyable lives. The conscious and subconscious stresses of constantly doing everything to suppress, addict, sicken, and even kill huge numbers of other beings eventually makes these

people numb, miserable, ill-tempered, unable to enjoy even the simplest pleasures, and eventually sick. The system only exists due to the fact that specific leaders are able to float on the addictive idea of their own importance. To do so they must use intense psychological denial of what they are really doing to themselves and others. Thus, though there is no one Big Brother, these people collectively constitute a Big Brother Culture of Power, by continuing to live in the lie, as Vaclav Havel might say.

However, America is the land where the individual stood up first and most forcefully in any human society. Some aspects of the Native American societies were actually more individualistic than the Europeans who came to replace them. Tom Jefferson, Ben Franklin, and their colleagues took a cutting from the tree of the Iroquois confederacy, grafted it on the sapling of Anglo feistiness, and created a democratic government. They prevented any one person from being king so kingliness could be an aspect of every person. They created a system that would be forced to keep itself in check. That gave individuals, at least of one dominant group, unprecedented freedom to develop as they wished. It was imperfect by not extending to other groups. But it began a process.

Our biggest problem lies within our own ambivalence. We have our own imperial streak. We are on the brink of stalling our drive to freedom, disillusioning the freedom-seeking people of the globe. If we continue wishful thinking about the kind of order kept by the Saddams and Dengs; if we keep failing to imagine an organic order, peaceful and durable because emerging from the hearts of free people; in short, if we keep letting the power culture dominate our society, we will turn our own society over to the lie.

Though we started a democratic revolution we have not mustered the resources on our own to finish it. We have not understood the real principles of a politics of enlightenment. We have not understood the Buddha and his cool revolution. We have not digested the vision of Gandhi, his deep insight and sophisticated discipline of cool heroism. We are puzzled by His Holiness the Dalai Lama and do not fully recognize the practicality of his social and political vision.

We have not found spiritual support for our habitual optimism and have let it be co-opted by ultimately unsatisfactory materialism.

What we need is a politics of enlightenment, a politics to bring on a Shambhala of peace. The politics of enlightenment can be said to have five principles:

1. *Transcendental individualism*: This is the principle that each individual has an absolute right and destiny to reach the pinnacle of his or her own evolutionary potential in perfect enlightenment, which is loving bliss and secure happiness. All collectivities exist to support all their individuals to realize their transcendent goal. Each one of us is here for each other and all others are here for each of us.

2. *Nonviolent pacifism*: This is the principle that each one, including non-human beings, has an absolute right to his or her life, which is his or her evolutionary earning and potential for fruition. Each life is ultimately sacred and all arrangements must be based on that principle.

3. *Educational universalism*: This is the principle that all societies must be organized to place evolutionary development of individuals as their top priority. Thus, neither production, possessions or power, but the lifelong education of individuals toward the goal of complete enlightenment is the supreme purpose of all societies.

4. *Compassionate democratism*: This is the principle that human beings intuitively recognize their own extraordinary value, recognize its roots in the extraordinary value of every other being, and themselves know best their own deepest needs. From the enlightened perspective, a human being is a living being who has individually evolved for billions of years to reach a high degree of intelligence and sensitivity. Therefore, humans on the whole will make decisions that enhance their mutual welfare and will strive to take care of all others.

5. *Decentralistic globalism*: This is the principle that, while management of societies along enlightened principles is most effectively controlled at the local level, no locality can flourish disconnected from all others. Thus, local liberty and creativity is guaranteed by a shared sense of univer-

sal responsibility expressed as a conscious and constantly monitored delegation of authority for certain functions to a global organization, such as a future, truly representative United Nations Organization.

The implementation of these principles lies within our power. The revolutions of 1989 and 1991 are the result of massive numbers of individual people putting something like these principles into effect. The twenty-first century could be the time for us finally to find the way to live transcendentally, non-violently, evolutionarily, democratically compassionately, and globally responsibly. No one can say that it is impossible. And anyone can see that we have to make it so in order to survive. That is why this new way of life is welling up out of the earth right now, so to speak. We can call it New Jerusalem, New Heaven and New Earth, Vaikuntha, Utopia, Shambhala, or whatever. Let us understand its clear possibilities and look for ways to reach it. Let us pray for it. Let us work for it.

Micheline Flak

NEW WAYS IN EDUCATION

Micheline Flak PhD, *international yoga teacher and trainer of teachers bringing yoga into public schools. Founder of RYE: Recherche sur le Yoga dans l'Education, recognized by the French Ministry of Education. She says: 'When the mind changes its outlook, it meets with consciousness. Then it is capable of creation and able to communicate on deep levels with people and the environment.'*

Writing here in the company of renowned contributors
Whose thought and action have rightly won
Credit and respect from a worldwide audience;
Realizing besides that among those,
Some great souls have been duly trained
To maintain an enduring link
With the all-pervading Force that shapes and rules
The various forms of our life on Earth –
I take advantage of their joint presence
To forward an urgent plea in favour of
Brave new ways of Training
The coming generations.

Let me introduce myself through an original experience which has been practised in the French educational context for fifteen years. However humble and limited at the start, it has gained impetus here and abroad. This is not only due to the efforts of colleagues motivated as I was, but to the urge the experiment had sprung from.

One day at the end of the academic year, 1973, I was quietly sitting in my classroom expecting children about twelve years of age to come to their English lesson. I heard and watched them coming as usual. There were about thirty breathless, crimson-cheeked, howling youngsters male and female, hurling their satchels and crashing down on their seats. They were coming from a Physical Training period unaware of the instinctive relief they felt on sitting after their exertions in the stadium.

It may be hard for outsiders to imagine the difficulties a teacher commonly encounters while handling the disrupted energies of childish minds in order to bring them to focus on the day's topic! Pupils are somehow dipped from morning to evening into various subject-matters ranging from languages, maths, and biology to swimming, history, geography, art, and so on.

'How is it then that you suddenly felt the necessity of a transition?' people have often asked me, when I later had to explain how I started to teach differently. The only reply I can think of is the following: my former training in yoga had come to a mature point. I was giving vent to it on this professional ground for the first time. In the volcanic occurrence I have just described above, I felt perfectly calm and heard myself saying gently in the midst of turmoil:

'Now while sitting on your chairs, you are going to relax for a little while. Put your elbows on your table and your palms on your eyes. You may keep them open if you like. Or if you feel like it, place your head in your folded arms, as birds do in their nests when they go to sleep; you will be feeling very heavy on your chairs but you are not going to fall asleep, just listen to your teacher's voice (pause). Now listen to the tiny sound of your breath in your nose, like the sound of waves rising and unfurling on the beach in sunlight.'

Incredulous at first, they yielded to this proposition and I experienced the beauty of an inordinate silence. Not the absence of noise only, as when the pupils leave the classroom after a tiring day, but a living silence inhabited by the joyful blending of vigilance and receptivity in the group. It evoked the repose of a band of passengers enjoying a spell of fine weather after a storm at sea: here I was the captain of a ship just out of Cape Horn!

It was clear to me they were quite attentive and this is not only a most pleasurable state for anyone – young or old – but a very essential condition for effective learning. So I chose to prolong this period of well-being into an opportunity for acquiring knowledge.

I told them I was going to read them the lesson. I would leave a silence after every sentence. They would just have to repeat each one mentally during the blank. I did it. I felt they were working inside their heads. Then I announced that in the same special manner, I would ask questions. They would answer these if they wished, in a silent manner still. I did it as planned. I could perceive the fine work they were doing while they sat immobile with closed eyes. Then I said:

'Now, it's very nice. Let's see! Feel your feet on the floor; feel you're here in Paris, in your school, in your own classroom. I am going to repeat the same questions again. This time you will enjoy answering them aloud. So hold up your hands, if you feel like it.'

And so they did! I saw a host of fingers up. Everybody wanted to participate. That was a moment of grace, when enthusiasm assumed the harmonious form it may take in innocence, when every learner becomes aware both of the thing learnt and of the process of learning. Then the common purpose is achieved in joy.

We were all impressed by this new state of being together between desks and chairs. The next class the children asked for it again. They realized they had made good progress. I told my colleagues about the experiment. A lot of them tried it in turn on the basis of their own practice of yoga – with the same success.

At last some tutors instead of shouting 'Pay attention!' 'Be careful!' could give their pupils *the means* to become attentive and careful.

Throughout repeated attempts it became clear that this research on yoga at school was like a river meeting other rivers. Various movements aiming at better education have since then come to join their efforts with ours in order to promote new educational values.

School is the archetypal place where the process of being civilized is enacted day after day in every country. It is obvious that teachers have to acquire and maintain a high level of academic efficiency; but this didactic purpose should be made to unite with methods of self-development. Knowledge cannot be confined to the handing over of masses of information. All the facts and data which are necessary for a professional – whether an executive, an employee, a politician, or an engineer – may be reached easily from computers, books, videos or various such sources.

Just as a library is a bank where you can borrow all you need to know about every subject, the use which is to be made of such knowledge depends upon the quality of the readers. Who are they and what are they going to do, once they leave the institution? We have the answer to that query when we understand that the real aim of education is plumbing the being itself to unfold its full potential. When the mind changes its outlook it meets with consciousness. Then it is capable of creation and able to communicate on deep levels with people and the environment. Then an individual becomes aware of his real needs and so becomes responsible for his own learning. The manifold eyes of science, literature, art and philosophy, useful as they are, seem less important than one speck of such self-knowledge.

Let us hope that such values will be transmitted at the speed of light through reformed educational systems, but above all through reformed patterns in the being of educators and students alike.

John Bradshaw

THE FAMILY

John Bradshaw MA, theologian, educator, counsellor. Author of *Bradshaw On: The Family* (based on his US television series), *Healing the Shame that Binds You*, and bestseller *Homecoming: Reclaiming and Championing Your Inner Child*. He says: 'Families, which once bonded on the basis of survival and work apprentice systems, must learn new skills which lead to emotional intimacy.'

The war crime trials which were held at Nuremburg, marked the end of an era.* Eichmann and Hess pleaded innocent on the basis of obedience to authority. They argued that they were not *personally* guilty – the guilt belonged to those giving the orders. Eichmann listened to the most moving accounts of his heinous brutality without the slightest trace of emotion. Yet he blushed with embarrassment when it was pointed out that he forgot to stand up when the verdict was read. This blind obedience and the repression of emotion were normal products of the strict authoritarian German family in which these men were raised.

A decade earlier, Caroline Playne had argued that, because

* Hess was sentenced to life imprisonment at the Nuremburg Trials. Eichmann was not present at the Nuremburg Trials, but was subsequently traced, tried and hanged for crimes against humanity in 1962.

of this rigid authoritarian structure in the German family, the Germans would have a hard time with the democracy of the Weimer Republic.

When we look at the German family of Hitler's era, it was an extreme caricature of the family rules that have dominated the Western world for centuries. This is why Erik Erikson warned: 'It is our task to recognize that the black miracle of Nazism was only the German version . . . of a universal contemporary potential.' In other words, Nazism is a potential in all Western nations because the Western rules which govern family life embody the same tenets – obedience without content, and the repression of emotion. These tenets are based on the deeper underlying assumption that parents *own* children and have all power over them. Such an assumption justifies physical abuse and often leads to incest. We are only now coming to see how widespread the practice of battering and incest have been.

The war crime trials at Nuremburg evoked what was called the natural law, an instinct-based individual conscience. This law, it was argued, supersedes any form of blind obedience.

After Nuremburg, it was clear that the Western family rules had an inherent potential toward cruelty and a group obsession with conformity. Theologians of all persuasions began to challenge the tenets of blind obedience and the repression of emotion.

Other phenomena pointed to the limitations and obstructive power of the Western family rules. One such phenomenon is our expanded awareness of the nature of addiction. According to Dr Pat Carnes at Golden Valley, there are presently 131 million addicts in the US. These statistics include addictions like eating, starving, vomiting, gambling, working, buying, loving, and the rituals acted out in sexual addiction. All addictions are rooted in what I've called toxic shame. Toxic shame is the feeling of being flawed and defective as a human person. Unlike guilt which is about actions that transgress our norms of value, toxic shame is about our personal being. Guilt says: 'I made a mistake', while toxic shame says: 'I am a mistake.' Toxic shame is fostered by norms which measure us, especially our sense of worth. Toxic shame is covered up by perfectionism, power, control, judgement, criticism, and blame. And these are the very qualities spawned by blind obedience.

Our massive addictions are abortive attempts to feel good and to transcend toxic shame. They are the only way a numbed-out person can find in order to feel. The *numbed-out* state of being is a direct result of the repression of emotion. In fact, toxic shame has been called the 'master emotion' since it is commonplace to shame all feelings in our Western model of parenting. Anger is one of the seven deadly sins; sadness is for the weak; fear is the result of a wimpy kind of childish immaturity; and joy must not be enjoyed since there are starving children in Latin America.

In short, the family rules we've inherited are directly shaming. They are the foundation and training-ground for addiction.

The good news is that, since Nuremburg, we are moving into a new state of consciousness. Like all evolutions in consciousness, we are struggling with the new forms that must be created. This is especially true of the family. The indissolubility of marriage has been challenged by serial monogamy. Many children now run away when their family abuse is intolerable. Blended marriages demand new skills in communication, emotional expression, getting one's needs met, and conflict resolution. We are realizing how emotionally endarkened our past has been, that we have truly been emotional primitives.

Families, which once bonded on the basis of survival and work apprentice systems, must learn new skills which lead to emotional intimacy. Emotional intimacy is the basic need of the family of the future.

The very recent advent of systems-thinking has had a major impact on our understanding of families as bonded units of overt and covert interaction. Like a mobile, a distress in one member of the family affects all other family members. This awareness is forcing us to discover new ways of forming social unity which will lead to greater individuality. Our emotions are no longer seen as weakness. They are part of our basic human power. Our anger is our strength; our sadness is our ability to finish the past in order to have full energy for the present; our fear is our discernment and wisdom; our joy is our ability to respond, our capacity to celebrate, our embracing of exuberance.

Families of the future may well be based on twenty-five year contracts which are open-ended and renewable. In that form, a couple can decide on a commitment to raise a family with a chosen number of children. They can participate in the creation of new life, while retaining the option to personally move on when their task is finished. My guess is that this form of marriage would be more durable and that the divorce rate would decrease.

All in all it is the worst of times and the best of times. In spite of all the dreary statistics about the family, never before in the history of humankind has there been a greater opportunity for family love based on true intimacy. I honestly believe that we are standing on the foundations which will open up an era of self-actualization and interpersonal co-creation – the likes of which we've never known. All transitions are difficult. We are in the open air between trapeze bars. The transition offers us an evolution of consciousness. Like all previous evolutions, growth and expansion are fraught with pain. But without pain there is no gain. We must all 'take the current where it serves, else lose our venture.'

Serge Beddington-Behrens

FROM VICTIMHOOD TO EMPOWERMENT

Serge Beddington-Behrens
PhD, psychotherapist, educator and
international seminar leader. Author of
Towards a Sacred Psychology. He says:
'We too can learn that it is possible
not to allow our spirit to be broken,
and that even in the middle of great
despair and crisis we can discover
a place deep within which is totally
beautiful, pure and powerful and
which is never victimized – it never
has been and never will be.'

> We do not become enlightened by imagining figures of light but
> by making the darkness conscious.
>
> Carl Jung

Tomorrow is created by how we live today, just as today is
influenced by how we lived yesterday. But if 'old agendas'
still tug at us and pull us back by darkening our perceptions,
then we can be hindered from moving ahead with proper
clarity and laying the foundation stones of a more humane
and balanced world.

The need to return – to acknowledge our old agendas – is
something which, in our zeal to move forward into a new
millennium, we often tend to dismiss. We are reminded by
the spiritual teachers that we are entering a New Age, and that
a new humanity is gradually being born. We are told we must

begin to wake up to deeper understanding and learn to become loving and peaceful. But it is not always made clear how we should deal with those parts of us which resist such advice – which refuse to move ahead – and which are still fixated into ways of being that seem to look backwards into some of the more endarkened and musty corridors of our often conflicting past. It seems easier simply to ignore these corridors than to enter into them.

However, I do not believe that we can ignore these parts and pretend they are not there, for we cannot grow beyond our past until we have understood, integrated and transformed it – that is, until we have 'brought it up' with us into our present. Only then can it work with us, as an ally, as opposed to against us, as an enemy. We cannot create a more workable world for ourselves and our children by ignoring or bypassing some of those old ghosts which still haunt us in the deep unconscious.

This seems to me quite appropriate. For obstacles can, and often do, make us grow taller as we tussle with them. Many of the old wisdom traditions emphasize this and inform us that the adversarial forces are yet another of God's many faces! St George's dragon, after all, was a great ally with its fire-breathing capabilities that evoked the most courageous and noble parts of him to come forward in order to defeat (transform) it. Evolutionarily speaking, then, the challenges which our resistances offer may be seen as helping spur our human and planetary unfoldment. 'Thank God,' wrote Christopher Fry in *A Sleep of Prisoners*, 'The time has come/When wrong comes up to meet us/Never to leave us 'til we take the longest stride of soul man ever took . . . The enterprise/Is exploration unto God.'

Among the many ghosts that are coming up to haunt us at this time is one which lies behind much of the pain and conflict in our world and which is present in a thousand guises. We call it victim consciousness. If we are to move forward and claim our humanity, then surely we need to recognize this for what it is and find ways to disengage ourselves from its hold over us?

The fact that victim consciousness is such an issue today is not all that surprising considering how much of our past history has been filled with the enacting of savage rituals of victimization – butchery and slaughter, war and martyrdom on a vast scale – and how little, thus far, we have managed to heal our ancient wounds or consciously activate our higher evolutionary potential. As a result, painful memories of helplessness in the face of powerful destructive forces still flourish in our collective unconscious. And, in accordance with the dictum 'As within, so without', so these are consequently manifested in our lives. The river of victimization has a multitude of tributaries; the more we learn to reduce its hold over us, the more opportunity there will be for many other human ills to evaporate. While the victim factor is naturally not responsible for *all* human suffering, it nonetheless plays a significant part in promoting much surplus pain and destruction.

At its root, I see victim consciousness as a symptom of our feeling separate from life – from ourselves, from other people – which in turn leads to an inability to trust life, consequently making us feel helpless in certain situations. Being a victim is a state of mind where we feel no sense of being the cause of the matter but rather experience ourselves as being at the mercy of our outer circumstances. In those areas of our lives where this is most prevalent (such as relationships/the State/parents/illness) we feel powerless to do anything to change what is happening. We tend to give our power away, abnegating all responsibility for determining the course of our lives to forces outside of ourselves and, unconsciously or consciously, imbuing those forces with the power to hurt us in some way. In so doing the victim creates a space for the victimizers – those forces which would crush and suppress – to flourish.

The victim is someone who has not yet discovered his or her essential 'innerness', that is, has not yet claimed ownership of their 'Kingly' or 'Queenly' energy – that inner power which, when tapped, opens up a deeper landscape within us. This allows us to feel secure in ourselves and at home in the world. The typical victim does not have any such sense of belongingness and consequently feels moved to derive his well-being from outside himself, with the result that he is forever dependent upon favourable outer circumstances. If the tides of life flow in a contrary direction, victim consciousness will result and the person concerned will feel hard done by.

'Poor me', the victim will say, 'look at how the world has treated me!'

What all victims have in common is that they never take responsibility for what happens to them. It is never their fault – always someone or something else's! And the price paid in terms of balance and harmony in our world is very great, for not only is victim consciousness highly contagious but it also prevents our deeper humanity from emerging. For example, if we happen to be old, poor, starving, small, gay, ugly, have cancer, AIDS, or a skin colour other than white (to name but a few categories), we tumble into an automatic, ready-made victim-coffin, in which many people lie throughout their lives, never managing to climb out of it. After all, it is easier to 'breathe in' other people's perceptions of us and to 'take them on board' than find out who we really are.

Victim consciousness fades the more we take a stand for those life-principles which give rise to genuine inner wealth, allowing us to operate in the world with more love and wisdom. Learning to honour ourselves permits us to feel more whole and when we feel this way we can then appreciate others. It is a state of empowerment. And this is essentially what all the great liberation movements in the world are about – people beginning to put the crown on their inner monarch and claiming their true inheritance, people choosing to rise up and push the nails up out of their coffins, people saying 'Yes' to those forces which build, heal and transform, and 'No' to those which attempt to reduce, limit and disinherit the human spirit. We must never forget that it was this kind of collective force that eventually brought down the Berlin wall; or that it was the blacks taking a stand to proclaim their beauty and their humanity which not only ended slavery and nearly put a black President into power in America, but is currently threatening the very roots of apartheid (the apotheosis of victim-consciousness).

This new kind of power-stand may be summed up in the following remarks by a gay man: 'I don't have to feel antagonistic to those who make me wrong or put me down. The darkness is in their gaze not mine. I realize that I am susceptible to that darkness only if I do not honour myself, only if I do not learn to love and appreciate my own humanity and validate my own uniqueness. If I do this, I feel strong and may touch my sacred depths. When I do this, nothing and nobody can harm me.'

Is there a way, then, that those very victimizing forces which at one level threaten to 'enfeeble' us, can also serve to empower and enhance us? I believe the answer is Yes. It is so painful to feel the victim, and so ennobling to be in touch with our inner strength, that there is surely a part in each of us pulling us towards discovering how to make that inner shift, how to ignite our inner royalty so it may burn within us as a bright and noble flame. People who have learnt to do this (often out of necessity) are wonderful to be around; they shine, and their light seems to reflect the contents of that other reality to which they have opened up – filled with joy and love and laughter and freshness and vision and inspiration – and which gives no space for victim consciousness.

What also helps this kind of awakening is the realization of how urgent our current situation is. We must stop deceiving ourselves; we must have the courage to look at the worst, both in ourselves and out in the world, not as victims but as spiritual warriors. There are great horrors that prevail, there is enormous cruelty, much barbarism, much unconsciousness in our world – and the antidote is a higher consciousness which we must bring forth within us. Simply eradicating tyrants or winning wars will not of itself change the victim pattern or prevent it from re-emerging. It needs to be accompanied by inner transformation.

One friend of mine who is dying of AIDS recently described himself as being 'more alive now, more conscious of the beauty of life and how much love there is, than before I had the disease and took life for granted.' Similarly, no one could be less a victim than my old paralyzed friend Charles who, for most of his life, has had no feeling or movement from the neck down. Despite his horrific limitations, he has not an iota of self-pity, retains a cheerful spirit, has helped a great many people through his wise counselling, continuing to support himself financially by dictating books from his horizontal position. No one could be less of a victim than the young Canadian Terry Fox who, with cancer and one wooden leg, walked across Canada raising money for cancer research before eventually dying.

What all these people share is the fact that, despite adverse circumstances, they chose to make their humanity come more alive and in doing so became greater human beings: greater of heart, greater of spirit, greater of soul. We too can learn that it is possible not to allow our spirit to be broken, and that even in the middle of great despair and crisis we can discover a place deep within which is totally beautiful, pure and powerful and which is never victimized – it never has been and never will be. It is this place which must be claimed, not just once but every day, over and over again, and often in the face of great opposition. As my friend Charles has said: 'Sometimes the sun shines and sometimes it doesn't, but you just get on with your life. Quietly. You don't go in for heroics; you are honest with yourself; you give up pretending. Never stop honouring every single part of life, everything that happens to you and never stop being grateful for the little things. If you do this, life is always a blessing.'

Vernon Kitabu Turner

ONE PEOPLE

Vernon Kitabu Turner, Zen practitioner, martial artist and journalist. Author of poetry books *Kung Fu: The Master*, *The Secret of Freedom*, and *Lovesong*. To be published: *The Art of Dancing to No-Music*. He says: 'For centuries the spirit of God, through the Church, sustained black people when there was no other hope. In the coming age may we strive to be vessels of that spirit.'

For centuries the spirit of black people in America was crushed by slavery, followed by a powerless freedom, but most of all by the denial of our humanity. Black people have always been treated as outsiders, never fully welcomed into the human race. It is hard to feel good about ourselves, our ideas, and our relationship to the world when we are aware that people routinely assume we are ignorant or inferior by nature. To be black is to fight two wars simultaneously. We have to struggle to believe in ourselves despite centuries of negative imaging, while also fighting to be recognized as viable, individual human beings.

Unless we can transcend the limiting concept of race we cannot understand what it means to be fully human. In the quest to realize who we are we cannot hold to the concept of race and embrace the Universal at the same time. Those who try are living a delusion. Black men and women will find their true place in the world, not through seeking greater cultural identity with Africa, but in the way all humankind must, by passing through the barrier of our sentient nature to embrace the God within. Then truth will be experienced. The journey starts with loving ourselves. As we black people learn to love ourselves as creations of God then we must also transcend the past and current politics to love all equally. When a human begins the spiritual journey, the concept of race must be burnt to ashes. Race has no value to God.

Generally we give only lip service to the thought of a power greater than ourselves. We approach that which is spiritual through the safety of the intellect, choosing to discuss and argue beliefs rather than surrender ourselves to the transformation inherent within those beliefs. Yet the improvement of society cannot be separated from the search for self. For society is simply a collection of beings. If the individuals within the group are out of harmony with their own beingness, how can they be harmonious with each other?

The path to God is through self-surrender. This is a frightening choice as we fear to lose our identity. Yet, by letting go, we can experience a far greater reality. By letting go of the limited self, we merge into a oneness and experience a universal love. This love is more than an emotion. It is an incomprehensible and unstoppable power. For one loving and focused person can do more than an army to change the world. The lives of Mahatma Gandhi and Martin Luther King both demonstrate the incredible force generated by selfless love.

To improve our world we need to discover our roots – not the original home of our ancestors but the original home of our soul. Black people, long persecuted and scorned for an inescapable difference, must transcend all desire for revenge, purging ourselves of anger. In accepting our suffering we can heal. Like the Christ who took the scorn and torment the world heaped upon him and only gave endless love in return, we can spiritualize our suffering so that we can rise above it.

The world needs people who can draw the love of God through their own hearts and minds and freely give it to all. For centuries the spirit of God, through the Church, sustained black people when there was no other hope. In the coming age may we strive to be vessels of that spirit. May our black skin be seen as a God-given robe. May our once defiant fist raised against the sky become but a single finger pointing the way to love.

Allen Ginsberg

COSMOPOLITAN GREETINGS

Allen Ginsberg, poet. Author of *Collected Poems 1947–1980, White Shroud Poems 1980–1985*, and *Howl*. Distinguished Professor at Brooklyn College, co-founder of the Jack Kerouac School of Disembodied Poetics at Naropa Institute, Colorado. He says: 'How do you *live* with the death of the planet, rather than how do you die with it? That seems to be the turning of the spirit ... To look at it steadily without hope or fear.'

Stand up against governments, against God.
Stay irresponsible.
Say only what we know and imagine.
Absolutes are Coercion.
Change is absolute.
Ordinary mind includes eternal perceptions.
Observe what's vivid.
Notice what you notice.
Catch yourself thinking.
Vividness is self-selecting.
If we don't show anyone, we're free to write anything.
Remember the future.
Freedom costs little in the US.
Advise only myself.
Don't drink yourself to death.
Two molecules clanking against each other require an observer

to become scientific data.
The measuring instrument determines the appearance of the
phenomenal world (after Einstein).
The universe is subjective.
Walt Whitman celebrated Person.
We are observer, measuring instrument, eye, subject, Person.
Universe is Person.
Inside skull is vast as outside skull.
Who's there in between thoughts?
Mind is outer space.
What do we say to ourselves in bed in the dark, making
no sound?
'First thought, best thought.'
Mind is shapely, Art is shapely.
Maximum information, minimum number of syllables.
Syntax condensed, sound is solid.
Intense fragments of spoken idiom, best.
Move with rhythm, roll with vowels.
Consonants around vowels make sense.
Savor vowels, appreciate consonants.
Subject is known by what she sees.
Others can measure their vision by what we see.
Candor ends paranoia.

POETRY FOR THE NEXT SOCIETY

Ordinary mind includes eternal perceptions. So how do you get
to those eternal perceptions? The slogan would be: *observe
what's vivid*, and the way of doing that would be to *notice
what you notice*, and the way you notice what you notice is
to *catch yourself thinking*.

And the question is, how do you know what's vivid? How
do you choose what's vivid? And the answer to that, another
slogan: *Vividness is self-selecting*. If it's vivid, it's vivid; otherwise you wouldn't notice it. *if we don't show anyone, we're free
to write anything*; that deals with the questions of shame and
showing your parents your confessions or your perceptions
that are vivid.

There is a further element of subjectivity. *Two molecules
clanking against each other require an observer to become scientific
data*: so in that sense there is no objective history and *the*

measuring instrument determines the appearance of the phenom-enal world after Einstein. Thus, *the universe is subjective.* Thus, *Walt Whitman celebrated Person.* We, ourselves, are the observer or the measuring instrument, 'I,' the subject, the person; so, our *Universe is Person: Inside skull, vast as outside skull.* From Chögyam Trungpa to determine what's vivid. *First thought, best thought.*

From Kerouac, *If the mind is shapely the art will be shapely,* this in terms of spontaneous recognition of our own minds for form.

Maximum information, minimum number of syllables. Syntax condensed, sound is solid, so the poet might – as the rapper – *Savor vowels, appreciate consonants.*

Subject is known by what she sees and *Others can measure their vision by what we see.*

So the social function of this accumulation of slogans returns to Whitman's measure, Candor, which he hoped would be the standard for future poets and orators. *Candor ends paranoia.*

In 1967 there was a convocation in London. R. D. Laing brought a number of scholars and thinkers together in 'The Dialectics of Liberation', and my speech on 'Consciousness and Practical Action' of July 27, 1967, at 3.30 pm in the Roundhouse in London contained the following page:

> This week I've been impressed more than anything else by Gregory Bateson's talking about the scientifical, apocalyptic aspect of the anxiety syndrome we suffer from. His thesis concerned the carbon dioxide layer over the planet. Is there anybody that has not heard of that? R. D. Laing gave a summary and then I checked with Bateson. He said that given the present rate of infusion into the atmosphere of carbon dioxide, the mammalian, human aspect of the planet had a half-life of ten to thirty years. In that time, the opaque, carbon dioxide layer over the atmosphere which emits heat but doesn't let it bounce out would build up, the temperature rising, in a process that would be irreversible after thirty years. The polar icecaps melt, and the continents inundated with 400 feet of water (this being only one of the threats to the human mammal). Though there was actually a charming, cheerful aspect, Gregory Bateson also being an expert on porpoises. He pointed out that porpoises have a nervous system as complex as ours, their language and brains complicated as well, and

most of their language concerns personal relations, that's what porpoises discuss all the time. So if there is 400 feet of water over the continents, it will leave more room for the porpoises. So, ultimately, the universe doesn't need our exhortative yowling for the continuance of its own life, like Porpoise Power.

That was 1967. As Ezra Pound said, it takes a geologic era for an idea to penetrate the public's head, but with the accumulated evidence of our own senses there seems in this last year or two to have precipitated in public consciousness and awareness the fact that our planet itself has AIDS, with a prognosis not much different from AIDS prognosis. Lesions in the surface of the planet: desertification, deforestation, poisoning of garbage dumps; pulmonary ills: of ozone layer depletion, acid rain, greenhouse effect (that Bateson described in great detail in 1967). From a poetic point of view, the four poetic elements, earth, air, fire and water, are tainted. Earth with desertification, industrial poisoning, primarily petrochemical and nuclear. The Air, as you know, has pulmonary problems with the atmosphere. The Water: eutrophication of lakes omnipresent in the landmasses, and the soiling of the oceans. And as for Fire: the tainting of the source of energy, both petrochemical and nuclear; our source of fire, or energy, has been, is, questionable, poisonous.

So what we have is a dominance over nature, as everybody's realized, both capitalist and communist, a rape of nature and her subjugation on the part of White Intellectuality, European and American mass production, Hyperrationalization, or what Blake would call the Urizenic element of our intellectuality. Not sweet science but a poisonous science. I've been recently reading W. E. B. Du Bois and noted for our own situation one interesting comment he made:

> What the black laborer needs is careful personal guidance, group leadership from men with hearts in their bosoms to train them to foresight, carefulness and honesty, nor does it require any fine-spun theories of racial differences to prove the necessity of such group training after the brains of the race have been knocked out by 250 years of assiduous education and submission, carelessness and stealing. After emancipation it was the plain duty of someone to assume this group leadership and training of the negro laborer. I will not stop here to inquire whose duty it was,

whether it was the white, ex-master that had profited by unpaid toil or the Northern philanthropist whose persistence brought on the crisis or the national government whose edict freed the bondsman. I will not stop to ask whose duty it was, but I insist it was the duty of someone to see that these workmen were not left alone and unguided, without capital, without land, without skills, without economic organization, without even the bold protection of law, order and decency. Left in a great land, not to settle down to slow and careful internal development, but destined to be thrown almost immediately into relentless and sharp competition with the best of modern workingmen, under an economic system where every participant is fighting for himself and too often utterly regardless of the rights or welfare of his neighbor.

So, the karmic shadow of the situation that W.E.B. Du Bois wrote about in his beautiful Melvillean prose casts its shade on our own decade: this year's economic crisis in NY schools where there were strikes i n the past week. Du Bois' *Souls of Black Folk* was published in 1903. The great insight of that book was his statement that the color line was one of the major or *the* major problem of the twentieth century in America and internationally. He amended that sixty years later in a Preface (1963) – writing:

> So perhaps I might end this retrospect simply by saying I still think today, as yesterday, that the color line is a great problem of this century, but today I see more clearly than yesterday that back of the problem of race and color lies a greater problem which both obscures and implements it and that is the fact that so many civilized persons are willing to live in comfort, even if the price of this is the poverty, ignorance and disease of the majority of their fellow men. And that to maintain this privilege men have waged war until today war becomes universal and continuous, and the excuse for this war, largely, continues to be color and race.

I thought that those ideas were perhaps too polemical twenty or thirty years ago, but they seem to make common sense now, to me, more than ever before, and it seems to me, as I said, that the karmic shadow of slavery and serfdom in the American cities is now more and more evident, the playing out of that earlier karma, which I don't think I realized, as a white and intelligent and sensitive, soulful poet interested in alternative cultures and my own gay alternative culture, among others. But it comes to me now as I'm getting older to be more and more a substantial insight than most of us in our dominant culture have acknowledged to ourselves, and I think the problem there, or at least with me, was the fear of recognition of that enormous grief and enormous distortion of our own presumptions and the distortion of history as it was taught to us. The fear that in looking into the pit we will find that the problem is too great for us to resolve.

If my proposition, which I borrowed from Jean-Claude Van Itallie, that the planet itself has AIDS, is anywhere near useful as a way of thinking about it, or that the four elements have been tainted, we would have to begin to look at the relation between our attack on nature and the dominance of white hyperintellectuality or hyperrationalization or hyperscientism on other cultures. If it is something that is insoluble, we should look at it without denial. I have been working with Alcoholics Anonymous concepts lately, because of family problems, and notice that one of the great problems both with AIDS, people dealing with AIDS, and people dealing with addiction, petrochemical or power or alcohol or drugs, has been this element of denial, of unwillingness to look steadily at the problem and acknowledge that it may not be so easy to solve, the turning around of thought. How do you live with AIDS? How do you *live* with the death of the planet, rather than how do you die with it. That seems to be the turning of the spirit. How do you *live*? . . . We have the notion of people *living* with AIDS, rather than people *dying* of AIDS, negatively, pessimistically, suffering it out. Some acknowledgement of the problem might help either resolve it or give us a way of cohabiting with our disease. To look at it steadily without hope or fear; and I think that the emergence of Buddhist thought and Buddhist dharma and meditation has been part of that movement in the twentieth century toward the recognition of . . . the conditioning of our consciousness and the need to transcend the forms of thought that we were used to as kids in high school. For your own generation these may be sort of obvious and they are obvious, I think. But I don't know if the grief of our situation, as whites, blacks or people of color, or gays, or women, or Jews or Nuyoricans, I don't think that the grief of that feeling of being left alone, hopeless, has yet been realized. And so I would guess that the poetry of the future would particularize the local evidence of our grief, not programmatically, but as it rises in us spontaneously, in the old tasks of poetry to reflect the consciousness and feelings of the individual – that won't change. I think, however, that given the massive destruction of our environment and the destruction of human trust that we've all experienced just walking the streets of New York, it has not yet been expressed in terms of sincerity of fear and grief, and I think that that would be the task of the poet.

So I want to end with recounting a dream I had, in which I had a long conversation with Henry Kissinger. We met and I said: 'The trouble with you is, the very tone of your voice is so heavy and authoritative, that there is this element of intimidation and force and violence in it, so that people are afraid even to argue with you, you seem to know everything. Or the assumption is that you know everything, that you "wrote the book," as you said, on Nuclear Determination and nobody knows any more than you, and so they can't have a conversation with you. And, yes, you may win your point but you win it by force, and as war is an extension of politics or politics is an extension of war, so your very tone of voice, your conversation and your discourse, is an extension of violence. And you can never create peace through violence, it's a contradiction in terms.' So he replied, 'Well, this insight may be true but I would like to tell you what my secret plan was.' And I said, 'Well, what was your secret plan?' And he said, 'My secret plan was to ensure that everybody in the world on reaching the age of two was to be empowered with trust by some parent or adult or authority, and was given response of feeling, trust, and support; this was my secret plan all along. I was trying to create those conditions.' So I said, 'Well, geeze, why didn't you say so? I never would have guessed. Why don't you write a little essay about it and I'll write a preface to give it some credibility.'

Rabbi Zalman Schachter-Shalomi

FROM AGING TO SAGING

Zalman Schachter-Shalomi, Rabbi, PhD. For thirty years he was Professor of Religion at the University of Manitoba. Founder and spiritual leader of the P'nai Or Religious Fellowship and the P'nai Or's Spiritual Eldering Project. Author of *The Dream Assembly*. He says: '[to] look death in the face and accept our mortality. This is the door through to the next phase. The key that opens this door is in the body, the heart, the mind and the soul. We need to open all four parts of the lock to move through the gate ...'

Let me say it in the most fantastic way: Souls coming over to the other side say, 'This has been my lousiest lifetime ever. As I grew older and could no longer do what I could when I was younger, nobody was talking about how to handle aging. If I have to come for another incarnation I'm not going to go until the aging thing gets handled right!' Just as midwives help with natural births, and the hospice movement helps with the dying, so someone needs to help with initiation into eldering. Much of the physical and custodial care for the aged has been humanized, but the preparation and psycho-prophylaxis for eldering has generally been ignored.

All the eldering stuff that every human being has to go through demands that we look death in the face and accept our mortality. This is the door through to the next phase. The key that opens this door is in the body, the heart, the mind, and the soul. We need to open all four parts of the lock to move through the gate marked 'fulfilment', 'completion', or whatever our word is for a worthwhile life. In inspired imagination it opens, and from the inside comes light and guidance for the next stage. When the fear of death is seen as part of the normal software for the preservation of life, then we can dare to open that door to completion.

However, up to now everything that threatened my life got an automatic knee-jerk response that pumped adrenalin, urging: run, fight, flight, 'I've got to save myself'. I became aware of a program which runs in the deep background of my consciousness. It repeats: 'I don't want to die. I don't want to look at death.' It's best life-affirming function is that it says: 'At all costs save your life.' In *Halakhah* (Jewish law) the same program is called: 'A human life is worth more even than the Torah.' What is Halakhically expressed is also part of the biological program written into our body: 'Save your life at all costs.' That response, which was essential in my earlier life, stands in the way of my walking through the door to true *eldering*. Because of the habitual and built-in response to save life, we naturally panic and do everything to avoid facing death. This blindspot also blocks conscious and deliberate spiritual eldering.

So I can't walk through the spiritual eldering door until I say: 'This program running in me is only a program. *I* am not the program.' I have to separate my self from my ego's automatic avoidance responses. As one gets older these responses are less and less energetic. This is natural and as it should be. The energy in the software of 'save your life at any cost' is running low.

Eventually this program wears out, even though younger people – and public policy – are still operating as if 'life at any cost' is the right way to be. The medical ethic of using heroic measures to save lives is quite proper in cases of accidental injuries, but it does not consider the possibility that what we are doing may be counter-natural and counter-productive at a later stage in life.

Let's look at this from our highest, most expanded mind. Part of 'fight and flight' is that I don't dare look at my own death. So when my death keeps coming up I get anxious and distracted . . . I'll move in any and every direction so as not to face it. But when I remain steadfast and don't flinch, then beyond my fears I see a wonderful potential to complete and round out my life.

Just as the child is father of the man, so the adult in his prime is the father of the elder. To perfect the knowing of one's inner 'sage', we need to look past death. And here the contemplative, philosophical, spiritual intuition work needs to be learned. Most people have learned how to run a spreadsheet or to write a letter, but they haven't learned to see life contemplatively. In other words, I can't say 'yes' to my life if I don't say 'yes' to my death. I have to be able to say 'yes' to the normalness of aging, and that aging makes me a special person. There is so much mileage left if we can understand *who* we are, *what* we can handle, and *how* we can yet grow and expand. The sage meets the conditions of aging rather than displacing them. The key is to live within the context and the conditions in order to maximize potential.

I asked myself what this eldering thing was doing to me personally, and that question brought me a vision. I saw every seven years of a lifetime as one month in the year. Imagine – from birth to age seven, until the second teeth come, is January. Seven to fourteen years, puberty, is February. Then to twenty-one, when we are fully grown in our body, that's March. April begins at this point, the true spring of our life, and is over when we are twenty-eight years and have our Saturn return. This is like cleaning up all the debris, a spring-cleaning. Then we go to thirty-five in May and to forty-two in June, during which we set ourselves up as social beings, as a husband or a wife, as a professional or a this or a that. But we are in our prime from forty-two to forty-nine, from forty-nine to fifty-six and from fifty-six to sixty-three, July, August, and September. These are the months when we are doing our work in the world. In order to have the prime of our life between forty-two and sixty-three right, we need a vision of how we want to spend our sixty-three to seventy, our seventy to seventy-seven, our seventy-seven to eighty-four years.

It works out that I am now in the October of my life. By putting it in this context I saw that this period arrives after the soul searching and examination of conscience of the High Holidays which occur in the fall. At this time one asks oneself about life – what will bring about its fulfilment? Taking the year this way, spring is when we are twenty-one years old. We go out of Egypt (winter) and it is Passover and Easter. When we are a bit older, at twenty-eight when we reach the Saturn return, we receive the Torah. In the middle of the summer comes the midlife crisis – Tisha b'Av, the destruction of the Temple. When we see the year this way, we find that the liturgical year and the lifetime are parallels which carry within themselves this deep mythic understanding.

I saw that while earlier libido was in sex and procreation and acquisition of space and owning things, now it is invested in preserving the distillate of my life's experiences. This is the truth behind the question: 'Are you saved?' I became aware that 'you must save life at all costs' is not the current program, but that we must save the joy and wisdom of our life and write into the global awareness what it is that we have accumulated in our lifetime and who we have become. I saw myself very much like a cell in the global brain. Each cell doesn't own its experience – it has to pour it back. I was supposed to do my job, to acquire my experience, but the experience was for the global awareness and not just for me. Someone who does not graduate from the automatic response in the face of death doesn't make it to sagehood. That person remains sidelined in June, July, and August, rather than entering into fall and becoming an excellent September, October, or November person.

Spiritual eldering is to do with initiation. We can look at our death, we can start saying: 'I'm not scared of you.' Once I accept my mortality I can have an abundant life and I can follow my bliss. All the options that I didn't have while I was in the world of *doing* – I had to do for my family, I had to do this and that – open up as they've never opened before to a world of *being*.

I was at the Sinai gathering in which about 150 people met in the Sinai Desert: Muslims, Sufis, Christians, Coptics, Palestinians, Israelis, Americans, Japanese, Native Americans, Jews, all were there. We started to climb Mount Sinai at one o'clock in the morning and made our way up to the top of the mountain to be there at sunrise, where we prayed. Somebody brought a stone on which was engraved 'Dona Nobis Pacem' which means 'grant us peace'. We left it on the top of the mountain. We all offered prayers and sang Halleluia . . . it was an amazing thing.

We had helped each other up the mountain. This old Japanese man and I helped each other over the tough places. We didn't even have to talk, there was such a fellowship. When the sun came over the horizon at the right moment all the Japanese shouted 'Bonzai!' greeting the sun, and each of us worshipped in our own way.

I sat with the old Muslims there, listening to what they had to say. What hit me was that, just as male and female are more different than Sfardi-Ashkenazi, so are younger and older more different than Christian and Jewish. I began to see that we need a whole new dialogue to cross the age barrier. We need to create an aging ecumenism so that the older people can gain inspiration and energy as well as the urge to continue to expand, and the younger people can gain sagacity, wisdom, experience, and counsel.

What do we call a wise person? A sage. I want to say 'saging not aging'. The best service of a grandfather, an elder, a Zayda, is to listen. The word *staretz* is interesting. *Staro* means 'old' in Russian, so *staretz* means 'the old one'. It is the name for the Russian Father Confessor, the spiritual director. It is very important for people to learn to be sages, ones who live in their wisdom.

I asked myself: If we take meditation out of the solo practice and socialize it, then it becames something that people do in twos and threes, and then what happens? The whole meditative process becomes a way to spend quality time together. When the Jews are saying: 'Adonai Melekh – Adonai Malakh – Adonai yimlokh l'olam va'ed, The Lord is, was and will be in charge', then the Muslims can say: 'Ya Rahim Ya Rahman Dhul Djalal w'al ikram', and the Christians can say: 'Glory Father, Glory Son, Glory Spirit, Three in One.' That way they can even do it simultaneously and rhythmically together. I did it once with three intertwined circles: the Muslims in one circle, the Jews in another, and the Christians in the third. The three groups chanted together. It was a wonderful experience of ecumenity.

And the point is that saging is not a special gift, it is only actualizing that with which we have been born, using the gift of life we already have. To accept life as the gift I have been given and to now give my body to the worms and my spirit to the Universal, I flow into the Godstream not with the pain of an unlived life but with the grateful joy of appreciated completion.

PART THREE

Dimensions of Healing

Kitaro

THE GREAT SPIRIT

Kitaro, best-known of all contemporary Japanese musicians. He has pioneered an evolutionary music that has crossed over classical, jazz and pop charts. Has made over fourteen albums and sold well over ten million copies worldwide. He says: 'We must choose which path to travel. We can continue along the present path paved with pollution and blood . . . Or we can make a conscious decision to veer off this road and on to a fresh one lined with a new consciousness.'

Great Spirit
All living things come face to face with the Great Spirit
And the Great Spirit dwells within all living things

Tree
Flower
Water
Earth
Wind . . . all things

At times the Great Spirit is severe
At times the Great Spirit is soothing
Encompassing all life

Everyplace the Great Spirit dwells
Is the source of a gentle crystalline light

And within that light we become one
Floating as if in our mother's warm body
Living together as children of the earth

Without time
Without end . . .

As we approach the close of this century, the human race faces a very serious test. We must choose which path to travel. We can continue along the present path paved with pollution and blood which we are now on – one of destruction of our planet and ourselves. Or we can make a conscious decision to veer off this road on to a fresh one lined with a new consciousness.

Deepak Chopra

UNDER THE WISHING-TREE

Deepak Chopra MD, former Chief of Staff at the New England Memorial Hospital, founding President of the American Association of Ayurvedic Medicine. Author of *Creating Health*, *Return of the Rishi*, bestsellers *Quantum Healing*, *Perfect Health – The Complete Mind/Body Guide*, and *Unconditional Life*. He says: 'We did not put the destructive power into nature. As a primal force, destruction is eternally linked to creation and is just as necessary. But we drove destruction beyond some invisible limit that was not foreseen.'

In India there is said to be an ancient banyan tree that will grant any wish to the person sitting under it. If a man ever found this wishing-tree, he would have to be careful. Too many good wishes have gone awry, leaving evil in their wake. We are presently living in someone else's idea of a brave new world, as it was wished for by past generations. Let us suppose, then, that the man sitting beneath the banyan knows all about the ravaged rain forests, the hole in the ozone layer, the stockpiled warheads. He doesn't want to assign blame for these horrors. He realizes instead how intimately his future is tied up with everyone else's.

How could he possibly make a wish only for himself? He would want to desire a world that everyone can share – and that poses a problem. There is no single happiness that applies to everyone.

Looking up from his seat under the banyan tree, our wisher would observe the bullock carts driving by, carrying farmers who have not changed their way of life for centuries. Perhaps a black Mercedes overtakes them, and the impatient industrialist inside scowls as he drives the carts out of his way. A jet breaks the silence overhead, scaring up a flock of kites who have nested in the same tree long before man first appeared.

How to satisfy the needs of the rich and the poor, the educated and the illiterate, the virtuous and the not-so-virtuous? How to permit humans their ingenuity and creativity without laying waste to the green planet and the animals and birds who accept their existence upon it so innocently? The wisher imagines the hateful conflicts that would arise from even the most benignly conceived future.

But he must wish for some better world! The one we now inhabit contains too much destruction. We did not put the destructive power into nature. As a primal force, destruction is eternally linked to creation and is just as necessary. But we drove destruction beyond some invisible limit that was not foreseen. The troubling truth is that unchecked creativity, far more than our greed or hate, tipped the balance of nature. We came to value our creativity over the enduring background that sustains life in all its forms. The same DNA gave birth to the rainforests, the animals, and man himself. Through man, the intelligence of life kept pushing its way into the future; it discovered how to unleash any force in nature, and at that point something broke down. Why has man's DNA turned against its own interests, threatening to topple everything?

'Ignorance,' our wisher thinks to himself. 'All this evil has come out of the potential for good – it is sheer ignorance.' In that thought, he would have the seed of his wish. The only survivable future is one in which ignorance has been abolished. Man is not a cancer let loose on the face of the earth; his DNA is the DNA of all life. Its interests have been safeguarded by nature for 600 million years, and its basic atoms have been protected from destruction since the Big Bang.

What we fail to grasp is a way to return to the broad, shining river of evolution that has sustained us for eons already. A return implies a path. This path is hard to conceive of, unfortunately, since there is nowhere to go. We are already in nature; the forests, however ravaged, are obeying the same laws as before. The plankton and whales and seals which we devastate have no way to live other than the way they have always lived. The root of the damaged world is in our own interpretation. We have this wounded world because of our divided vision of ourselves. A grim Roman saying – 'Man is the wolf to man' – tells us the origin of war, degredation, prejudice, rivalry, and hate. The same holds true for any other evil in the world: it is the visible evidence of an invisible conflict within us.

'To restore nature,' our wisher concludes, 'I must restore my own nature.' Certainly he is right – the path out of ignorance begins and ends in our minds. At this point I believe we must take a leap and place our trust in the resilience and final goodness of the life in us. To change human nature seems like the most impossible task of all unless this mounting nightmare in the world has all been a mistake. The Upanishads, the most ancient record of man's self-knowledge, declare that this is so: 'Of bliss these creatures were conceived, in bliss they live, and into bliss they will merge again.' The horror of history may not confirm these words, but man's aspirations do. We are not just wolves; we are free intelligences who have chosen to be wolves when our true nature is love.

What I have been saying here I try to convey on a personal level to my patients. They come to me wanting to heal, but most of them have turned this wish into a huge struggle. They fight against their pain as if attacked by a foreign enemy, instead of seeing that pain can be a signal of where healing needs to begin. 'As long as you see healing as a struggle,' I tell them, 'you will be the prisoner of pain and fear. You will constantly identify with your illness and measure yourself by its ups and downs.'

'But I can't help it,' they say, 'I want to survive, and fighting is the only way I know how. Do you want me to give up instead?'

This inability to see any other way but fighting or giving up is the real obstacle to all healing. Our old conditioning tells us that we must work hard to survive, and the harder we work the more we will be rewarded. But healing is not like that. It involves no work, only the courage to be ourselves, and then the rewards are immense. The basic question, at every level of healing, is how to stop struggling. When the old hurts are released, new life rushes in to fill the gap!

'The future generally turns out to contain one of two things,' I tell patients; 'a repetition of what we know today or a surprising turn into the unknown. It could be that everything you long for – a cure from this disease, freedom from fear, the return to a meaningful life – is biding its time in the unknown, ready to present itself when you give the right signal.'

'Then what should I do?' they ask.

'First, be willing to let the old boundaries fall away. In that willingness, unexpected powers can awaken. Remember, nothing you already know is going to free you. Getting beyond the mind's boundaries is a much more profound goal than the mind can grasp. If you begin this investigation into your deeper nature, you will find that real, lasting healing comes just from being yourself and watching what happens. If you have a sincere willingness, what will happen will be an inner unfolding; the tightly furled bud will open into a flower.'

Health means not just a sane mind in a sound body (the classical ideal in the West), but a full expansion of man's inner potential. 'I am the universe' is the primary intuition of a healthy man. The ideals of love, compassion, and freedom are fully alive in him; his comprehension of the human situation includes all life around him.

If I were the wisher under the banyan tree, I would wish for every person to know his own nature. Then, without coercion or pressure, every person would reach his own ideal of happiness, for what can make a person happier than to be himself, breathing life in freedom?

We do not necessarily have to perform the heroic task of saving nature. Nature is self-sustaining, once we cease to interfere. The same pulse of life flows through the whole world, emanating from the gods or God. This unimaginable force created the galaxies and at the same time preserves the most fragile mountain flower. All around us life gushes forth and meets itself coming back, curving in joy on to itself and leaping in jubilation at its own infinite strength. We are part of this stream too. We issued from it, and our destiny continues to ride its crest.

Gerald G. Jampolski and Diane V. Cirincione

CHANGING OUR ATTITUDES ABOUT AIDS

Gerald Jampolski MD, psychiatrist, founder of The Center for Attitudinal Healing, California. Author of bestseller *Love is Letting Go of Fear, One Person Can Make a Difference*, and with Diane, *Love is the Answer: Creating Positive Relationships*. **Diane V. Cirincione**, international lecturer, co-director of Children as Teachers of Peace. They say: 'The AIDS crisis has engendered a tremendous amount of fear which has created hostility and isolation. In all probability soon there will not be one of us who does not personally know someone who has AIDS or is HIV-positive. If ever there was a time to light our hearts with the fire of compassion, it is now.'

Just for a moment, try to imagine what it would be like to be the parents of a five-year-old boy who has AIDS and who probably was infected with the AIDS virus from a blood transfusion he received when he was three-and-a-half years old. Can you identify with the initial shock, agony, and disbelief? Can you imagine what you would do when your son reaches school age and is ready to attend classes? Do you keep the fact of that illness a secret from school officials, your relatives, and your community, or do you tell the truth?

Try for a moment to identify with the parents of Ryan Thomas, a five-year-old boy from California, whose family found themselves in this situation. They were well aware of the Surgeon General's report and the findings contained in the bulletin of the Federal Centers for Disease Control, as well as other reports from medical authorities throughout the world, that you don't get AIDS from casual contact, from hugging, from kissing, or from living in the same house with someone with AIDS; that you can only contact AIDS from sexual intercourse or having blood-to-blood interaction.

The Thomas family knew what the medical, educational facts were; at the same time, they also understood what fears, doubts, and uncertainty can do to a community to close off their hearts, to isolate and to ostracize a family with AIDS. They struggled with the decision about whether or not they should make their son's illness known. They decided they should. Their hearts told them to tell the truth.

The result was that the community and the school responded with fear and attack. Ryan and his older brothers, Robert, and Richard, aged thirteen and ten, were subjected to the teasing of other children, who called them 'AIDS monsters.' However, after a community-education program and pertinent legal maneuvers, the situation became quite different. Ryan went back to school, and other children began playing with the Thomas boys, and a compassionate and helping attitude by many in the community replaced the taunts and jeers.

There is, of course, really no one to blame for the AIDS crisis. But there is much that we can do. We can do our best to be well informed about the medical facts and to take the responsibility for informing others. Rather than closing off our hearts and focusing on our own self-interest, we can begin a new era by taking the same interest in others as we do in ourselves. We can reach out and help those affected by this devastating disease, by allowing the fear in our own hearts to be transformed by a compassionate, caring, and loving attitude. It means living this instant as if it were the only time there is – an instant of joining and not separation. We need to remind ourselves of what our purpose in life is. Is it just to protect our own self-interest and to think of ourselves first? Or is it to live a life where we are demonstrating Creation's love flowing through us to all others, regardless of the circumstances?

Let us tell you about the transformation that took place

in Jeannie White's family. We first met Jeannie White, her son Ryan, and her daughter Andrea at the height of public outcry over Ryan's attending school while his AIDS was in remission. Ryan, a haemophiliac, had acquired the disease through a blood transfusion prior to the institution of current blood-testing regulations. Nevertheless, he has been called a 'faggot', 'queer', and other homophobic epithets. On one of those days when he had the strength to get up and go out, he was asked to leave the shopping mall, as well as restaurants amidst stares of arrogance, anger, and rejection. His sister and mother quietly left with him and decided then and there to take a stand on his right to go to school, a battle they eventually won in court. While the family has undergone extraordinary pain and cruelty because of the ignorance and fear of others, there is something about them that seems to have risen above it. Out of the tragedy of having AIDS there is great potential for personal transformation.

When Ryan was first diagnosed, Jeannie couldn't believe it. The diagnosis was so rare that it took almost a year to confirm. Jeannie's disbelief turned to anger – hostility and rage towards all homosexuals, even though Jeannie had rarely encountered a gay man. So how are we to explain the shift to the inner peace we now observe in this very exhausted mother? She explained that while on a trip to New York early in Ryan's illness to do a morning talk show on the controversy, someone suggested that she visit the AIDS ward at Bellevue Hospital. While doing so, her anger and judgment began to dissipate. She felt a common bond with the patients she met there and their families, who were similarly suffering and had as much to fear as she did. In their shared pain, they all found a way to join together.

Shortly after returning home, she was further transformed while watching the local news. On the TV screen she saw mothers, fathers, children, and teachers arguing about whether or not Ryan should be allowed to enter their school district. Suddenly, instead of hating them, she felt compassion for the conflict they were undergoing, the separation the issue was causing with the other families, and she found herself identifying with their confusion and pain. Although she knew that she would never agree with their views, nevertheless she could empathize with them on another level.

Jeannie's final transformation at that time took place when a local mother whom she had never met called her and shared the following: first, she had a son who had just told her he was gay; second, he was diagnosed as having AIDS; and third, he wanted to come home to die. She asked Jeannie what to do. Without hesitating a moment, Jeannie advised the mother that if she wanted to give herself an incredible gift, she would invite her son home. The woman did, and Ryan subsequently befriended him.

The White family's healing came about by finding and accepting a way to join others and to help them even when the outside world said otherwise. Jeannie White has also found a space in her heart to forgive. She has since networked with numerous families who find themselves experiencing similar situations and problems. She has been active in The Center for Attitudinal Healing AIDS Hotline.* At the same time Ryan was active as national spokesperson, along with Elizabeth Taylor, for the National AIDS Research Foundation, and spoke on behalf of other children with AIDS. There is still, however and unfortunately, a lot of fear around this issue. On more than one occasion Ryan White's grave has been maliciously desecrated.

For a moment let us try to identify with Mr and Mrs Clifford Ray, formerly of Florida, who are the parents of three young sons with haemophilia, ages eight, nine and ten, and one healthy daughter, age six. They are faced with the fact that their boys are carrying the AIDS virus but do not have the disease. After much inner struggle their hearts dictate that they tell the truth to school officials. As in the cases of Ryan Thomas and Ryan White, fear in the community leads to the ruling that the children not be allowed to attend school. And although that decision is eventually reversed, the Ray boys are

---

* The Center for Attitudinal Healing in Tiburon, California, has an AIDS Hotline for Kids, telephone number: (415) 435–5022. It is both an information and a support network. The Center also has a Phone/Pen Pal program to link together those people who are unable to come there. The Center offers free services both to adults and children with AIDS, and support groups for families and friends. They also have a poster on which a child is saying: 'I have AIDS. Please hug me, I can't make you sick.' Center for Attitudinal Healing, 19 Main Street, Tiburon, CA 94920.

put in a special class in a special school where no other children are in attendance. The children are isolated; no one wants to play with them. Adults also begin to shun both the parents and their youngsters.

The tension gets so great that they decide to relocate to Alabama, where the same thing happens again, and so they return to Florida. Then they find a doctor and a lawyer who are both willing to offer their services free to help in a legal battle to get the children into school. But when the fall semester gets underway the court victory becomes little more than a paper triumph as the Rays spend the first week of classes subjected to bomb and death threats, and a boycott led by classmates' parents.

Fear and lack of education are causing similar untold anger in many communities throughout the US. And while all the incidents are not of the magnitude of hostility directed towards the Rays, the fact remains that there are an estimated 5,000-plus children in America who carry the AIDS virus from blood transfusions, and that there is a vast need and challenge for all of us in dealing with their suffering that goes beyond medical concerns. As Seigne Post wrote in a letter to the editor of 'Time' magazine: 'As important as finding a cure for the disease is finding a cure for people who are turning their backs on AIDS victims.'

There is a beautiful story at our Center for Attitudinal Healing we would like to share with you. It has to do with a mother who found that her husband was dying of cancer. Later she learned that both of her sons were gay and that her elder boy had AIDS. She, her elder son, and his lover all came to our Center. After her first son died, her second son was diagnosed as having AIDS. The mother found that the best way she could heal herself was to volunteer her services at County Hospital in San Francisco, where she now helps other mothers who come to the city from other parts of the country to see their sons, oftentimes for the first visit, knowing that they are gay and have AIDS. She is a beautiful light. And while one might expect that she would be depressed, she is not. Her work in service has made her strong and given her peace. She has tremendous faith in God.

We have seen great personal and spiritual transformations

take place in many ways for the families with AIDS with whom we have worked. We have met parents who have told us that their child has taught them what courage, patience, faith, and unconditional love are all about.

More recently, we have begun to see remarkable foster parents who have volunteered to take care of children who have AIDS, AIDS-Related Complex, or who are carrying the HIV antibody. These courageous persons have no fear of being infected with the disease; their biggest problem is their own fear of social isolation. When one foster couple told their landlord what they were doing, he agreed to let them remain on the premises on the condition that they do not tell others at the complex about their child. They can only go out themselves when their best friends, in whom they have confided the facts and the truth, volunteer to babysit because the couple is still trying to keep it a secret. One of the foster mothers we are seeing decided to adopt the child she is caring for. These people are beacons of light and are teachers of unconditional love for all of us.

Although the Center for Communicative Diseases only reported 3100 cases of children with AIDS by the end of June 1991, many paediatricans feel that the actual number is closer to over 20,000 cases when you combine both AIDS and HIV infections together. In addition, there is probably a higher number of children with haemophilia who have not been tested but who are HIV-positive.

The figures for AIDS as projected by the World Health Organization are staggering and overwhelming. They project that by the year 2000 there will be over 10 million children in the world who either have AIDS or are HIV-positive. They also project that by that same year there will be over 10 million children who will have been orphaned by their parents dying from AIDS.

The AIDS crisis has engendered a tremendous amount of fear which has created hostility and isolation. In all probability soon there will not be one of us who does not personally know someone who has AIDS or is HIV-positive. If ever there was a time to light our hearts with the fire of compassion, it is now.

We have great hope that a cure for AIDS will happen. But in

the meantime there is a great need for all of us to reach out to each other with helping hands and hearts. To this day there has not been one report of anyone being infected in the family of a child who has AIDS. Rather than isolation, it is our feeling that there needs to be more joining. In every and any way possible it becomes important for us to reach out to help others in every encounter and ask the question: 'How can I be helpful?'

Perhaps things would be different if each of us would take on the educational task with others as our own individual responsibility. Many of these children can use the help of a big brother or big sister. The parents often need friendship and support. We can always call our local AIDS organization and offer help.

The AIDS crisis offers each of us an opportunity to face our own fears, our own purpose on this planet Earth, and allows us to look once again at other ways of thinking about life and death. We personally, as well as the many volunteers who have worked at our Center with families who have been affected by the AIDS virus, have received the gift of having our lives transformed as we have been witnesses to faith, love, compassion, and coming together that has resulted in a life that has new meaning. Won't you join us in the challenge that remains for all of us, to face our fears and let our hearts be transformed by the Creative Love Force of this universe into compassion, caring, and love?

Bernie and Bobbie Siegel

A TORCH TO LIGHT OUR WAY

Bernie Siegel MD, pediatric and general surgeon. Founder of Exceptional Cancer Patients. Author of bestsellers *Love, Medicine and Miracles* and *Peace, Love and Healing*. International teacher with his wife **Bobbie Siegel**. They say: 'We have heard of individuals whose lives have been saved by saying "I love you" to those who are threatening them. We must see beyond the act to the part of us that is shared by all creation and come together in this.'

From our experience there seem to be only two significant issues in the world today. They are the preservation of the planet in its physical sense, and the raising of children who are loved. These two issues are really one and the same, as at the present time we are capable of destroying both the planet and also the life it contains.

The outcome of our life here therefore stems from the use of free choice. In the Garden of Eden there were no choices, there was just love. There was no notion of destruction. In fact it was meaningless to say 'I love you' because there were no other options, there was nothing but love. However, in order to have purpose and intent, free will was added. Then an expression of love became significant as it was the result of making a choice. Yet with the awakening of this consciousness of choice there arose both a risk and a challenge – we can choose to be either creative or destructive.

The real challenge is to create a world of lovers, people who instinctively and intuitively make choices which heal themselves, heal their society, and thus the planet. We are already surrounded by and imbued with creative, intelligent energy. The choice is to become one with this. Native Americans had this sense of belonging and being a part of nature. They made decisions based upon the seventh generation to come after them. That is what true lovers do. They make choices which express the depth of their love for all beings that naturally include conservation and preservation so that life may continue.

We believe in a God without qualities; an intelligent, loving energy that created the universe and that communicates with us through dreams and visions. If we tap into this awareness we become one with creation, we become co-creators. If you question the existence of such an energy, let me refer you to ice or to band-aids as symbols and reminders of its existence! For instance, when a liquid is frozen it becomes denser, solid and sinks, except for one liquid – water. Ice floats. Why? Think for a moment what would happen to our planet if the oceans, lakes, and rivers froze from the bottom up. Death would come to all the life they contain, and eventually it would come to the planet. Nature is thus created in such a way that it does not self-destruct if left to itself. Interesting, isn't it?

Band-aids were created to stop us from interfering with our innate ability to heal. We cut our finger and cover it. A week later there is no cut present, it is healed. How did that happen? Who directed the healing? How did the body know how to do this? Quite mysterious, isn't it? As a physician I (Bernie) can tell you that we have no idea how a wound heals or how a single cell knows how to create a human being. What I do know is that if we love and nurture ourselves and our children, we grow to our full potential. In this way we give this intelligence a powerful message of life that stimulates healing to its fullest extent.

We are all products of parents who had parents and it is not an issue of blaming anyone but of stopping the dysfunctional process by deciding to love. Then healing of all the generations can start. When we accept our own mortality, we may at last begin to make our time here really precious and realize our unity with the creative intelligence. We cannot live forever. Death is not a failure to be fought, but a natural culmination. In the meantime we can be very much alive.

We have made enormous strides in a mechanistic way but we cannot cure every problem by artificial means. If we destroy the self-healing mechanisms of our planet, then we die with it. Our present actions tell it we are more interested in dying than in living. For instance, in medicine I see what I call the 'rise and walk' approach. This is one that focuses on replacing organs, maintaining and repairing, rather than healing; where, as long as we can walk, we are presumed to be healed. The Bible tells us that Jesus healed a paralyzed man by saying: 'Your sins are forgiven.' He did not do it by saying he should rise and walk, for he knew the innate ability that went with a healed heart, with a healed life. Without healing the pain we cannot be healed within.

We must come together to realize we are one family of man, to sit in groups and listen to each other so that we can heal our pain and therefore our lives. Helen Keller, blind and deaf from the age of nineteen months, told us: 'The happy busy noises of community, the voice of a friend, the imagination of Mozart – life without these is darker by far than blindness.'

We know what love in the face of adversity can do. We have seen the human body heal when people have found their true path in life. We have learned that the real reports are not just pathology reports but are reports on whether we are on our path in life or not. We have heard of individuals whose lives have been saved by saying 'I love you' to those who are threatening them. We must see beyond the act to the part of us that is shared by all creation and come together in this. Our lives are but an opportunity to participate in creation. Our actions manifest on all levels. We are at the center of a circle with no circumference, yet which intersects with all other circles.

What can we do to light the way? It is our belief that we each can become a torch and burn up with the love that lights it. We commonly hear about people who burn out. They are not living their life in love, and sadly they die with that capacity still unused. We want each of us to burn up with love; to be used so fully that there is nothing left when we go. We all have the potential for this, it is not limited to our physical ability. We know quadriplegics who paint with a brush held in their mouths and contribute tremendous beauty and love to the world.

When I (Bernie) teach at schools I tell the children the most important professions are those of the elevator operators, the bus drivers, and the subway conductors. When they look puzzled I tell them in these professions you have a trapped audience and can really love them! Then you can have them spread that love like ripples over the earth, to all beings. We are all elevator operators of life! See the people around you, listen to each other and make room for love to come into your life by putting the garbage out. No one is untouched by pain. Viktor Frankl, in *Man's Search for Meaning*, said: 'To live is to suffer, to survive is to find meaning in the suffering.' Share together, heal and light the way ahead.

The Bible tells us: 'He who seeks to save his life will lose it, but he who is willing to lose himself will save it.' We need to let the untrue self die and thereby save our lives. If we live this kind of life we can die laughing. Laughing over the joy we create and the love we have experienced, and what we have accomplished for all beings. Again the Bible speaks: 'For the son of man comes not to be served but to serve, and to ransom his life for the good of many.' Is it a coincidence that Isaac does not protest when Abraham is about to sacrifice him? Is it a coincidence that the name Isaac means 'He will laugh'? We think not. We think Isaac knew he could make an enormous contribution with his life. It was an act of deep faith and compassion, as well as an understanding of the impermanence of the body.

Let us open our wounds to each other and let the healing begin. In *The Bridge of San Luis Rey*, Wilder writes: 'And we ourselves shall be loved for a while and forgotten, but the love will have been enough. All those impulses of love return to the love that made them. Even memory is not necessary for love. There is a land of the living and a land of the dead, and the bridge is love, the only survival, the only meaning.'

> Peace, love, and healing lie ahead of you.
> Pick up the torch and light the way!
> Your sins are forgiven.

Mickey Hart

THE MAKING OF THE DRUM

Mickey Hart, musician, percussionist with The Grateful Dead for twenty-five years. Author of *Drumming at the Edge of Magic* and *Planet Drum*; executive producer of 'The World' music recordings. He says: 'To have built a drum together is probably to be bonded for life; but then to have ridden that drum together – there are no words for that.'

I had been given an invitation from my old friend Hugh Romney, better known as Wavy Gravy. I'd known him since joining the Grateful Dead. He was running a summer camp for children between seven and fourteen, some of them under-privileged kids from the Oakland ghetto, and he wanted to know if I would come and spend three weeks teaching the kids about drums.

Camp Winnarainbow. What do you do at camp? You make things.

I borrowed one of the Grateful Dead's trucks, and Ram Rod packed it with instruments from my collection. *Berimbaus*. Bull-roarers. Slit gongs. Thirty hoop drums. Enough for every kid in camp who wanted to really experience rhythm and noise.

I didn't want to bore these kids with music lessons – it takes years to master an instrument like the *berimbau*. I wanted to give them a taste of something larger, the spirit side. I had jotted down a quote by the Sufi master Inayat Khan that expressed what I was after:

> There are different ways of listening to music. There is a technical state when a person who is developing technique and has learnt to appreciate better music, feels disturbed by a lower grade of music. But there is a spiritual way, which has nothing to do with technique. It is simply to tune oneself to the music.

I wanted to take these street kids and tune them to the groove. I wanted to see how fast they'd entrain.

There were close to a hundred kids at Camp Winnarainbow, most in their early teens, both sexes. They lived in huge tipis located around a firepit. The firepit was the camp's meetingplace, where we did exercises every morning and sang songs at night.

The first thing I did after I arrived at Winnarainbow was walk the whole camp, carrying a *berimbau* with me, looking for the perfect spot. I knew there had to be a perfect spot somewhere among the acres of giant oaks and red woods or near the lake. There had to be a spot that contained magic, power, a place of such presence that all your senses start tingling, where you feel high, as if suddenly the volume has been turned up, inside you, outside you, everywhere.

No place seized me like that. I ran into Wavy and asked him whether he knew any power spots and he said I might try the hay barn, but it was pretty far. He pointed past the lake, toward the crest of a distant and very steep hill, upon which sat an immense old redwood hay barn. The edge.

It was the most isolated spot in the camp. It felt good to be in this abandoned cathedral-sized building, particularly in the late afternoon when the sun fell at just the right angle revealing all the dust motes and hay chaff dancing in the warm afternoon air.

At the noon gathering I stood up with a hoop drum and announced that I had brought to camp some of our species' earliest musical instruments. Instruments that had been used in very special ways, for very special purposes, and if anyone wanted to learn about these instruments they should meet me there, and I turned and pointed toward the barn.

After lunch I drove the truck up to the barn and carefully unpacked the instruments and placed them around the barn. I wanted to create a garden of percussion. I wondered how many would make the hike. There were a hundred kids in camp; about twenty-five showed up. I demonstrated some simple rhythms and then told the kids to relax, just play, forget being nervous, let the instruments take them where they wanted to go.

It's interesting how long it takes people to entrain. These kids locked up after about twenty minutes. They found the groove, and they all knew it. You could see it in their faces as they began playing louder and harder, the groove drawing them in and hardening. It lasted about an hour. These things have life cycles – they begin, build in intensity, maintain, and then dissipate and dissolve. When it was all over everyone started laughing and clapping. They were celebrating themselves and they were also celebrating the groove. Although they had no words for it, they knew that they had created something that was alive, that had a force of its own, out of nothing but their own shared energy.

When they calmed down I handed them all bullroarers, explaining that this was the first ritual instrument that we had any real information on. The bullroarer is not a quiet instrument. Some bullroarers bark, some howl, others emit terrifying shrieks – the strange, unsettling sound quickly overpowers all your senses. We took the bullroarers outside to play. Their sound was incredible, and the kids quickly got lost in it. But as I observed them, I wondered if anything else was happening. Was the door opening for any of them? Were they feeling it? It occurred to me that I had become a recruiter for the tradition, that the art was using me as a vehicle to reach this next generation of drummers, some of whom were starting to smile.

That's how it begins. Something triggers it and for the rest of your life you are possessed by rhythm and noise. Zakir heard it while he was still in his mother's womb. Airto started dancing to it before he could crawl. I discovered it the first time I hit my father's practice pad with one of his snakewood sticks. It was as if someone had tweaked the pleasure center in my brain. I smiled. I hit the pad again. Although I haven't heard the sound of my father's practice pad in years, I've never forgotten it; at some level of consciousness it is always resonating, it's part of my code.

On the morning of my second day at Camp Winnarainbow, I stood up at breakfast and proposed that we build a camp drum, one that would be played for years to come at ritual occasions. Anyone who wanted to participate in this project, I said, should see me this afternoon because that's when we were going to kill the steer.

I had arranged with a local slaughterhouse to do the killing. About a half dozen of us watched as the butcher shot the steer with a 30–30. He'd been patient with us, standing around with an amused smile as we made tobacco offerings to the animal's spirit, assuring it that its meat would feed the poor and its skin would become the voice of a great and powerful drum.

Obtain hide of two-year-old steer.

That's a simple sentence to read, but it doesn't even begin to convey the reality of a sixty-pound hunk of steerhide, dripping with blood, with big gobs of fat still clinging to it. The kids didn't blink an eye, but it nearly made me sick, and it sure depressed me as I contemplated the amount of work it was going to take to reduce this formless bloody mass into a finely stretched and tuned membrane.

I set up operations in a creek bed about a hundred yards from the kitchen. The kitchen was the most popular place in camp – one thing these kids did a lot of was eat – and I intended to lure as many of these hungry street kids as I could over to my drum pit. The creek we were working in was nearly dry. What made it the ideal spot was a big fallen tree that spanned the creek. We could drape the hide over the trunk and work on it standing up.

So began the long, hot, smelly, endless task of scraping, soaking, stretching, shaving the hairs off, then the fat. By the third day the hide began to stink and the odor attracted bees, who went back and told their hivemates about us. A couple of times we had to grab the skin and run. This added an element of danger that excited the kids even more. I'm afraid we developed a street gang attitude toward the bees. As soon as one appeared he would be assaulted and chased away. Word quickly got back to the hive not to visit our creekbed.

As we worked I told the kids the story of the drum we were making, the Ojibwa pow-wow drum. I told them how a vision had come to a Sioux woman named Tailfeather Woman at a moment of profound grief and terror. White soldiers had just massacred her village, killing her four sons and almost killing her. She had managed to escape by hiding in a lake. For four days Tailfeather Woman hid under the lilypads. While she was hiding, the Great Spirit came to her and told her what to do. On the fourth day she emerged from the lake and walked to her village to see who had survived the attack. When the survivors had gathered around her, she told them that the Great Spirit had commanded them to build a drum, saying 'That is the only way you are going to stop the soldiers from killing your people.'

This was the beginning of the pow-wow, for the Great Spirit had not just given the Sioux a drum, but also a rhythm and dance to go with it – a ceremony. The ceremony spread rapidly among the Indian tribes. We were now building a power drum, one put on this earth by the Great Spirit.

Every day the crowd in the drum pit grew. Without the limitless energy of the kids I might have given up. I spent mornings in the drum pit, afternoons in the hay barn with the instruments. And very gradually I found myself talking almost as much as I was playing. I couldn't help myself, it just came flowing out: stories, myths, bullroarers howling in the jungles of Papua New Guinea as the boys underwent the ritual that turns them into men, talking drums calling the *Orisha* down into the bodies of the dancers, Gene Krupa massaging the backbeat.

And as I told these stories and watched the kids absorb them in their tough, suspicious, fourteen-year-old ways, I realized that the Yoruba were right: to keep a spirit alive in this world you need only mention its name. By sharing my feelings about the bullroarer and my stories about it, I was not just feeding these kids, I was also feeding the bullroarer, strengthening its spirit hold on this world. The Yoruba have the idea of the crossroads, the point where the spirit world and this world intersect. Certain things attract the spirits to a crossroads. One is music, another is stories. The spirits love to listen to both.

One morning I left the drum pit early and hiked up to the

barn to sit and think. I wanted something special to consecrate the drum we were making. A ritual of some sort. One that would be both fun and strong enough to link the drum and its spirit side in these kids' minds. I sat in the silence waiting. What came through the door was Joe.

The last time I saw Joe Campbell, a few months before his death, was at the Jung Institute in San Francisco. For some reason he began telling me the story of the buffalo maiden, a story he had told thousands of times before. I had heard him tell it superbly, but now he was having trouble remembering the details; he was groping for the opening lines. Suddenly the rhythm of the myth came back to him and before I knew it Joe had stood up and was shuffling through the steps of the buffalo dance, his eyes closed, chanting out the myth as he danced. After he died, it occurred to me that this had been Joe's dance of death. It was as if he had caught a final wind and had ridden it out in glory.

Now I was the one telling the stories. And the story I decided to tell these kids at Camp Winnarainbow was the one Joe had so loved, the story of the shaman's journey, the story of how the shaman rides his drum to the World Tree, summons his allies, and does battle with the dark forces.

It took over a week to reduce the steerhide, using serrated scrapers, to the right thickness. When it was perfect we soaked it in water, then stretched it over a shell and hung it in a nearby tree for four days. As the moisture evaporated from the drumhead, the skin slowly tightened, a process that was intently observed by the kids. Each day the crowd around the drum grew.

I had intended to follow a similar process with the drum body, but it became apparent that we wouldn't have time to chop down and hollow out a tree. It also didn't seem right to take a whole tree for one drum. So we did it the way it had been done by the Ojibwa.

Obtain one wine barrel. Cut in half.

We placed the wine barrel on the skin and marked how big the two heads should be. Then we stitched the heads together using laces made from the hide. Out of some cloth we made a skirt for the drum – the Ojibwa dress their drums – and decorated it with symbols representing each of the Camp

Winnarainbow tipis. The camp had some fine embroiderers
who made wonderful trees and animals.

Then we named our drum. All the Ojibwa drums have the
names of their keepers. The Whitefeather Drum. The Pete
Sam Drum. The Johnny Matchokamow Drum. Ours was the
Winnarainbow Drum.

I began rehearsing the shaman's ritual during the last
week. One of the camp counselors became the shaman, and
I recruited a number of kids to play percussion. This was
one shaman's ritual that was going to be heavy on drums,
but otherwise I wanted the kids to imagine that they were
somewhere on the North American plains, four hundred
years ago. An Indian family has brought a sick relative into
the shaman's tipi. The tipi is dark. The family lays the sick
person on a cot and retreats. Then the shaman enters and the
drumming begins.

We performed the shaman ritual on the last day of camp, just
before the kids went home with their parents. What had started
out modestly had grown much grander by opening night. We'd
driven at least seventy miles to locate some dry ice, so we'd
have a nice smoky fog. We had stiltwalkers in the wings and
an actual tree that grew next to the stage – the World Tree. But
in the center of it all was the Winnarainbow Drum.

The risk in making a drum is that even though you follow
directions exactly, you can still end up with an instrument
that sounds like a boot scuffing the pavement. The voice of
the drum is a spirit thing, which is why the Ojibwa go to
elaborate lengths to infuse their drum with the proper voice.

There was a moment of silence as the lights went down,
then the drum spoke, a strong, throaty, tenor sound, filling
the little amphitheater with a slow, pulsing, booming beat that
was soon joined by an orchestra of rattles and hoop drums.

The counselor who played the shaman was wonderful. He
danced on and mimed falling into trance, calling his allies to
come and guide him to the World Tree. They came out on stilts.
As everyone watched, the shaman climbed the Tree and then
went into its roots to battle with the forces of disease.

By this time the percussion orchestra had a wide and thun-
derous groove going, which I like to think played a part in what
followed. One of the counselors had rented from a magic store a

theatrical prop that makes a body appear to levitate. When the shaman shouted for the sick person's body to arise healed, the body really *did* rise, and so did the kids in the audience, who all jumped to their feet, their mouths wide open.

For them it was suddenly real. Something had happened that they couldn't explain. It was a trick, of course, but it shattered their expectations and charged their imaginations. Who was going to tell them that a person couldn't rise into the air – hadn't they just seen a steer transformed into a drum?

I still meet some of these kids backstage at shows or on the street. We usually just nod or give each other the high five, rarely stopping to talk. To have built a drum together is probably to be bonded for life; but then to have ridden that drum together – there are no words for that.

Jill Purce

RE-ENCHANTING OUR LIVES

Jill Purce, international teacher of Inner Sound and Voice workshops, author of *The Mystic Spiral.* She has studied in the Himalayas with the chantmaster of the Gyuto Tibetan Monastery and Tantric College. She says: 'How do we create a sense of balance with a resonant universe? One of the best ways is by resonating with it, by re-enchanting our lives, for the heart and the voice are one and if we open the voice, we open the heart.'

There has been no other time in history when people did not sing as we do not sing. In the 1930s G.K. Chesterton, the English writer, was looking at a series of sculptures showing medieval peasants working in the fields and in all the activities of daily life. He wondered why in each scene the people had their mouths open. Then he realized they had their mouths open because they were singing. We rarely have our mouths open. We do not sing any more. We not only don't sing any more, but we don't realize we don't. We've forgotten to do it, and we've forgotten that we've forgotten. We're suffering from a double amnesia.

In all traditional societies chanting is the principal way of communing with the Divine, and of keeping society in tune with itself. In the Christian world, to take one example, until fifty or sixty years ago everyone went to church. People didn't

sing in church because they sang well, it was simply the way
to achieve and maintain harmony. By singing, chanting, and
intoning together in church, people tuned themselves. Our
body is a vibratory system with many different kinds of
resonances. If we stop chanting, we no longer keep ourselves
in tune. At church people are surrounded by their family. So
they would not only be tuning their own body, soul, and
spirit, but would also be tuning with their own family. The
family would be in tune with itself. In addition, since the
family would be surrounded by the people of the village,
all the village would be tuning itself together. The whole of
Christendom, to its furthest reaches, would be in resonance
with itself by tuning in similar ways at similar times. This
great resonant network would be tuned with the overall Divine
purpose.

Since all the great churches and cathedrals were built on
already sacred sites, this resonant tuning of the whole community would in turn be tuning itself to its *place*. When people
chanted together, they did not do it just anywhere, they came
to their local sacred place to do it, a place where there is
a mediation between, and therefore a greater permeability
between, the different realities or worlds, a place where the
tuning is more effective.

In a similar way, it was not just done at any *time*, but at the
sacred times, the cracks in time, when all things are accessible
in the moment, where all time is present. These were the
old festivals, later assimilated into the ecclesiastical calendar.
Each person's life would not only be related to its immediate
needs, requirements, and desires, but it would be put into the
context of its family, its village, its local community, its place
and time, and then related to something much greater still.
Through sonorous means every thing or being was resonantly
embedded in a greater meaning.

This kind of sacred chanting is now the preserve of a few
professionals and a negligible number of people. Our society
has gone silent.

Traditional societies have always encouraged a reciprocal
relationship with those forces that are greater than us and
which seem to have control of our life and destiny. In the
sixteenth and seventeenth centuries we began to find that

machines seemed to provide this greater degree of repeatability and predictability, and thus the kind of control of our circumstances that we had been trying to promote through invoking, praising, and petitioning God. As the sense of control became greater, we got increasingly confident, until our spiritual lives became marginalized.

This newly mechanized world was also a very noisy world. So we shifted the whole emphasis from a natural world full of natural sounds – birds, the wind in the trees, and, within it, ourselves singing and chanting as we praised the Divine – to a noisy world within which we ourselves are silent.

However, because it still seems right that some people should use their voices, we have empowered a few people out there, whom we have professionalized to make the sounds on our behalf. They make the sounds for us while we pay and then sit back and listen. Maybe inspired by some atavistic memory, we still have an unconscious desire to have the sounds back inside us. Since we have this dependent relationship with machines, we put the sounds of these professionals inside a machine, and then, excluding all human, environmental, and contextual sounds, put the machine over our ears, as close to our brain as possible. Then, unfortunately, since headphones impair our hearing, we end up silent *and* deaf in a noisy world!

In medieval times people talked about the sonorous nature of the soul. When we lose our voices, maybe we lose our souls. To *enchant* means to make magical through chant. So by rediscovering our voices, we may both find our souls and re-enchant the world.

There needs to be some readily available opportunity for people to be able to sing where they do not feel they have to sound like other people or necessarily sing in tune, so they can actually find their own voices. When people come together in this way to find their own voice, and have an opportunity to do this with others, it is as if they have been reborn. There is a sense of tremendous liberation.

When we do not sing, we are not in tune physically, we are not in tune emotionally or spiritually, nor are we in tune with others.

So I see the future as a time of re-enchantment where,

instead of going round with our mouths closed, as we have become accustomed to do, we will go around with our mouths open again, chanting and singing with each other. The balance of sounds will change. The mechanized world will diminish its noisiness and our song will again float on the atmosphere and rectify our lives emotionally, psychologically, and spiritually. We will become literally sound in mind and body.

This re-enchantment which can come through all of us finding our voices and expressing them together, also needs to be part of the greater re-sacralizing of art in general. It is not just music that should become revivified, but all our arts should again become sacred. Then every building that we create will have a sacred function and will take into account the proportions which make us feel good and which give us space for our souls to expand, and space for the sounds which come out of our mouths, for our breath or spirit to soar. The art world needs to change so that art is no longer just an expression of individuality and the state of mind of the person doing it, but becomes an expression of divine participation. Theatre could again become ceremonial and initiatory. Like the other arts, dance has also changed. Originally we danced in circles, so that the whole community danced together around the centre, then gradually we danced in threes and fours, in quadrilles and so on, then we waltzed in pairs, and now we dance alone.

The whole notion of resonance is now coming, not just as a musical metaphor or a mythological story, but into the very heart of science. Within every discipline, whether it be physics, chemistry, mathematics, biology, or brain physiology, we now find that resonant fields are the way that we have of best understanding and describing the world.

What we have also found is that the kind of control we thought we were getting by mechanizing and technologizing the world, in a desperate attempt to feel safe, has actually had the reverse effect. In some ways the more we have tried to control the world, the more we have made it a very dangerous place to live in. We have completely upset the balance. All the forces we were trying to control are now threatening our very existence. We have discovered that it's not possible to control the world through control. We have found that the only way we can have of living safely in a sustainable world is by reciprocity and creating a state of balance.

How do we create a sense of balance with a resonant universe? One of the best ways is by resonating with it, by re-enchanting our lives, for the heart and the voice are one and if we open the voice, we open the heart.

Paul and Linda McCartney

IF IT HAS A FACE DON'T EAT IT!

Paul and Linda McCartney, musicians. Paul is a former member of The Beatles, both are members of Wings. Campaigners for vegetarianism and the end of cruelty to animals. They say: 'Our point is that we have won the race on earth. Humans have won. There are no other species that will ever give us a problem ... Any time we want to remove a species we can do it. But we are not noble in our success.'

For us, becoming vegetarians was really only down to one thing – that we both grew up being great nature-lovers.

Linda, on her side of the world, was looking under rocks for salamanders in posh Scarsdale, New York, where she grew up. She had found a little patch of disused land between two houses and that is where she always used to go. Meanwhile, Paul was in Speke, Liverpool, out looking for frogs and sticklebacks. Paul used to go out with friends a lot, but when being with nature he was always on his own, walking and feeling poetic. And all the while Linda was doing the same in America.

By the time we got together, Paul was already with The Beatles and had lost touch with nature. He thought that was just his youth and now it was time to leave it all behind. But he already had a farm in Scotland. He had never done anything to it, just bought it and then wondered why it wasn't running so well, why the sheep were dying. It never occurred to him that as the owner he needed to be looking after it.

Linda suggested we repair the place and get it back into working order. So over the years we did, until we were the ones looking after the sheep, repairing the fences, riding the horses.

One day we were eating roast lamb. It was the lambing season so there were all these beautiful young lambs gambolling around the fields, running and playing in gangs together. And we looked at the lambs playing and we looked at the lamb on our plates and we suddenly realized that we were eating leg of lamb. And we looked at them running around outside again and saw leg of lamb, running and playing. And we said: 'Wait a minute, maybe we don't want to do this.' And that was it, the great turning point!

And now it has all changed. What started out just because we both loved animals has come to mean so much more to us. Some people think we are really odd! When we were kids, being vegetarian meant eating curry; in the sixties it meant having a lettuce sandwich! We see these signs in America saying things like 'Real meat for real people.' It's funny! It's like saying: 'Keep America beautiful – get your hair cut.' It's unnecessary. What excites us now is that being vegetarian is catching on. We notice the 'Real meat for real people' campaigns and know that it implies that people like us are wimps – but we know we're not. Traditions are changing, and it's good, it's allowing people to decide what they want to do.

There are three main reasons for becoming a vegetarian. Firstly, because it is better for your health – there is far less risk of heart attacks, high cholesterol, and so on. Secondly, there is the moral reason, to stop killing so many animals and subjecting them to incredible pain and suffering. We have all the food we want, with all the nutrition we could possible need, without having to eat meat. And thirdly, there are environmental reasons. Raising animals for meat uses up an enormous amount more land than growing grains and vegetables does. Forests are being razed to graze cattle, we feed the animals the grains while humans are starving. Giving up eating meat is the most important thing we could do to help the environment.

People don't realize that when they are eating meat they are eating an animal that had its throat slit, or that has been reared and died in pain, that it has been hung upside down and bled. People want their chicken pre-packed and clean – they don't want to have to pull out the giblets any more. They try to hide the fact that what they are eating had a face and a heart, was once alive.

Animals are like us. They can't talk or read or write, but they have feelings and instincts. They know when they are going to die. Slaughterhouse attendants testify that almost all pigs, forced up the ramp to the killing room, do one thing – they scream. The average Westerner will eat twenty cows, fourteen hundred chickens, twelve pigs and thirteen sheep in his or her lifetime. That is a lot of lives.

It is only by demand that things change. As each person demands vegetarian food and stops buying so much meat, so it will change. The demand has fallen off for fur coats because less people want to wear them. Have you ever seen a factory-farmed chicken in its cage, with half its feathers missing and its talons bent and its beak gone? It doesn't look too appetizing! Or a veal calf, crammed into a box so tight that it cannot turn around to lick itself? Fish and chicken are not vegetables, they have faces, they have babies, they have nervous systems, they have feelings, and they do not grow in fields. They have to die for you to eat them.

Charity begins at home. If we can clean up our own house then it will affect others. We can all make a difference. If each individual became a vegetarian it would make for a much happier and more peaceful world. Have we not had enough of the murder and slaughter and vivisection?

It was all brought into focus one day by our youngest daughter, Stella, coming home from school and saying how they had been having a debate about eating meat. She said that when she came to talk about it she had a really clear conscience. That was very powerful – a child having a clear conscience.

And so we really got into it and started becoming activists because we realized that what we were doing was helping to save those poor animals from getting shunted into a slaughterhouse, and we were helping to save the environment at the same time.

And so the spiritual side of our life changed too. Our point is that we have won the race on earth. Humans have won. There are no other species that will ever give us a problem. No elephants will ever rule us, we've got guns to stop them. Any time we want to remove a species we can do it. But we are not noble in our success. We look forward to the time when, as a race, we can have nobility in our success and relax a bit, when we do not have to keep hating and fighting.

People say that fish don't have feelings. Come on. People think that animals don't have souls. How does anyone know that? Has someone got inside an animal's head and found out? It is so convenient to think an animal has no soul. It makes it OK to eat it then. But what if it has? The human race really is the most pompous thing going!

But we have faith things will change.

Larry Dossey

DOING MORE BY DOING LESS

Larry Dossey MD, physician with the Dallas Diagnostic Association. Author of *Space, Time and Medicine, Beyond Illness, Recovering the Soul: A Scientific and Spiritual Search,* and *Meaning and Medicine: A Doctor's Stories of Breakthrough and Healing.* He says: 'The Earth *is* together; it is we who are fragmented. If we hope to play any lasting role in what occurs on our planet, we must recover our lost unity.'

In recent years we have learned some surprising lessons about predicting the future. We know that it is impossible to foresee accurately what will happen in most situations in nature, from the behavior of electrons to global weather patterns. However, our inability to know what lies ahead is not due to our ignorance, of not having enough facts to make accurate predictions, but the way the world inherently works.

This understanding is part of the emerging science of chaos dynamics, which tells us that, even if we know all the initial conditions that make up certain situations, we are nonetheless unable to know what will develop in the future. This is a far cry from the causal, linear formulations of classical science, in which 'A leads to B leads to C' and invariably does so whenever 'A' is initially present.

In addition, chaos science tells us that nature holds many

happy surprises. Disordered situations often give rise paradoxically not to additional chaos but to greater order and
complexity. In certain situations, disorder is in fact *required*
for the development of more highly organized future states.

If ever our global society was in chaos, that time is now. Does
this mean, consistent with chaos theory, that we could be on
the threshold of a great leap forward into a more intricately
organized and highly ordered future? This is where I place
my hope for the future because I believe we have a greater
ally in nature than in the best schemes of our most brilliant
thinkers.

One of the most consistent results of human attempts to fix
global problems is our unerring ability to make them worse.
Attempts to 'civilize' native peoples have repeatedly brought
about their near destruction, as when smallpox, measles,
venereal diseases and other maladies decimated the Native
American and Hawaiian populations. The widespread use of
DDT to control 'pests' almost wiped out certain avian species,
which was totally unforeseen. The introduction of modern
medical measures into many cultures has led to population
explosions with resultant social disruption and hardships that
were completely unanticipated. These attempts reveal again
and again that our knowledge about how to 'improve nature'
is tragically incomplete and frequently backfires.

What, then, are we to do? We can continue to act with good
intention and with as much foresight as we can muster. And
we can take advantage of the inherent tendency in nature
for order and healing to emerge from the chaotic situations
that confront us. And we can help set them in motion – not
by *doing* anything in particular, but paradoxically by *being*
a certain way.

Evidence for the power of being as opposed to doing
comes from many sources. Numerous studies in meditation
conducted over the past decade have repeatedly shown that
when a certain number of people enter into a particular state
of consciousness, the world around them quite simply changes
for the better.[1] Interestingly, participants in these studies do

1. Larry Dossey, 'The Maharishi Effect', in *Recovering the Soul* (Bantam,
New York, 1989), pp. 256–63

not meditate with a particular outcome or goal in mind. They are not intentionally willing, for example, that a war diminish in intensity, that atmospheric pollution fall, or that the level of violent crime in the surrounding community abate. They simply come together and meditate. This approach is in marked contrast to the widespread notion that one must hold the preferred outcome of one's prayers, images, and meditations 'in consciousness,' that one's wishes be highly specific.

Similar results have been demonstrated in an extensive series of experiments by the Spindrift organization. They discovered not only that prayer works but that the most effective prayer strategy is a *nondirected* one. In a nondirected approach the praying person simply asks that the best outcome for the situation in question occur, without implying what that might be. This prayer strategy avoids telling the Universe what to do. It does not presume that we know how to 'fix' a situation. It employs perhaps the simplest prayer strategy possible, a 'Thy will be done' or a 'Let it be' approach. The presumption underlying this perspective is that the Universe at some level already knows what to do.[2]

If this is so – if the natural world may improve when we assume certain ways of being – then our robust, rough-and-ready attempts to 'fix nature' may be extremely misguided. If the world works best when we get out of the way, then it is not surprising that our aggressive efforts so frequently backfire and make matters worse. And if there is an inner perfection waiting to happen, our current dilemmas do not depend on us for answers. The solutions already exist and are just waiting to occur. The world already knows what to do.[3]

Ironically, thus, our best approach may be to learn how to *be*, not *do*. But how? Pierre Teilhard de Chardin, the Jesuit priest and scholar, once said,

2. See Larry Dossey, 'How Should We Pray: The Spindrift Experiments', in *Recovering the Soul* (Bantam, New York, 1989) pp. 54–62
3. Renée Weber, 'Philosophical Foundations and Frameworks for Healing', *ReVision* 2:2, Summer/Fall 1979, pp. 66–77

> For men upon earth, all the earth, to learn to love one another,
> it is not enough that they should know themselves to be
> members of one and the same *thing* [such as the Earth]; in
> 'planetising' themselves they must acquire the consciousness,
> without losing themselves, of becoming one and the same
> *person.*[4]

Teilhard realized that a new way of defining ourselves is
necessary if we are to live harmoniously with each other
and the Earth. This transformation must involve, he tells us,
a sense of unity. We cannot act wisely as long as we believe
we are isolated individuals disconnected from each other and
the world. The sense of a thoroughgoing individuality sets
the stage for viewing the world as an 'out there' completely
separate from ourselves. As long as we feel cut off from the
world, we are likely to be unaware of its innate intelligence
and regard it as an unthinking organism that is wholly brute,
mute, and blind. Yet there is another attitude we can take. It is
exemplified by those who learn to change the universe by ways
of being – meditators who come together and merely enter a
certain state of consciousness, praying persons who ask only
for the 'right thing' to be done, sick persons who learn to 'just
be' and who experience a cure. These persons seem to have
gone beyond a sense of rigid individuality. They are 'beyond
duality,' as some religious traditions put it.

It may seem that the oneness spoken of by Teilhard is
hopelessly mystical and impractical, as skeptics frequently
charge. I believe this is not the case, and that modern scientific
research has demonstrated in various ways the essential unity
of the mind and consciousness of all peoples. What does
this evidence look like? Human consciousness at some level
appears to be *nonlocal* – i.e. minds cannot be localized or
confined to specific points in space, such as individual brains
or bodies, or to specific points in time, such as the present
moment. Some aspect of the psyche of all persons is at some
level unbounded in space and time.

The spiritual implications of this picture of the mind are
unmistakable. Because minds are unbounded in space and

4. Robert Wright, *Three Scientists and their Gods* (Times Book, New York;
1988), p. 271

time, they appear to be *omnipresent* and *immortal*, descriptions we have always attributed to the Absolute. There appears, thus, to be an inner, imperishable, *divine* quality in every human being. And if this part of us is genuinely nonlocal and unbounded, there cannot be five-and-a-half billion separate minds on the face of the Earth, but a *single* mind – what is called the Universal or One Mind. This point of view was expressed by Nobel physicist Erwin Schrödinger, whose wave equations lie at the heart of modern physics:

> The mind by its nature is a *singulare tantum*. I should say: the overall number of minds is just one.[5]

The vision of a unitary consciousness that envelops all persons has been affirmed throughout history by countless mystics and poets. W. B. Yeats' statement is typical:

> The borders of our minds are ever shifting
> And many minds can flow into one another . . .
> And create or reveal a single mind, a single energy.

The intrinsic unity of all minds, when acknowledged, could create an action based on being, not on doing. A sense of unity with each other is only a short step from a sense of unity with the living Earth, of which we are a part. This relationship leads naturally to the wish to attune and align with the natural world instead of dominating, utilizing, or 'fixing' it.

Will this relationship come to pass on a scale large enough to make a difference? Will we learn to *be* in ways that facilitate the self-healing tendencies of our planet? As in all situations that are governed by the laws of chaos dynamics, we cannot say with certainty what lies ahead. But if these views were once thought to be only dreamy mysticism, that time has changed.

On the back cover of the Whole Earth Catalog, that magnificent publication that was a clarion call of the hippie movement in the late Sixties, was a stunning NASA photo of the Earth floating in the black immensity of space. Under this image was the caption:

> You can't put it together. It is together.

5. Erwin Schrödinger, *What Is Life? and Mind and Matter* (Cambridge University Press, London; 1969), p. 145

The Earth *is* together; it is we who are fragmented. If we hope to play any lasting role in what occurs on our planet, we must recover our lost unity. If we want to be around to witness the outcome of our current dilemmas, our efforts toward healing had best be directed inward to ourselves, instead of only outward, as is generally the case today. This means discovering the right way to *be*.

And what if we should fail? If there is truth to the messages of chaos dynamics, a higher order may yet arise on our planet in spite of our appalling stupidities and ineptitude. If there is an inherent perfection in the world, perhaps there is no failure.

For which, it seems to me, we should lift up our voice in praise to the Cosmos.

PART FOUR

The Ecological Relationship

Rick Fields

THE DREAM CORRIDOR

Rick Fields, author of *How the Swans Came to the Lake: A Narrative History of Buddhism in America*, *Chop Wood, Carry Water*, and *The Code of the Warrior: in History, Myth and Everyday Life*. His poems have appeared in many publications, including 'Dharma Gaia'. He says: 'Impeccable, attentive, intent, not wavering, *This is how to look at the world . . .*'

Yellowjacket bite on bare belly
Wakes me up
Sky clears
Human going wrong way,
I run into doe with two yearlings
on hoof-cut deerpath.
Her eyes are deep pools. Watching,
Unafraid, she steps calmly
Down and around me, the young ones
Skittering after.

This world is absolutely pure
As is. Behind the fear,
Vulnerability. Behind that
Sadness, then compassion.
And behind that the vast sky.

Crossing the stream to leave
A snake, upright, S-curved,
Slit eyes a-glitter
Stares straight ahead,
Tiny black red-tipped forked
Tongue flickering like flame.

We sit eye to eye.
Seconds, minutes, ages pass.
Snake doesn't blink.
I do.
Impeccable, attentive, intent, not wavering,
This is how to look at the world
You are returning to.
Snake doesn't move. I do.
I bow, inhaling sweet pine resin of the earth
And pass back over the rushing stream
To the other side.

Václav Havel

POLITICS WITH CONSCIENCE

Václav Havel, President of Czechoslovakia, and internationally acclaimed playwright. Formerly jailed for four years for being a co-founder of the Charter 77 human rights movement. Author of *Living in Truth*. He says: 'No evil has ever been eliminated by suppressing its symptoms. We need to address the cause itself.'

As a boy, I lived for some time in the country and I clearly remember an experience from those days: I used to walk to school in a nearby village along a cart track through the fields and, on the way, see on the horizon a huge smokestack of some hurriedly built factory, in all likelihood in the service of war. It spewed dense brown smoke and scattered it across the sky. Each time I saw it, I had an intense sense of something profoundly wrong, of humans soiling the heavens. I have no idea whether there was something like a science of ecology in those days; if there was, I certainly knew nothing of it. Still that 'soiling the heavens' offended me spontaneously. It seemed to me that, in it, humans are guilty of something, that they destroy something important, arbitrarily disrupting the natural order of things, and that such things cannot go unpunished. To be sure, my revulsion was largely aesthetic; I knew nothing then of the noxious emissions which would one day devastate our forests, exterminate game and endanger the health of people.

If a medieval man were to see something like that suddenly on the horizon – say, while out hunting – he would probably think it the work of the Devil and would fall on his knees and pray that he and his kin be saved.

What is it, actually, that the world of the medieval peasant and that of a small boy have in common? Something substantive, I think. Both the boy and the peasant are far more intensely rooted in what some philosophers call 'the natural world', or *Lebenswelt*, than most modern adults. They have not yet grown alienated from the world of their actual personal experience, the world which has its morning and its evening, its *down* (the earth) and its *up* (the heavens), where the sun rises daily in the east, traverses the sky and sets in the west, and where concepts like 'at home' and 'in foreign parts', good and evil, beauty and ugliness, near and far, duty and work, still mean something living and definite. They are still rooted in a world which knows the dividing line between all that is intimately familiar and appropriately a subject of our concern, and that which lies beyond its horizon, that before which we should bow down humbly because of the mystery about it.

The natural world, in virtue of its very being, bears within it the presupposition of the absolute which grounds, delimits, animates, and directs it, without which it would be unthinkable, absurd and superfluous, and which we can only quietly respect. Any attempt to spurn it, master it or replace it with something else, appears, within the framework of the natural world, as an expression of *hubris* for which humans must pay a heavy price, as did Don Juan and Faust.

To me, personally, the smokestack soiling the heavens is not just a regrettable lapse of a technology that failed to include 'the ecological factor' in its calculation, one which can be easily corrected with the appropriate filter. To me it is more, the symbol of an age which seeks to transcend the boundaries of the natural world and its norms and to make it into a merely private concern, a matter of subjective preference and private feeling, of the illusions, prejudices and whims of a 'mere' individual. It is a symbol of an epoch which denies the binding importance of personal experience – including the experience of mystery and of the absolute – and displaces the personally experienced absolute as the measure of the world with a new, man-made absolute, devoid of mystery, free of the 'whims' of subjectivity and, as such, impersonal and inhuman. It is the absolute of so-called objectivity: the objective, rational cognition of the scientific model of the world.

Modern science, constructing its universally valid image of the world, thus crashes through the bounds of the natural world which it can understand only as a prison of prejudices from which we must break out into the light of objectively verified truth. The natural world appears to it as no more than an unfortunate left-over from our backward ancestors, a fantasy of their childish immaturity. With that, of course, it abolishes as mere fiction even the innermost foundation of our natural world; it kills God and takes his place on the vacant throne so that henceforth it would be science which would hold the order of being in its hand as its sole legitimate guardian and be the sole legitimate arbiter of all relevant truth. For after all, it is only science that rises above all individual subjective truths and replaces them with a superior, trans-subjective, trans-personal truth which is truly objective and universal.

Modern rationalism and modern science, though the work of man that, as all human works, developed within our natural world, now systematically leave it behind, deny it, degrade and defame it – and, of course, at the same time colonize it. A modern man, whose natural world has been properly conquered by science and technology, objects to the smoke from the smokestack only if the stench penetrates his apartment. In no case, though, does he take offence at it *metaphysically* since he knows that the factory to which the smokestack belongs manufactures things that he needs. As a man of the technological era, he can conceive of a remedy only within the limits of technology – say, a catalytic scrubber fitted to the chimney.

Lest you misunderstand: I am not proposing that humans abolish smokestacks or prohibit science or generally return to the Middle Ages. Besides, it is not by accident that some of the most profound discoveries of modern science render the myth of objectivity surprisingly problematic and, via a remarkable detour, return us to the human subject and his world. I wish no more than to consider, in a most general and admittedly schematic outline, the spiritual framework of modern civilization and the source of its present crisis. And though the primary focus of these reflections will be the political rather than ecological aspects of this crisis, I might, perhaps, clarify my starting point with one more ecological example.

For centuries, the basic component of European agriculture had been the family farm. In Czech, the older term for it was *grunt* – which itself is not without its etymological interest. The word, taken from the German *Grund*, actually means ground or foundation and, in Czech, acquired a peculiar semantic colouring. As the colloquial synonym for 'foundation', it points out the 'groundedness' of the ground, its indubitable, traditional, and pre-speculatively given authenticity and veridicality. Certainly, the family farm was a source of endless and intensifying social conflict of all kinds. Still, we cannot deny it one thing: it was rooted in the nature of its place, appropriate, harmonious, personally tested by generations of farmers and certified by the results of their husbandry. It also displayed a kind of optimal mutual proportionality in extent and kind of all that belonged to it; fields, meadows, boundaries, woods, cattle, domestic animals, water, toads, and so on. For centuries no farmer made it the topic of a scientific study. Nevertheless, it constituted a generally satisfactory economic and ecological system, within which everything was bound together by a thousand threads of mutual and meaningful connection, guaranteeing its stability as well as the stability of the product of the farmer's husbandry. Unlike present-day 'agro-business', the traditional family farm was energetically self-sufficient. Though it was subject to common calamities, it was not guilty of them – unfavourable weather, cattle disease, wars and other catastrophes lay outside the farmer's province.

Certainly, modern agricultural and social science could also improve agriculture in a thousand ways, increasing its productivity, reducing the amount of sheer drudgery, and eliminating the worst social inequities. But this is possible only on the assumption that modernization, too, will be guided by a certain humility and respect for the mysterious order of nature and for the appropriateness which derives from it and which is intrinsic to the natural world of personal experience and responsibility. Modernization must not be simply an arrogant, megalomaniac and brutal invasion by an impersonally objective science, represented by a newly graduated agronomist or a bureaucrat in the service of the 'scientific world view'.

That is just what happened to our country: our word for it was 'collectivization'. Like a tornado, it raged through the Czechoslovak countryside thirty years ago, leaving not a stone in place. Among its consequences were, on the one hand, tens of thousands of lives devastated by prison, sacrificed on the altar of a scientific Utopia about brighter tomorrows. On the other hand, the level of social conflict and the amount of drudgery in the countryside did in truth decrease while agricultural productivity rose quantitatively. That, though, is not why I mention it. My reason is something else: thirty years after the tornado swept the traditional family farm off the face of the earth, scientists are amazed to discover what even a semi-literate farmer previously knew – that human beings must pay a heavy price for every attempt to abolish, radically, once and for all and without trace, that humbly respected boundary of the natural world, with its tradition of scrupulous personal acknowledgement. They must pay for the attempt to seize nature, to leave not a remnant of it in human hands, to ridicule its mystery; they must pay for the attempt to abolish God and to play at being God.

The price, in fact, fell due. With hedges ploughed under and woods cut down, wild birds have died out and with them a natural, unpaid protector of the crops against harmful insects. Huge unified fields have led to the inevitable annual loss of millions of cubic yards of topsoil that have taken centuries to accumulate; chemical fertilizers and pesticides have catastrophically poisoned all vegetable products, the earth and the waters. Heavy machinery systematically presses down the soil, making it impenetrable to air and thus infertile; cows in gigantic dairy farms suffer neuroses and lose their milk while agriculture siphons off ever more energy from industry – manufacture of machines, artificial fertilizers, rising transportation costs in an age of growing local specialization, and so on. In short, the prognoses are terrifying and no one knows what the surprises the coming years and decades may bring.

It is paradoxical: people in the age of science and technology live in the conviction that they can improve their lives because they are able to grasp and exploit the complexity of nature and the general laws of its functioning. Yet it is precisely these laws which, in the end, tragically catch up with them and get the better of them. People thought they could explain and conquer nature – yet the outcome is that they destroyed it and disinherited themselves from it. But what are the prospects for man 'outside nature'? It is, after all, precisely the sciences that are most recently discovering that the human body is actually only a particularly busy intersection of billions of organic microbodies, of their complex mutual contacts and influences, together forming that incredible mega-organism we call the 'biosphere' in which our planet is blanketed.

The fault is not one of science as such but of the arrogance of man in the age of science. Man simply is not God, and playing God has cruel consequences. Man has abolished the absolute horizon of his relations, denied his personal 'pre-objective' experience of the lived world, while relegating personal conscience and consciousness to the bathroom, as something so private that it is no one's business. Man rejected his responsibility as a 'subjective illusion' – and in place of it installed what is now proving to be the most dangerous illusion of all: the fiction of objectivity stripped of all that is concretely human, of a rational understanding of the cosmos, and of an abstract schema of a putative 'historical necessity'. As the apex of it all, man has constructed a vision of a purely scientifically calculable and technologically achievable 'universal welfare', demanding no more than that experimental institutes invent it while industrial and bureaucratic factories turn it into reality. That millions of people will be sacrificed to this illusion in scientifically directed concentration camps is not something that concerns our 'modern man' unless by chance he himself lands behind barbed wire and is thrown drastically back upon his natural world. The phenomenon of empathy, after all, belongs with that abolished realm of personal prejudice which had to yield to science, objectivity, historical necessity, technology, system and the *'apparat'* –

and those, being impersonal, cannot worry. They are abstract and anonymous, ever utilitarian and thus also ever *a priori* innocent.

And as for the future? Who, personally, would care about it or even personally worry about it, when the perspective of eternity is one of the things locked away in the bathroom, if not expelled outright into the realm of fairy tales? If a contemporary scientist thinks at all of what will be in two hundred years, he does so solely as a personally disinterested observer who, basically, could not care less whether he is doing research on the metabolism of the flea, on the radio signals of pulsars or on the global reserves of natural gas. And a modern politician? He has absolutely no reason to care, especially if it might interfere with his chances in an election, as long as he lives in a country where there are elections . . .

A Czech philosopher, Václav Bělohradský, suggestively unfolded the thought that the rationalistic spirit of modern science, founded on abstract reason and on the presumption of impersonal objectivity, has, beside its father in the natural sciences, Galileo, also a father in politics – Machiavelli, who first formulated, albeit with an undertone of malicious irony, a theory of politics as a rational technology of power. We could say that, for all the complex historical detours, the origin of the modern state and of modern political power may be sought precisely here, that is, once again in a moment when human reason begins to 'free' itself from the human being as such, from his personal experience, personal conscience and personal responsibility and so also from that to which, within the framework of the natural world, all responsibility is uniquely related, his absolute horizon. Just as the modern scientists set apart the actual human being as the subject of the lived experience of the world, so, ever more evidently, do both the modern state and modern politics.

As Bělohradský points out, the depersonalization of power and its conquest of human conscience and human speech have been successfully linked to an extra-European tradition of a 'cosmological' conception of the empire (identifying the empire, as the sole true centre of the world, with the world as such, and considering the human as its exclusive property). But, as the totalitarian systems clearly illustrate, this does not mean that the modern impersonal power is itself an extra-European affair. The truth is the very opposite: it was precisely Europe, and the European West, that provided and frequently forced on the world all that today has become the basis of such power: natural science, rationalism, scientism, the industrial revolution, and also revolution as such, as a fanatical abstraction, through the displacement of the natural world to the bathroom down to the cult of consumption, the atomic bomb and Marxism. And it is Europe – democratic western Europe – which today stands bewildered in the face of this ambiguous export.

The contemporary dilemma, whether to resist this reverse expansionism of its erstwhile export or to yield to it, attests to this. Should rockets, now aimed at Europe thanks to its export of spiritual and technological potential, be countered by similar and better rockets, thereby demonstrating a determination to defend such values as Europe has left, at the cost of entering into an utterly immoral game being forced upon it? Or should Europe retreat, hoping that the responsibility for the fate of the planet demonstrated thereby will infect, by its miraculous power, the rest of the world?

I think that, with respect to the relation of western Europe to the totalitarian systems, no error could be greater than the one looming largest: that of a failure to understand the totalitarian systems for what they ultimately are – a convex mirror of all modern civilization and a harsh, perhaps final call for a global recasting of that civilization's self-understanding. If we ignore that, then it does not make any essential difference which form Europe's efforts will take. It might be the form of taking the totalitarian systems, in the spirit of Europe's own rationalistic tradition, as some locally idiosyncratic attempt at achieving 'general welfare', to which only men of ill-will attribute expansionist tendencies. Or, in the spirit of the same rationalistic tradition, though this time in the Machiavellian conception of politics as the technology of power, one might perceive the totalitarian regimes as a purely external threat by expansionist neighbours who can be driven back within acceptable bounds by an appropriate demonstration of power, without having to be considered more deeply. The first alternative is that of the person who reconciles himself to the chimney belching smoke, even though that smoke is ugly and smelly, because in the end it serves a good purpose, the production of commonly needed goods. The second alternative is that of the man who thinks that it is simply a matter of a technological flaw, which can be eliminated by technological means, such as a filter or a scrubber.

The reality, I believe, is unfortunately more serious. The chimney 'soiling the heavens' is not just a technologically corrigible flaw of design, or a tax paid for a better consumerist tomorrow, but a symbol of a civilization which has renounced the absolute, which ignores the natural world and disdains its imperatives. So, too, the totalitarian systems warn of something far more serious than western rationalism is willing to admit. They are, most of all, a convex mirror of the inevitable consequences of rationalism, a grotesquely magnified image of its own deep tendencies, an extremist offshoot of its own development and an ominous product of its own crisis. Those regimes are not merely dangerous neighbours and even less some kind of an avant-garde of world progress. Alas, just the opposite: they are the avant-garde of a global crisis of this civilization, first European, then Euro-American, and ultimately global. They are one of the possible futurological studies of the western world, not in the sense that one day they will attack and conquer it, but in a far deeper sense – that they illustrate graphically to what the 'eschatology of the impersonal', as Bělohradský calls it, can lead.

It is the total rule of a bloated, anonymously bureaucratic power, not yet irresponsible but already operating outside all conscience, a power grounded in an omnipresent ideological fiction which can rationalize anything without ever having to brush against the truth. Power as the omnipresent monopoly of control, repression and fear; power which makes thought, morality and privacy a state monopoly and so dehumanizes them; power which long since has ceased to be the matter of a group of arbitrary rulers but which, rather, occupies and swallows up everyone so that all should become integrated within it, at least through their silence. No one actually possesses such power, since it is the power itself which possesses everyone; it is a monstrosity which is not guided by humans but which, on the contrary, drags all persons along with its 'objective' self-momentum – objective in the sense of being cut off from all human standards, including human reason and hence entirely irrational – to a terrifying, unknown future.

Let me repeat: it is a great reminder to contemporary civilization. Perhaps somewhere there may be some generals who think it would be best to dispatch such systems from the face of the earth and then all would be well. But that is no different from an ugly woman trying to get rid of her ugliness by smashing the mirror which reminds her of it. Such a 'final solution' is one of the typical dreams of impersonal reason – capable, as the term 'final solution' graphically reminds us, of transforming its dreams into reality and thereby reality into a nightmare. It would not only fail to resolve the crisis of the present world but, assuming anyone survived at all, would only aggravate it. By burdening the already heavy account of this civilization with further millions of dead, it would not block its essential trend to totalitarianism but would rather accelerate it. It would be a Pyrrhic victory, because the victors would emerge from a conflict inevitably resembling their defeated opponents far more than anyone today is willing to admit or able to imagine. Just as a minor example: imagine what a huge Gulag Archipelago would have to be built in the West, in the name of country, democracy, progress and war discipline, to contain all who refuse to take part in the effort, whether from naïvety, principle, fear or ill-will!

No evil has ever been eliminated by suppressing its symptoms. We need to address the cause itself.

HRH Prince Philip

A NEW VISION IN BUSINESS

HRH Prince Philip, The Duke of Edinburgh. He says: 'Vision generates hope; hope that we will be able to halt and eventually reverse the destruction of nature that we can so clearly see all around us . . . "Where there is no vision, all life will perish."'

The question that I would like to pose is whether people involved in business and commerce can develop a code of conduct which allows them to be productive and profitable, while at the same time being concerned about the source of raw materials, what is produced, how it is produced, and whether the whole process is in accord with the need to treat the natural environment with respect, making use of it in such a way that it can be sustained over a long period of time.

Corporations have many responsibilities, but I would suggest that responsibility for their impact on the natural environment has become by far the most important. Since this is a subject outside the traditional scope of business management, I would suggest that there is an urgent need for specialist assistance from both conservationists and moral philosophers in what will certainly prove to be a major reappraisal of priorities and responsibilities.

I would question whether it is possible for companies or associations, as such, to develop standards of ethics or responsibility. I believe that the initiative has to come from individuals in positions of authority within these organizations. Furthermore, if they are to influence the policies of their organizations in the right direction, they need to have a personal comittment to promoting action; not any action, but the right action.

Since the majority of such people have inevitably grown up in urban conditions, and since the education system includes little or nothing about the working of the global or natural environments, and even less about ecology, and since the churches are only now beginning to include conservation among their list of ethics, this is not as easy as it sounds.

The first priority is to see nature not simply as a storehouse of materials or as a place for human recreation, but as a vital interrelated web of life of which we humans are only a part, although a very important part. There can be no doubt at all that unless some serious rethinking takes place, the future of all life on earth will be at great risk and, as the apex species, humanity will be at greatest risk.

I would suggest that responsibility goes beyond individual companies. In a football match, it would be hopeless if only a few of the players played by the rules. Whole industries need to tackle these issues together. National and international trade and industry associations will need to develop policies and practices relevant to their industries and for all their members.

It is easy enough for the older members to shrug it all off on the score that nothing serious can happen in our time, but I believe that we all have a responsibility to future generations not to gamble with their quality of life. One thing is absolutely certain; this over-burdened earth of ours cannot conceivably sustain even the present human population for more than a very limited number of years. Even without further growth, it is barely able to sustain the increasing per-capita consumption in the rich countries and the increasing number of subsistence consumers in the poorer countries.

I firmly believe that a new conservation ethic in business and private life could have a decisive influence. There may still be just enough time to ensure that reasonable standards of living could be achieved for all, but only by the exercise of restraint in reproduction and by the intelligent use of ecologically and environmentally sensitive industrial methods.

This in turn would depend on the use of the power of modern research techniques to develop such methods; but first there must be a motive. These matters are not about economic development, they are to do with comprehension and conviction. Fortunately there are welcome signs that the great faiths are searching for a new vision and a new motive. I hope that industry and commerce will do the same.

In many ways vision is the most important. Vision generates hope; hope that we will be able to halt and eventually reverse the destruction of nature that we can so clearly see all around us. As the writer of the Book of Proverbs puts it: 'Where there is no vision, the people perish.' Had he been alive today, I think he might have written; Where there is no vision, all life will perish.

Helen Caldicott

CREATING A SANE AND CARING SOCIETY

Helen Caldicott MD, founding President of Physicians for Social Responsibility, member of the 1986 Nobel Prizewinning International Physicians for the Prevention of Nuclear War. Author of *Nuclear Madness: What You Can do? Missile Envy*, and *If you Love This Planet*. She says: 'We are really at a turning point now as we move towards the next millennium. We have few choices about what has to be done. And it can be done because we can handle the dark, the lies, and the pollution, just as we can handle the light and the forces of good. It is our task in life to make this planet a beautiful place to be, that is why we are here. I know we can do it, I know we will.'

We've got about ten years in which to save the world. If we don't act now, then within that period of time many of the earth's species will be extinct. Mankind has a huge brain which has developed very fast in evolutionary terms and which enables us to make and hold on to things like guns. In this way we dominate the earth. We are the only species that destroys other species for our own purposes. We think nature was put there purely for our convenience because it says in Genesis that man was given dominion over the earth. But who wrote Genesis? Did the koalas write Genesis, did the elephants write Genesis? It would appear that there are approximately thirty million other species of which we have detailed only 1.5 million. A biologist who went to the forests in Peru found as many species of ant on one tree as there are in the whole of the United Kingdom. So the number of species is enormous and we are destroying them.

There are only ten thousand elephants left. There used to be millions when I was a child. They have become endangered because we like to wear their tusks on our wrists and on our ears. The scientists say it's OK because when the elephants have gone we will put their genes in a gene bank. So I suppose the elephants could say: 'It's OK. If Homo sapiens disappears then we'll put their genes in a gene bank and then one day we can try to reconstruct a human being.' Makes sense, doesn't it?

We have to feel for the animals: for the lions, tigers, whales and elephants. I surf with the dolphins every morning in Australia. They have brains as big as ours, they can count and speak in funny phonetics. They are as intelligent as us but they just don't communicate in the same way. They don't think how they would like a nice steak that night so they should go and kill a human and take out the fillet steak from beside the vertebrae and cook it up just right. But we kill them in drift nets sixty kilometers long in order to eat tuna fish sandwiches.

One third of the fresh water of the world is in the Amazon. Every afternoon there is a huge thunderstorm because the trees transpire thousands of gallons each day to create their perfect climate. It rains and the leaves fall creating humus, then the bacteria rot the humus and the trees take up the rotting humus again as necessary nourishment. The rainforest is being chopped down to create land to raise cheap beef to give us hamburgers which are no good for our health anyway, producing hypercholesterolaemia, arteriosclerosis, hypertension, strokes, heart attacks, and colonic cancer. We did not evolve eating meat – we evolved eating grain. The amount of grain that is now used to feed cattle in America alone could feed all the starving people in the world. Meantime, two thirds of the world's children are malnourished.

When we chop down the forests to make room for grass then after two years nothing grows because the soil is basically sterile without the rotting humus coming from the forest. So then the grass dies and more trees get chopped down to make room for more grass. There are plans to put a hundred dams in the rainforest and to put a road right through the center for development. Open up the forest like this and the whole thing soon goes. These beautiful cathedral-like trees get chopped down or they fall down and lie rotting on the ground. Small, spindly banana trees are planted between them.

The Amazon is the lungs of this hemisphere. The earth is dying as we fill up the atmosphere with carbon dioxide from all the cars we are driving and the electricity we are burning and there aren't enough trees left to take in that carbon dioxide and replace it with oxygen. So we add to the global greenhouse effect simply by getting in our car to go and get some milk. Trees are upside down lungs, the lungs of the earth, our earth.

How do we use paper? The Japanese use the equivalent of one forest a day in disposable chopsticks. We use trees to blow our noses on. It is medically contra-indicated to use trees to blow our noses because if we do this then we are killing the earth. It is medically contra-indicated to kill the earth because then we all die. I watched a television advertisement recently. There were soft, beautiful, out-of-focus pictures of young mothers with their little babies. The mothers were drying their babies' tears with paper tissues – with their babies' futures.

Let us not buy unnecessary paper products, magazines, or newspapers. Magazines that are made from glossy paper are made from eucalyptus trees, depriving the koalas of their homes. Most of these magazines are full of advertisements telling us that if we put certain stuff on our faces, at maybe $50 a bottle, then we will live happily ever after, wrinkle-free and having great sex! I urge you to think carefully about how you use paper in your life because paper is from trees and trees are our lungs, our life.

The ozone layer is three kilometers thick up in the stratosphere, but if we bring it down to the high pressures at the earth's level it is only three meters thick. Before there was ozone there was no complex life. The plankton absorbed carbon dioxide, utilizing solar energy, creating oxygen that floated slowly up to the stratosphere where it reacted with ultraviolet to form ozone. The ozone then started filtering out, like a pair of sunglasses, the ultraviolet light from the sun. That meant that multi-cellular organisms could develop because ultraviolet light is phototoxic: it kills cells. In other words, without ozone there is no development of life.

We recently discovered that there is a hole in the ozone layer over the south pole, and the ozone layer over the north pole is getting thinner. Why? Years ago they discovered this gas called chlorofluorocarbon (CFC), which was inert and did not react with other chemicals and did not seem to hurt us. So it was used for refrigeration, air conditioners, and the propellant in the spray cans which we use when we spray our hair, our armpits and so on. We spray spots on our carpets and spray clean our ovens. Styrofoam also has CFC in it.

CFC rises very slowly, then, when it gets to the stratosphere, the chlorine atom breaks off and it turns into an ozone-eating pac-man. It starts gobbling up the ozone molecules. As it eats them it is released to eat more, and so on for years and years. Meanwhile we keep making more styrofoam. For each one per cent decrease in ozone there is a six per cent increase in skin cancer. The dermatologists in Australia have seen a doubling of malignant melanoma in the last ten years. The ozone is pretty thin in Australia. We have to wear a hat and have our skin covered when we go out in the sun. When we were children the sun was our friend – we drew pictures of it with a smiling face. It is now causing cancer.

The ozone layer is disappearing faster than was predicted. If we stop producing CFCs now it will take eighty-five years to get the ozone layer back to 1985 levels. But the manufacturers say they can only reduce production by fifty per cent by the year 1995. They say they cannot do it any faster because they will lose too much money. That's like my saying to you that you have an overwhelming septicaemia – a bacterial blood infection – and I can only afford to get rid of half of the bacteria but no more or I will lose my profit. So you will die just as the earth is dying. We cannot treat a biosystem like the earth in this way because as the ozone goes so the plankton get killed and the plankton make the oxygen that replenishes the ozone. Then the trees die and the earth heats up and even more plankton die. Everything relates to everything else. If we get liver failure then the heart fails. If the heart fails then the kidneys will fail. Every organ function is dependent upon every other organ. That is why the earth, which is a living organism, has to be protected. We thought it was infinite but it is not.

The earth is dying from global warming because we are driving cars all the time and burning electricity. The way we make electricity is either by burning uranium and making toxic waste that lasts millions of years and causes cancer, leukaemia, and genetic disease; or we burn coal which pushes up the carbon dioxide that then hangs around the earth like a blanket heating it up. We should all have solar houses. There should be a law that every building is a solar building: solar panels for hot water, for heating, for electricity. The technology is here and it is cheap.

Never turn on a light switch! Just use one light if you need to but do not leave lights on unnecessarily. Throw away your hair dryer and let your hair dry naturally. Every time we turn on a switch we are adding to the global warming because the generation of electricity produces carbon dioxide. It is really easy: no clothes driers, no hair driers – a return to a more basic and simpler way of life.

Plastic is made out of oil. When we make plastic we produce hundreds of toxic, disposable carcinogenic compounds which no one knows what to do with. The corporations give them to the Mafia to dump in the lakes and sewage systems at night when nobody is looking. They put them in ships and try to sell them to the third world. 'How would you like a shipful of toxic waste and we will pay you to take it?' The third world is starving and needs all the money it can get so it says 'yes'. Thus the third world has become a depository for the first world's toxic and nuclear waste.

This is a true story. A man I know had heard about a lake that had turned blue. Next to the lake was a big building and he discovered that blue toxic waste was dealt with in this building. The company was paid to remove the waste. He was told that if the blue waste was mixed with some other chemicals then it made a nice paste that was sold to the mortuaries. When we do autopsies we cut open the body and take out all the organs which leaves a hollow cavity inside. Then we stuff the cavity with old gloves and newspapers, sew it all up and dress the corpse in its best clothes and with lots of make-up so it looks good for us to say goodbye to! But this building was selling toxic waste to stuff in the bodies and then the bodies got buried full of it. The man I know wondered what to do. Should he tell Mrs Brown that her husband, Ralph, who died last year, is a toxic waste problem, so that he has to be disinterred and buried in a toxic waste facility? Toxic waste is all around us. No American lives any more than about twenty or thirty miles from a toxic waste facility. It's reaching into our underground water systems and into the food chain. Our foods are sprayed with weedicides, pesticides, herbicides, insecticides, and fertilizers, so we cannot get away from it.

Fast food is not about food. It is about packaging and processing. Packaging is killing the earth because it is made from trees, and from plastic that lasts for 500 years and produces by-products which are synergistic with radioactive by-products that cause cancer. We are filling the earth up with carcinogens.

Next time you go to the supermarket take your own jars and bags. Get to the check-out counter with all your purchases and unpack them all into your own bottles and baskets. Put the eggs in one basket and the flour in a jar and the onions in a bag. Then leave all the packaging behind. Soon you will be on the front page of 'Time' magazine and you will find yourself leading a revolution! There is no civil disobedience in this – you are simply refusing all the packaging.

We have to start in communities. We have to take down the fences that divide us. We have to start buying our food together, caring for each other, helping young mothers with their children, and the old folks with their shopping and gardening. Each block should have a couple of cows to milk and to graze the grass. A biology professor in New York state took some college students out to see where milk comes from. They did not know. They thought it came from cardboard cartons and plastic bottles. One girl fainted when she saw a cow defecate. We are so out of touch with nature.

So we need to form communities and grow vegetables together and share our food. We can do away with huge supermarkets and buy our food straight from the sacks, putting it into our own bags. We need to start loving and caring for each other, regardless of our colour or race. Compassion starts at home and leads to compassion for the nation, to a compassionate society and a compassionate world.

If we continue to grow exponentially as we are, then within fifty to a hundred years there will be fourteen billion of us humans and we could eat and drink for maybe a hundred years more and then that would be it – there would be no more food or space after that. Would that be such a bad thing? The towns would grow over with grass, Manhattan would be covered in trees, the bears would come back. Maybe it is time that we saw ourselves in perspective on the evolutionary scale and started valuing all lifeforms, not just ourselves. If we can really love all life then we see that the butterfly has as much right to live and to survive as we do.

We were born for one reason – to save creation. It is as clear as daylight and we have about ten years left to do it in. So we have to change – to change our way of life and our habits. To have the courage to feel uncomfortable with what is happening and to feel the pain of the earth. Because that is the start of love and compassion. We may even get mad and angry and not want to accept what is happening. But in accepting we can transform and become active.

We are really at a turning point now as we move towards the next millennium. We have few choices about what has to be done. And it can be done because we can handle the dark, the lies, and the pollution just as we can handle the light and the forces of good. It is our task in life to make this planet a beautiful place to be, that is why we are here. I know we can do it, I know we will. God bless you and God help you.

Jeremy Rifkin

THE GLOBAL ENVIRONMENTAL CRISIS

Jeremy Rifkin MA, President of the Foundation on Economic Trends and the Greenhouse Crisis Foundation, Washington DC. Author of, among many, *Beyond Beef, Biosphere Politics* and *The Emerging Order*. He says: 'By living an ecological lifestyle we set a prophetic example for the rest of the community, and provide a new vision for a post-modern world. Transforming ourselves, recasting our world view, remaking our institutions, and restoring the earth are all part of the same process.'

Our generation faces the first truly global environmental crisis in recorded history. While our ancestors experienced traumatic environmental threats, they were limited to specific geographic regions. Now as we near the second millennium, a new environmental threat is emerging so enormous in scope that we find it difficult even to fathom. We have no equivalent past experience from which to mount an appropriate response.

Only in the last few years has the public been introduced to the greenhouse effect, ozone depletion, acid rain, and mass species extinction. This new genre of environmental threats is global in scale and could affect the very viability of life on earth.

Some scientists now predict a four to nine degree Fahrenheit rise in the earth's surface temperature over the next fifty years as we continue to spew chlorofluorocarbons (CFCs) and nitrous oxides into the atmosphere, blocking solar heat from escaping the planet. Just as every living species lives within a narrow temperature band, so does the earth. The earth's temperature has not varied more than about four degrees Fahrenheit since the last ice age eighteen thousand years ago. Now, scientists project a change in temperature in less than one human generation that may well exceed an entire geological epoch in world history.

The implications are far-reaching and potentially catastrophic. Thermal heat expansion may result in a three to five foot rise in sea water, imperilling coastal regions and the very existence of low-lying countries. Radically fluctuating weather patterns could turn the midwest farm belt and other agricultural regions into giant deserts. Cities like New York and Chicago may be transformed into tropical climates in a few decades. Mighty lakes and rivers like the Mississippi could turn into giant mud-flats.

While the greenhouse gases accumulate in the earth's atmosphere, man-made products containing CFCs are tearing an even wider hole in the delicate ozone layer that forms a protective shield around the planet, blocking deadly ultraviolet radiation from reaching the earth's surface. The EPA estimates that up to 170 million human beings may develop cancer in the coming decades from exposure to deadly ultraviolet radiation. This radiation also undermines the immune systems of living creatures, making them vulnerable to a broad range of bacterial and viral diseases.

At the same time, fossil fuel burning plants are spewing out ever greater amounts of sulphur dioxide and nitrogen oxide, contaminating the rain water over much of the planet. Acid rain has seriously damaged over fourteen per cent of the forest cover in Europe and polluted thousands of streams, rivers, and lakes in North America.

As the earth's atmosphere continues to deteriorate, the flora and fauna of the planet are being destroyed at a breathtaking pace. Millions of acres of tropical rainforest in Central and South America, Africa, and Asia are being razed to provide lumber and paper products and rangeland for cattle. Scientists now estimate that we destroy a species every sixty minutes. Between now and the end of the century we may destroy upwards of fifteen per cent of all the remaining plant and animal species on earth. The environmental and economic consequences of this mass genocide are beyond calculation.

However, global warming, ozone depletion, acid rain, and species extinction are not simply by-products of poor management decisions or callous government policies. Today's crisis is the inevitable result of a unique way of thinking about humanity's relationship to nature. To understand this we need to examine the philosophy of the man that gave rise to it.

In 1620, Francis Bacon, the founding father of modern science, wrote a small tract entitled *Novum Organum*. In this tome, he claimed that we could detach ourselves from the environment and, acting as disinterested observers, manipulate the workings of nature to advance human ends. Bacon viewed the environment as an exploitable medium. He stripped nature of any sacred value, reducing all earthly phenomena to quantifiable standards that could be easily manipulated to serve human economic interests. Bacon's philosophy and method of science provided Western civilization with both a vision and a vehicle to advance the short-term material interests of human beings on a scale never before imaginable.

Bacon declared that 'knowledge is power'. Successive generations of scholars relied on this dictum to reframe their respective disciplines. Adam Smith argued that material self-interest is the essential motivating factor behind human activity. While Bacon turned nature into an exploitable medium, Smith provided Western man with a socially redeeming rationale for selfish exploitation of the earth's treasures. The political philosopher John Locke then elevated this new self-centered materialism on to the metaphysical plane, arguing that the new era of utilitarian greed placed humanity on an irreversible sojourn toward an earthly cornucopia. Material progress became the banner of a new secular regime as Locke and his contemporaries championed the virtues of an earthly Eden over the vision of an otherworldly paradise extolled by the Church. This new way of thinking about people, nature, and history helped usher in a fundamental change in the temporal values of Western civilization.

Today, Americans have the highest standard of consumption in the world. Such material success, however, has been purchased at the expense of the rest of the planet. While the American population is little more than six per cent of the world population, it consumes over thirty per cent of the earth's resources. Americans use twice as much energy per capita as other industrial nations and are the major contributors to both global warming and ozone depletion, being responsible for twenty-five per cent of carbon dioxide emissions and twenty-seven per cent of CFC emissions.

Through a profligate way of life, America has squandered the earth's environment, stripped the forest to feed an insatiable demand for lumber and paper products, overgrazed rangelands to feed meat addiction, and poisoned the air with the exhaust fumes of over 120 million cars. We boast that we are the first consumer society in history and even tout a consumer movement, apparently unaware of the irony implicit in the word. The term 'consumer' dates back to the fourteenth century and, in both its English and French form, has meant to devour, to lay waste, to destroy, and to exhaust.

Only in the past several decades of the twentieth century has this word been elevated to its present lofty status. Today, the consumer is someone who participates in the good life and enjoys the material benefits of the Age of Progress. We have refused to acknowledge the relationship that exists between over-consumption and the pollution of the earth around us.

Americans have embraced the modern world view with abandon. We have conquered and subdued nature, harnessed its riches to advance material self-interests, and revelled in the belief that we are securing an ever more progressive vision. Our missionary zeal, however, has finally become tempered by a growing awareness of the global environmental crisis that has ensued from our unrestrained passion for consumption.

As environmental destruction begins to impact the biosphere, we are coming to realize that the environment is not merely a factor or externality. Nor is it simply an issue to be weighed and quantified. The environment is the primordial context: it is the place where we live, work, and sustain the process of life.

A new, more sophisticated vision of science is now called for if we are to heal our relationship to the earth. The postmodern view of science must be based on empathy with the environment as opposed to subjugation of it; on respecting the delicate and complex evolutionary wisdom of the natural world and working with it as a participant rather than as a usurper and detached observer. We can extend ourselves to the environment as we do to our loved ones, meeting nature as a partner, accepting and respecting the natural world on its own terms. The great challenge that lies before the next generation is to expand the bounds of human inquiry, to create a new approach to scientific pursuit that is inclusive and respectful of the myriad layers and vast network of relationships that animate the natural world of which we are an intimate part.

A new ecological world view *is* beginning to take form; and accompanying this transformation in the consciousness of the culture is a newly emerging environmental politics. The theme of this new movement is 'Think Globally, Act Locally.' It is as concerned with changing personal lifestyles as with changing the political and economic priorities. Many Americans are incorporating part of this new ecological vision into their personal lives, providing the framework for a deep cultural transformation away from the rank consumerism of the 1980s towards a green lifestyle in the 1990s. Empathy, partnership, sustainability, indebtedness, and re-sacralization capture the spirit of the green way of living. Changing our relationship to the earth is seen as both a personal and a societal mission.

By living an ecological lifestyle, we set a prophetic example for the rest of the community, and provide a new vision for a post-modern world. Transforming ourselves, recasting our world view, remaking our institutions, and restoring the earth are all part of the same process.

The term 'ecology' comes from the Greek word *oikos*, and means 'the household'. Ecological responsibility, then, begins at home and expands to fill the entire planet. This is what thinking globally and acting locally really means.

Rennie Davis and Sasha White

CAMPAIGN FOR THE EARTH

Rennie Davis is a prominent activist. He was national coordinator of the US anti-war movement in the 1960's and one of the Chicago 7, America's most celebrated political trial. He is presently campaign coordinator for the Campaign for the Earth. **Sasha White** is founder of the Campaign for the Earth. She has organized three international conferences for the Campaign. They say, 'One small step on one person's part can create transforming changes on the earth if we do it together. We are the generation to make this dream of humanity our daily practice and this historic undertaking our enduring triumph.'

Out of the extraordinary march of civilization, humanity has crossed into a deep and perplexing crisis without historic precedent. The Earth is pressing home the lessons of a long misunderstanding. The workings of time have revealed human fumblings with the laws of nature, placing the land, sea and air at great risk. The nations of the world now face a great decision – whether to make the heroic effort to put things right or meet overwhelming consequences. The urgent task before this generation is to undertake a unifying response – a Campaign for the Earth – for it is the condition of the Earth that is the unifying crisis. The choice will involve crossing every human barrier – race, religion, sex, nationalism, class

– and committing wholeheartedly to the moral equivalent of war. Not a war of destruction and not a world in conflict, we must mobilize an extraordinary convergence of resources in which all nations are allies and the efforts of all people are united towards a great common good.

People in every culture sense the transformative moment, the acceleration of world service that is coming. Once a focus of ancient prophecy, now the subject of modern forecasters, the gateway to the coming millennium has been flung open. Never in history has the opportunity to evolve our understanding been greater. Never has any generation set out with such promise to awaken its memory of wholeness and bring forth humanity's highest expression.

The cause of the Earth need not be defeated by the belief that time has run out. There is time to complete this undertaking. The option for delay, however has all but expired. Only a brief window of opportunity remains – perhaps fifteen to twenty years – to reverse conditions and cease the human quest to dominate life upon Earth. For this generation the sun will rise or set on humanity based on what we do, or fail to do, this decade.

Perhaps the condition of the Earth had to reach this junction point where critical numbers of human beings were pressed into responsibility for the ecological devastation and our passion for the Earth could authoritatively demand a human quantum leap and great citizens' initiative.

The Campaign for the Earth can not be an organization or coalition of organizations. Rather it is an invitation to partnership for all people, an unprecedented social experiment in human cooperation. No group or nation can own or control a campaign of this nature. The concept envisions millions of independent initiatives aligning on a scale unlike any other in history.

This does not mean the Campaign should be without structure or organization. Organizations or coalitions can be created to undertake any positive initiative. Resources can be pooled to underwrite global projects. Great planatary councils can emerge while thousands of Campaign 'hubs' or local centers are established for people ready to make a new commitment.

As the condition of the Earth becomes more apparent to
the world's people, the Campaign for the Earth will unfold
in natural stages like winter shifting to spring. Certain regions
of the world may proceed more rapidly through these cycles
creating resources and experience that can serve other regions
when they begin their transition.

Five stages are envisioned:

Preparation Phase: Individuals, organizations, and global networks establish structures in anticipation of the world response
to the condition of the Earth. Broad strategic objectives are
identified, community models are designed that others can
adopt, and local hubs are established to serve in a grass
roots coordination capacity as public momentum begins. Global computer and interactive two-way video communication
systems are developed for linking local centers. International
conferences are convened for enrolment of volunteers and
development of initiatives. Broad visions for Campaign activity are defined from politics, health, and arts to technology,
business, and agriculture.

Communication Phase: As understanding deepens that the
condition of the Earth must be comprehended beyond the
halls of UN conferences, environmental organizations, and
multi-national agencies, a great media campaign emerges to
communicate this extraordinary world-story – a vast educational project that assures humanity has the information
about the condition of the Earth and understands the window
of opportunity to act. From pulpits to stadium events, this
global communication project unites the grass roots and the
electronic media in public dissemination of civilization's current reality. Certain initiatives are dedicated to the purposeful
activation of the world's communication systems on behalf of
the Campaign. Earth scientists are brought to center-stage in
this early phase, broadcasting their reports and conclusions.
This is the stage that inspires workable, grass roots action
plans. This is the stage of great assemblies of pre-eminent
scientists focusing world attention on particular action plans.
This essential media focus allows millions of people to align
with the powerful purposes of the Campaign.

Mobilization Phase: As public understanding about the Earth's condition swells, a critical mass is achieved, unleashing volunteers and diverse activities in an outpouring of support for the Campaign. The worldwide environmental network is flooded with new support and resources. Great energy ignites the large stadium gatherings led by entertainers and visionary speakers. The mobilization stage has power and speed – a movement of rolling thunder. Major action centers are set up and declare themselves in service to the exploding network of local self-organizing groups. Financial resources become available to the Campaign on a large scale. This is the stage of great morale-building, public declarations of alignment with the Earth, and an unprecedented expansion of hope and promise.

Implementation Phase: The work of the Campaign involving specific platforms for action begins in earnest. Broad visions and goals are converted into local real-time strategies and projects. Understanding that the Earth expresses herself in regional bio-systems, five thousand bio-regions are defined as humanity's essential focus for work. New social models and eco-cities are created which excite thousands of communities with new possibilities. The concept of local empowerment and non-dominating communities is the common denominator of Campaign organizing. There emerges a purposeful reorientation of the artistic community on behalf of the planet. The largest multi-national corporations shift to environmental practices and new technologies that align with the action plan of the Campaign. World-changing Earth technologies are introduced to international markets. The public announcement of these great inventions instills a new level of conviction that the toughest environmental hurdles can be cleared. Global computer and interactive video communication networks go on-line, linking local Campaign hubs. Earth situation centers monitoring the planet's condition and the Campaign's progress from satellites open an extraordinary information resource for planning capabilities for every hub. Sustainability in all endeavors and reverence for the Earth become the guiding principles of Campaign undertakings.

Regeneration Phase: Natural alliances are developed wherever information and resources should be shared or coordinated. Local hubs throughout the world now have direct communication. Globally unified networks emerge. This phase begins the implementation of Campaign goals on a world scale. The shift of civilization out of fossil fuel into clean, inexpensive energy begins in earnest, involving the power of sun, water, wind, and sources of electricity that were always natural to the atmosphere. Foundations for the Earth join in vast networks to create financial resources on the scale of European governments. This alliance of private funding institutions can underwrite large-scale regeneration projects. A planetary Earth Corps enrols millions of volunteers who commit themselves to eradicate illiteracy, poverty, and homelessness from the Earth. It is now widely understood that where hunger rules, the Earth cannot be restored and unity cannot be fashioned. In the regeneration stage, sustainability is established as the principle in people's daily routines. Human needs are addressed with a new maturity. Indeed, the whole field of human awareness begins to shift. The world enters an era of co-creation. Rapid progress in human development is experienced. Global family becomes the heartbeat of the Campaign as access opens to the deeper wisdom encoded in all people. Earth celebrations – victory rallies – sustain the public momentum and evolving vision. This is the age that gives voice to the hawks, bears, rivers, and mountains, and to the principle that nature should be respected and its essential processes left alone.

We can never underestimate the power of imagining. The energy of millions of minds for regeneration can create deep and lasting change. The ability to imagine is far more than just a helpful tool on the way to making something happen. Imagining is what makes it happen. People can imagine both extraordinary beauty as well as dark and disturbing fears. That is why imagination is said to be both the gift and curse of the human race.

Imagination is the vital key to challenging and transforming a darkened world. That understanding underlies the great quest of the Campaign – to create a transforming, mythic vision from which we can restore the human-Earth relation and lay the foundation for the coming great age. The Campaign for the Earth is an invitation to participate in that quest – the next step of human evolution.

If each person who is now awakening and understanding this historic moment could be seen from space as a point of light, we would see the world as millions of lights enveloping the globe. The Campaign for the Earth is a connecting project for points of light, weaving a new circuitry of cooperation into one community. Creating this 'body of light' is all that is needed to empower humanity to experience this historic regeneration.

The Campaign for the Earth is the decision of the human community to change. We are the generation to do this. We possess the understanding to do this. The Earth is aligned with those who commit their hearts and perseverance to this sacred purpose, this mobilization of all human energy in service to world transformation.

The Campaign for the Earth is history's most daring adventure. It will be nourished most by openhearted vision. It will be expanded furthest by the theme of forgiveness. Its greatest strength will come by unleashing the talents of all people. One small step on one person's part can create transforming changes on the Earth if we do it together. We are the generation to make this dream of humanity our daily practice, and this historic undertaking our enduring triumph.

Sun Bear

THE TIME OF EARTH CHANGES

Sun Bear, international teacher, Native American of Chippewa descent, founder of The Bear Tribe Medicine Society. Author of seven books, including *Black Dawn/Bright Day*, and founder of 'Wildfire' Magazine. He says: 'The Earth changes long prophesied by Native peoples are here. I am glad they are because they are necessary for the survival of the planet ... And as human beings come into their full power, they will realize the generous and loving nature that is theirs just as it is a part of all creation.'

The Earth changes long prophesied by Native peoples are here. I am glad they are because they are necessary for the survival of the planet. This is what Native peoples were told long ago and what Spirit tells us today. We've been living in this time of Earth changes since 1973. According to all my beliefs and visions, the changes will go on past the year 2000 with ever increasing intensity.

My people see this time of great change as a period of cleansing and moving forward. During it, humankind is being given a wonderful opportunity to make a major breakthrough in consciousness and awareness. But though the Earth has gone through major changes throughout her history – and the current ones are part of a foretold sequence – they are coming more quickly and severely now because of the human role in them. There are even those who worry whether the planet will survive.

As I look around, I see that many humans are not yet willing to make the necessary changes in themselves and their actions which could prevent the most severe consequences. They will not stop polluting, they will not stop consuming the Earth's resources as if those gifts were theirs alone; they will not stop acting toward nature and all her creatures – including other humans – as if they were only a backdrop for their activities. They simply will not learn to walk in a sacred manner on the Earth.

To Native people the Earth is a living, intelligent being. She is capable of making the necessary changes for her own survival. These changes might not be convenient for humans, but the Earth will make them anyway. There may be drastic climatic changes, earthquakes, volcanic eruptions, economic and political problems, and other problems that humans have caused for themselves. I see that the planet will survive, although perhaps many people will perish. Predictions from different people vary regarding how many people will survive the cleansing – what the Native Americans call 'The Great Purification.' Some people believe that up to ninety per cent of the present population will perish. I feel that about one quarter of the world's population will survive.

Think about that. In the next ten to fifteen years, you're going to see such major changes at all levels that you won't recognize the world afterwards. And those changes are happening now. It's not a little 'maybe' thing any more – it's for real and growing in strength. Every day the papers bring the news of weather changes, natural disasters, man-made disasters, hungry and homeless people moving around the world. These are all part of the Earth changes, and they are all related.

The 1990s will be hard because the changes will be accelerating. But it will also be a time of rapid growth for people who are willing to reach out to a higher level of consciousness. This is what the cleansing is all about. All the prophecies of Native peoples speak of a time when the human beings will face a choice between continuing on a path of greed and destruction, or going toward spirit. Now is the time when we face that choice.

I get to travel all around the world these days and I see a great many people waking up. They're starting to realize that reality is not what happens in New York City, or Berlin or Tokyo; it's not what happens on Wall Street or in the Common Market. People are beginning to realize that reality is forests and trees, reality is clean rivers and oceans and air. More and more, people are asking before they turn a bulldozer on to the land so they can put up a new shopping mall – 'What does this do to the Earth? What does this do to the animals that live there? What does it do to us?' This is good because it shows that people are beginning to reach out and really feel the Earth as a whole being, and take responsibility for their relations with it.

At the same time, I also see many kinds of tragic things happening that continue the destruction of the Earth. Many people are still not willing to consciously make the changes in themselves and the way they treat the Earth that are needed now. So even though the old system is falling apart, people are clinging to it and continuing the destruction. When I travel in Europe these days, I see the break-up that has happened there as being very positive. People have the opportunity to make more of their own decisions now, and they are reaching out to new knowledge that was kept from them before. But many of the old dinosaurs are still in place. In large areas, the land is severely depleted, the waters are poisoned, the forests are dying. Consequently, I see major food shortages and famine in Europe this decade, and hordes of people migrating to find food sources. This is one of the ways the changes will be happening.

In my life I have had many, many dreams and visions that showed the coming of the Earth changes. I've dreamed of things before they happened. I've had these dreams and so have other people. Before any major change occurs on this planet then, there are warnings. I'd like to tell you of one from the Iroquois people that concerns the situation in the Middle East. This prophecy was given to me by a spiritual elder of the Iroquois named Mad Bear Anderson, who told me to share it with people.

In the Iroquois medicine societies there are staffs. Carved on some of these staffs are three serpents. There's a white and a red serpent with the same tail, indicating they have the same purpose toward humanity: domination, conquest, and control. The prophecy given me by Mad Bear Anderson says that the white and red serpents would wrestle until the rivers boiled and the fish turned up dead. Then the third serpent, a black one, would come and wrestle with and defeat both the white and red serpents. Then the black one would look around to see if there were other people to fight with. He would see the Native people gathered in the hilly country, along with all the other people who gathered with them wanting to understand and live in the spiritual way of the Earth. The black serpent would turn as if to fight with them, but then he would see coming the bright light of Deganawida, the great teacher of the Northeast Indian people. He would become frightened, flee, and never bother the people again.

The interpretation of this prophecy that was given to me by Spirit is that the white and red serpents represent the United States and the Soviet Union. They wrestled for a long time, until the rivers boiled and the fish turned up dead from their atomic weapons testing. They wrestled in the Cold War, supplying weapons to get other people to fight each other. They wrestled until they exhausted almost all their resources, until they were in so much debt from their wrestling they couldn't afford to continue any more.

Then the black serpent comes into the battle. The black serpent is the Moslem nations. The Moslem nations have gotten both the United States and the Soviet Union into wars they didn't know how to fight. They defeated the Soviets in Afghanistan, and the United States in Lebanon. Even though the United States won a clear military victory in the Persian Gulf War, there's still a lot of unfinished business there and it seems the United States is going to get in a lot deeper than it thought at the outset.

And now we're coming into the second stage of the wrestling of serpents: the war of the Moslem nations. This war can affect all the nations of the world; its battlefield will be the gas pumps. The Moslem nations control most of the world's petroleum and they can make quite a noose for Western civilization from their fuel lines.

There is another old Native prophecy that was recently fulfilled by events in the Middle East. This speaks of a time when the sun and the moon would be blacked out. Since the Iraqis torched those six hundred oil wells in Kuwait, black, billowy clouds regularly block out the sun and moon. Oil rains fall on the Persian Gulf and for hundreds of miles around.

And something else happened over there that I would like to share with you. Around the time of the invasion of Kuwait, several elders of the Lakota Nation had powerful visions in which they saw the sun blacked out by clouds. In August of 1991, a group of these elders, led by Garfield Grassrope, traveled to Iraq. They tried to warn the Iraqi leaders of what they had seen. Of course, the Iraqis didn't listen. Now we have a catastrophe there on such a large scale that no one knows what the effects will be.

Too often people think of prophecies and visions as little 'maybe' things. But we Native people know that this is the way Spirit communicates with us. During this time of Earth changes, a large part of the stretching-out of consciousness will be learning to listen to Spirit again. It will be learning to listen to the Earth. She is talking to us all the time, but humans have become deaf to her voice. It's really sad that we don't tune into the Earth and to all of creation. So many times, when we have the possibility of catching a bit of knowledge that might push us forward and help us tremendously, we don't bother to reach out for it. That's something to be aware of because there are many millions of people in the world who are dying or will die because of their prejudices, fears, and their unwillingness to look at something new and open up to it.

I'm often asked if I foresee a nuclear war happening. I don't see one between the United States and the Soviet Union. I do see the possibility of a nuclear war in the Middle East in the years between 1993 and 1997. If one happens, most likely Israel will be involved. Back in 1978, I had a very powerful dream about Iran. In the dream I saw a map of Iran, and then the word 'Iran' vanished. I asked what this meant and Spirit told me Iran would be completely destroyed by earthquakes and by its neighbors. So I see a lot of conflicts continuing in the Middle East throughout this decade. But my greatest concern for all the countries over there is that water will become increasingly scarce. The richer ones will have some comfort in their money for a time, but when water and food become scarce, their money will be small comfort. However, here, as all over the world, the people who learn to return to the land in balance, who reach out to each other with respect and cooperation, will survive.

I see the United States experiencing an economic recovery that will continue until about 1993. I strongly urge people to use this time to get their act together and become more self-sufficient. If you're still living in a major city, now is the time to relocate. I see life in cities all over the world becoming more difficult. As the Earth changes increase, you're going to see big disruptions in the dominant systems. So one of my major emphases these days is that people develop land bases where they can ensure their own food and water and shelter. But whether you're living on your own land or sharing it with others, it's important to reach out and form networks with other people.

I also encourage people to begin storing food. Many of the prophecies speak of a time when we will be able to grow hardly any food on this planet for three years. But don't just take on the attitude of the survivalist and think that sitting over your pork and beans with a 30–06 rifle will take care of things. The people who will survive the Earth changes are going to have to reach out and grow on all levels – spiritual, emotional, and physical.

In times past, all peoples knew they had a connection and responsibility to the Earth and to all the other beings upon her. They recognized the circle of life. They were aware of the gifts that their relations gave them. And they knew that by praying, by doing ceremony, they could give back some of their energy to the plants and the animals and the waters. You can't just take all the time. It's important to remember that. When we do ceremony, we are giving energy back to the Earth and to creation. We are saying thanks for their giveaway and returning what we can. This helps keep the life-energy circulating upon the planet in a good way; it helps keep the balance.

People often ask me how to change the world. I tell them, 'If you don't like the world you live in, create the one you like.'

It's time now for every individual to take real responsibility for his or her own life. I feel the purpose of humanity now is for each of us to grow to our highest level of consciousness and power, and then use that knowledge to help others and the Earth in these times. To do that, you have to develop a philosophy that 'grows corn.' By that, I mean it has to work here and now *every day* of your life. It has to help you walk in a sacred manner and give you the backup power that you need for your survival on the planet now. If it doesn't, then you'd better recheck your circuits.

As I've said, I've had many dreams and visions which showed major Earth changes and great destruction happening on this planet. There are going to be many things that are here now that will no longer be around when the cleansing is completed. But I've also seen that some of the people will grow from the changes. They will learn to use their gifts and powers in a positive way. They will put aside the 'isms' that now separate them from each other. There will be a relearning of the language of nature and a restoration of the damage that has been done to the Earth. And as human beings come into their full power, they will realize the generous and loving nature that is theirs just as it is a part of all of the creation.

Back in the 1880s when Wovoka, the Paiute Ghost Dance prophet, saw his vision, he spoke of what would happen after the Earth changes. He said: 'When all the little dreams of Buffalo, Man, and Horse are gone . . . we come together as one.' When this happens, we will look again upon a beautiful and unspoiled land.

Ho! It is good.

Jonathon Porritt

THE GREEN SPIRIT

Jonathon Porritt, ex-Director of Friends of the Earth, now Special Adviser. He wrote the Green Party UK manifesto in 1979 and 1983. Author of *Seeing Green, The Coming of the Greens,* and editor of *Save The Earth*; presenter of BBC television series 'Where on Earth are We Going?' He says: 'Ecology is a process of healing, a way of providing meaning in an otherwise sterile and empty world ... salvation lies in opening our spirit to the presence of the divine ... acknowledging joyfully a sense of wonder and humility before the miracle of creation.'

I remember some years ago, at the Second International Green Congress in Dover, England, that the Bishop of Lewes, Father Peter, opened the proceedings by giving a message that many people found hard to accept. What he said was: 'I must say this to you: you haven't a hope in a million years of changing anything by political methods unless you concentrate on changing attitudes, changing thought-forms deep, deep down in society, or at least understanding the need to do this.'

In my own arena – the environment movement – it is a matter of great concern that so many environmentalists are still so reluctant to reach out beyond their single-issue campaigns, beyond their passionate indignation about this or that cause. As yet few realize that they're not really campaigning about single issues at all, but about something much deeper.

In his book, *Natural Alien – Humankind and the Environment*, Neil Evernden wrote: 'For although they seldom recognise it, environmentalists are protesting not at the stripping of natural resources, but the stripping of earthly meaning . . . We call people "environmentalists" because they are moved to defend what we call the environment; but their action is actually a defence of the cosmos, not of scenery.'

However, we have become so used to separating our politics (in this case, environmentalism) from our spirituality – in a society that for the last three centuries has been dominated by the principles of individualistic, scientific materialism – that it is hardly surprising that so many people now seek to slot their spiritual concerns neatly into so cloistered a pigeon-hole that they never impinge on the rest of their lives at all.

The thing to understand is that politics and spirituality need not be, and in fact are not, separate. They are, if anything, two sides of the same coin. As Gandhi said: 'I claim that the human mind or human society is not divided into watertight compartments called social, political, religious. All act and react upon one another. I do not believe that the spiritual law works on a field of its own. On the contrary, it expresses itself only through the ordinary activities of life. It thus affects the economic, the social, and the political fields of life.'

So let us be clear about one thing. No one is proposing a gleaming, brand new, ecologically pure religion! We are not summoning people to genuflect at the altar of Gaia, or to abandon all that has provided spiritual or transcendental meaning up until now. To propose any such spiritual artefact would be a meaningless and arrogant exercise. To that extent, the spiritual dimension of the Green Movement consists simply of two essential components:

Firstly, the endeavour to promote ecological wisdom in all existing religions and spiritual traditions, by drawing out the teaching practices already inherent within those traditions.

Secondly, the need to find ways of letting people reconnect with the Earth, especially people who are otherwise untouched by religion, and possibly even embarrassed by the use of the word 'spiritual'. Pitched at the simplest level, when we look at what is going on throughout society, one can only conclude that we no longer know how to sing the song of the Earth. We are no longer at home in our earthly home. To heal that alienation we must now seek to re-present the abundance of the diversity of the natural world as the primary revelation of the Divine on Earth.

Let us take each of these two components in turn. As regards what is already inherent in our established religions, I am going to look at Christianity.

There has been a pretty lively debate for some years now about whether or not Christianity is itself partly responsible for the ecological mess that we are in. This is no mere academic argument! This is an extremely important debate about the whole future of Christianity in the late twentieth century, which revolves around an essential polarity. On the one hand, there is the theory that God created man 'in the image of God', and gave us 'dominion over all the fish of the sea, the birds of the heaven, and all the wild beasts and all the reptiles that crawl upon the earth.' It is the confusion between 'dominion' and 'domination' that has provided Christianity with a licence for participating, often with uncommon enthusiasm, in the wholesale exploitation of the planet, suppressing a sense of reverence for God's creation and any residual hint of pagan or animist traditions.

In his book called *Continuous Harmony*, Wendell Berry puts it very clearly in perspective: 'Perhaps the greatest disaster of human history is one that happened to religion, that is the division between the holy and the world, the taking out of the Creator from creation. If God was not in the world, then quite obviously the world was a thing of inferior importance, or of no importance at all . . . A man could aspire to heaven with his mind and heart while destroying the earth and his fellow man with his hands.'

So that is one side of the debate: that Christianity, by taking the divine out of all that is earthly and lodging it in some distant, divorced, and comprehensively male Godhead, has managed only to endorse and indeed accelerate the pattern of ecological destruction that we see now.

Against that there is a very different interpretation, based on the understanding that 'The Earth is the Lord's and the fullness thereof'. That all we have actually been given is the stewardship, not the control, of that creation. Here, of course, the whole concept of ecological interdependence finds an important biblical resonance in the covenant that God made with Noah after the flood: 'This is a sign I am giving you for all ages to come, of the covenant between Me and you and every living creature with you.' That text underpins the progressive Christian concept of stewardship. It has been taken up throughout the years by many people who found in it the absolute essence of their Christianity.

This understanding of the relationship between the planet and its Creator is, of course, very close to the sense of spiritual fellowship of many American Indians. But we do not have to live in the wilderness in order to share such an understanding. Consider the words of Archbishop William Temple: 'The treatment of the earth by man the exploiter is not imprudent, it is sacrilegious. We are not likely to correct our hideous mistakes in this realm unless we recover the mystical sense of our oneness with nature. Many people think this is fantastic. I think it is fundamental to our sanity.'

To a certain extent, this debate may seem to be relatively dry, academic stuff, light years behind what is really happening in people's hearts and minds. That is the real difficulty: how each one of us puts together his or her own spiritual vision when there are no structures, few models, and almost no enlightened guidance.

My own 'prescription' is neither terribly elevated nor terribly startling. First, we must take courage. We may already be accustomed to working against the tide. But to walk alone can be lonely work, however good the tune. Few of us are strong enough to make it without the right companions. So secondly, we need to take care. To pick those companions with care. For we can be easily manipulated. Courage and care. And thirdly, celebration:

> To see a World in a Grain of Sand
>   And Heaven in a Wild Flower
> Hold Infinity in the palm of your hand
>   And Eternity in an hour.
>
> William Blake

The answer to the question: 'Where does one start with meta-physical reconstruction?' must surely be with Earth itself. And in order to be at home in the world we must be fully of it, experience it directly as mud between our toes, as the rough bark on a tree, as the song of the world awakening every morning. The Earth speaks to something in every person, even when we are imprisoned by concrete and steel. Beyond that, learning how to celebrate is a very personal thing. For me, it has always been through trees. I have encountered many trees, many woods, many forests, and fashioned many intimate rela-tions with them. I have found myself replenished, enriched, enthused in more ways than I could describe. Through this I have become part of a spiritual community that embraces people of every culture, every country, every creed.

In *The Tree* by John Fowles, we read: 'No religion is the only religion, no church the true church; and natural reli-gion, rooted in the love of nature is no exception. But in all the long-cultivated and economically-exploited lands of the world, our woodlands are the last fragments of comparatively unadulterated nature . . . the last green churches and chapels outside the walled civilisation and culture that we have made . . . There is a spiritual corollary to the way we are currently deforesting and denaturing our planet. In the end what we most defoliate and deprive is ourselves.'

It is in the heart of nature that I find the hard conceptual divide between myself and the rest of life on Earth dissolves most easily. I am, there, wholly of the Earth, and as such feel no special joy, no gratitude to a benevolent Creator, but just an uncomplicated sense of Earth-bound identity. Only there can I bring the two perspectives together.

I particularly do not want to make a mystery out of this because the whole point is that there is no mystery to it. I believe that to relate to the Earth in this way is natural, ordinary, and theoretically accessible to everybody. The spiri-tual can and often should be utterly mundane. The problem of course is that fewer and fewer people have access to the Earth in this way, because they are bound by the constraints of conventional education, religion, or politics.

And that, of course, brings us back to the synthesis between the spiritual and the political with which I started. There remains in many people the suspicion that to be spiritual means to drop out, to disappear inwards, or to devote one's life to meditation. There is a time and even, on occasions, a critical need for such contemplative practice, as a part of one's spirituality. But it seems clear to me that too exclusive an emphasis on the unworldly, on withdrawal from this industrial culture of ours, has merely reinforced the parody of spirituality as a morally superior way of dropping out. I would rather suggest that the world we are a part of is as much spiritual as it is political. It is the moving spirit of the community which provides for me a compelling call for action. That is why the most powerful political messages often come from spiritual leaders. That is why I feel both privileged and frightened to count myself as more than a nominal Christian, knowing the gap between how I live and the actual words of Christ.

As we seek to create a harmonizing of the political and the spiritual, we must above all avoid being dogmatic about what shape this is likely to take. We must see beyond our own narrow, contemporary cultural assumptions and values, and allow ourselves to remain open.

Ecology is a process of healing, a way of providing meaning in an otherwise sterile and empty world. As with the body, so with the spirit. And that is where the synthesis can be created. It is the wisdom of ecology that re-instructs us now about the importance of balance and the interrelatedness of all living things on Earth. And it is the wisdom of religion that allows us to transcend our material confines and maintain contact with the source of meaning itself. That is why we can believe that salvation lies in opening our spirit to the presence of the divine in the world, acknowledging joyfully a sense of wonder and humility before the miracle of creation. Then we can go out and take action to put things right, inspired by that vision. It lies, quite simply, in learning to sing again the song of the Earth, and singing it again and again and again until we all sing in harmony.

John Seed

DEEP ECOLOGY AND THE COUNCIL OF ALL BEINGS

John Seed, Director of the Rainforest Information Center, Australia, international seminar leader and activist for deep ecology. Co-author of *Thinking Like a Mountain: A Council of All Beings*. Co-producer of 'Earth First' television documentary. He says: 'To deep ecology the world is seen not as a pyramid with humans on top, but as a web. Humans are but one strand of that web, and not only do we have no right to destroy other strands (species), but we do so at our own peril.'

Deep ecology is the name of a new philosophy of nature that has been exerting a profound effect on environmentalism in the last decade. To deep ecology the world is seen not as a pyramid with humans on top, but as a web. Humans are but one strand of that web, and not only do we have no right to destroy other strands (species) but we do so at our own peril. Indeed it would not be going too far to say that deep ecology offers a religion of environmentalism confirming the awe that many of us experience in the glory of nature and affirming that God/Nature/Humanity form an ultimately seamless whole.

The term was coined by Arne Naess, Emeritus Professor of Philosophy at Oslo University, to describe an approach to nature not unlike that held by most tribal peoples. In this respect we may consider the following statement from Luther Standing Bear:

We do not think of the great open plains, the beautiful rolling hills and winding streams with tangled growth as 'wild'. Only to the white man was nature a 'wilderness' and only to him was the land 'infested' with 'wild' animals and 'savage' people. To us it was tame. Earth was bountiful and we were surrounded with the blessings of the Great Mystery. Not until the hairy man from the East came and with brutal frenzy heaped injustices upon us and the families we loved was it 'wild' for us. When the very animals of the forest began fleeing from his approach, then it was that the 'wild west' began.[1]

Deep ecology may be contrasted to reform environmentalism which sees the world as basically composed of human beings and resources for those human beings. Obviously a responsible person wants to see these resources used wisely, sustainably, so that they remain for future generations. However, deep ecology is highly critical of this 'anthropocentrism' (human centeredness) and compares it to an earlier view where the earth was seen as the centre of the universe with everything revolving around it.

Perhaps we can blame many of the land-raping practices laying the earth to waste on the Judeo-Christian tradition with its injunction that we 'subdue' the earth which is there for man's use: 'And the fear of you and the dread of you shall be upon every beast of the earth, and upon every fowl of the air, and upon all that moveth on the earth, and upon all the fishes of the sea; into your hands they are delivered.'[2]

This attitude permeates all aspects of our society, our language, even our psyche. Growing up in a culture with this arrogant view of ourselves, we are isolated and separated from nature. As long as we maintain a self-image created in the matrix of such views, a shrunken and illusory sense of self that does not include the air and water and soil, we experience nature as outside, and fail to recognize that the nature 'out there' is one and the same as the nature 'in here'.

Under these conditions it requires a highly developed sense of duty, responsibility, and altruism to sacrifice our apparent self-interest by seriously committing ourselves to the defence

1. T. McLuhan (ed.), *Touch The Earth*, 1971
2. *Genesis* 9:2

of the earth. As Arne Naess has pointed out, this is a treacherous basis for conservation as so few of us are capable of such sacrifice.

If, however, we experience the profound interconnectedness, the interpenetration between ourselves and the Sacred Earth, that the earth is our very body, then it becomes merely a matter of self-interest to protect her, and no more nobility of spirit is required for us to take strong action than if we were to perceive somebody attacking our own body or family.

Ecological thinking – holding correct views, rooting out the attitudes of anthropocentrism – is a necessary part of moving towards such a shift. However, intellectual changes do not easily lead to major changes in lifestyle and action. So how do we allow these realizations to penetrate more deeply into our being and begin to influence our self-perception?

It was in answer to these questions that, in 1986, Joanna Macy and I developed a series of deep ecology rituals which we call the Council of All Beings. Basically we weave together three themes.

We begin with a *mourning* ritual. It is only to the extent that we will allow ourselves to feel the pain of the earth that we can be effective in her healing. As Joanna Macy points out: 'Deep ecology remains a concept without the power to transform our awareness, unless we allow ourselves to feel, which means feeling the pain within us over what is happening to our world. The group serves as a safe place where this pain can be acknowledged, plumbed, released. Often it arises as a deep sense of loss over what is slipping away – ancient forests and clean rivers, birdsong and breathable air. It is appropriate then to mourn, for once at least to speak our sorrow and to say goodbye to what is disappearing from our lives. As we let this happen there is a hopelessness expressed. There is also something more: a rage welling up and a passionate caring.'[3]

The energy previously locked up in the denial of these feelings is released and becomes available to us. The sense of numbness and paralysis evaporates and we can prepare for action.

3. Joanna Macy, *Deep Ecology and The Council of All Beings, Awakening In The Nuclear Age*, 1986

Then we move on to exercises which assist the *remembering* of our rootedness in nature. For instance, in the evolutionary remembering, we use guided visualization and movement to recapitulate our entire evolutionary journey and release the memories locked in our DNA. We invite the experience that every cell in our body is descended in an unbroken chain from the first cell that appeared on the earth four billion years ago, through fish that learned to walk on land, reptiles whose scales turned to fur and became mammals, evolving through to the present.

We further extend our sense of identity in the Council of All Beings itself where, after finding an ally in the natural world and making a mask to represent that ally, we discover that we can indeed give voice to the voiceless ones. In Council, we lend our voices to the animals and plants and features of the landscape and are shocked at the very different view of the world that emerges from their dialogue.

One of the defining characteristics of deep ecology is that as we make the transition to ecological self, extending our identification to include the natural world, we 'fall in love outwards' (Jeffers), and action on behalf of nature follows surely and inevitably. These deep ecology rituals should not be seen as a substitute but rather a preparation for action. When our strategies are formed and informed by a larger context than our narrow selves; when we realize we are acting not just from our own opinions but on behalf of a larger Self – the earth – with the authority of four billion years of our planet's evolution behind us, then we are filled with new determination, courage, and perseverance.

Rupert Sheldrake

DISCOVERING THE SACRED

Rupert Sheldrake PhD, biochemist and teacher, Fellow of Clare College, Cambridge. Past principal plant physiologist at the International Crops Research Institute for the Semi-Arid Tropics in India. Author of *A New Science of Life, The Presence of the Past,* and *The Rebirth of Nature.* He says: '... let us rediscover the sacred ... in our lives ... and re-establish our relationship with the planet as a sacred relationship. In this way we may be able to continue to be here.'

One thing we can be certain of: even if all human beings were wiped off the planet, the planet itself is not going to be rendered extinct. If everyone in England died tomorrow, in ten years time London would be green all over. There would be grass growing up through the streets, there would be trees in the gardens. There would be crumbling buildings covered with ivy and other plants growing on top of them. The planet will regenerate. It has survived appalling catastrophes in the past, like those that wiped out the dinosaurs, and when seventy-five per cent of animal and plant life was rendered extinct. Ten thousand years ago much of England was under ice. There were no trees at all and northern England was a desert. By the time people started settling in England a few thousand years ago, they found a richly forested country with a rich ecology and many animals. There had been incredible regenerative growth.

So the planet can survive. Whether we save ourselves or not is another matter. Perhaps we glorify ourselves too much if we think that we hold the destiny of the planet in our hands, for the regenerative capacities of the natural world are very great.

It would appear that science is now pointing us back towards a sense of wholeness – the interconnectedness of life, the relationship of humankind to the larger life of the planet. There is a pointing to a holistic or a mystical perspective, as science transcends the mechanistic world view. Individually and collectively we now need to recognize our connection with the larger life of nature through sacred places, sacred times, and through the sense that our life is part of the larger life – the life of the ecosystem, the life of the planet, the life of the cosmos.

Change is not going to happen just through human intervention. The materialists would say that the greater forces in change are just impersonal natural laws, together with chance and necessity: there's nothing you can do about it. Yet if we see that the world is alive, that there is a psychic or animate aspect to it and also a spiritual or conscious aspect, then one thing we can do to enhance this is through forming connections and opening ourselves to inspiration. All people and all societies throughout human history have seen that the way of forming a relationship with the larger powers that dominate our life is through prayer and sacrifice, through coming together for worship and praise.

The idea of dissolving traditional religion until there are just free individuals making all the decisions was, I think, a liberation for many after a rather restricted religious upbringing. But the result of it is that we have a society with no particular common goal, no spiritual dimension, no basis for social coherence; a world in which first the community fragments into nuclear families and then the nuclear families into broken homes and separated individuals. Finally we end up with a completely fragmented society where the only identity people have is with being consumers, and the only freedom they have is to choose which kind of video recorder or soap powder to buy.

I believe the only way to move back to a greater sense of cohesion and community – a greater sense of the relation of our life to our location, our locality, to our countries, to the planet – is through the rediscovery of the sense of community and of common spiritual goals. This has to come about through a religious revival, through a rediscovery of the sacred.

It is extraordinary how our lives are dominated by an attempt to recapture some lost vision from childhood which is enormously important to us and yet usually forgotten and not accessible to the conscious mind – some moment of epiphany or revelation. Or how many people spend careers as scientists trying to discover or fathom some mystery – something that intrigued them early in life – which they have since forgotten?

I remember as a young child, near the family farmhouse I saw a row of young willow trees with rusty wire hanging between them. I asked an uncle why there was this wire in the trees and he said: 'Well, we made a fence out of willow stakes and the stakes came to life and grew into these trees.' This vision of dead stakes coming to life and turning into trees made a tremendous impression on me, and I realized that since then I had spent years of my life obsessed with death and regeneration.

Then I think of the times when we have had moments of revelation later in life, moments on mountain tops or in woods or wherever we have had a sense of connection with the natural world. Our usual reaction is to say this is very fine, but essentially it is subjective; it has no part to play in objective, real life situations where what really matters is science, technology, human welfare, and so on. For one of the problems that has arisen from a mechanistic world view is the idea that our minds are inside our brains; that nature is essentially soulless or inanimate and that the only psychic life that happens is inside the human brain. If, therefore, we have an experience of intense participation or communication with nature, this has no objective validity or reality.

Almost everybody has some sense of connection with nature, but it is usually part of their private lives, at weekends, in the evenings, with lovers or family while on holiday. These experiences don't enter into official life, into business or commerce from Mondays to Fridays. These things are rigorously excluded from our lives. And it is the Monday-to-Friday mentality that sets the agenda for the development of tropical rainforests, the exploitation and ruin of the earth, and profit above all things. Growth of the national economies is the great good to which everything else must be subjugated.

So I think that recovering a sense of direction is something we can achieve individually, but also we need to recover our collective relationship as a society to the larger natural world. There are two ways this can happen. One is through a recovery of the sense of seasonal change, of sacred time, that the whole year in all societies has its festivals which link the life of the community together. The changing seasons, in turn, reflect the changing relationship between the earth and the heavens. So Jewish festivals, for example, like Hanukkah and Passover, are related to a lunar calendar. They are related to the solar seasons but also to the phases of the moon. The Christian sacred calendar has that character too. Easter and all related movable festivals – such as the beginning of Lent and Pentecost – are related to the moon and the sun. Easter is the first Sunday after the first full moon after the Spring Equinox. Other great festivals are solar festivals, including Mid-summer, Mid-winter, Christmas Day just after the Winter Solstice, and St John's Day which is the 24th of June.

We can also relate to the sacred through the rediscovery of pilgrimage. Pilgrimage is a basic human need to connect our lives to places of power. There are places with power because of the way they are: mountain tops, for example, are often places of revelation partly because there is a sense of being up above everything and looking down on it, and partly because they are where the earth reaches up to the heavens. Then there are places which are sacred because of what has happened there: where someone has had a vision, some great historical event has taken place, some act of healing, or maybe where some great man or woman has been born or died. The great churches, cathedrals, and temples, and almost certainly places like Stonehenge and Avebury, are located at very special places. Such places are like great outdoor temples through which you relate the community to the life of the heavens.

When pilgrimage was suppressed by the Protestant Reformation in the sixteenth century, this natural way of moving in relation to sacred places was cut off and tourism was invented to replace it. So tourism is a kind of secularized pilgrimage! You still go to the ancient sacred places – the cathedrals, the pyramids, the great henges, the Holy Land – but you no longer go explicitly because you want to connect with the spirit and power of the place. You go there to observe it in some kind of detached way and to take photographs of it to show your friends.

When tourists enter a sacred place of worship they are slightly embarrassed because they can't really take part otherwise they would not be tourists, they would be pilgrims. When you visit a place as a pilgrim you go with the intention of connecting with the place and you go with some kind of offering. You go there to pray and to seek some vision or blessings. You take back something of the power of the place to share with those around you at home. Most tourists would actually prefer to be pilgrims – they would enjoy it much more!

The traditional way that the sacred is brought into people's everyday lives is through the making sacred of space and time, and in all traditional households the home itself is considered a sacred place. In Chinese homes they have pictures of the ancestors and a little stove where they light joss-sticks and pray to the ancestors. There is a sense in which the house is a place where the ancestors are honoured. The places from which water comes, traditionally wells or streams, are also honoured as sacred places. Now we find in the modern home that water comes from taps, and the fire is there but it is hidden away in some invisible boiler which provides central heating but gives no focus. The Latin word for 'focus' means 'hearth', so the fire or hearth in a house is a central means for focus, for the family to focus together.

So let us rediscover the sacred in our homes, our lives, and the community around us, and re-establish our relationship with the planet as a sacred relationship. In this way we may be able to continue to be here.

Colin Wilson

EARTH FORCES

Colin Wilson, philosopher. Author of numerous books, including the bestseller *The Outsider, Necessary Doubt, The Philosopher's Stone, Access to Inner Worlds, The Magician from Siberia, Beyond the Occult*, and *Written in Blood*. He says: 'Now I am aware, beyond all shadow of doubt, that the earth itself contains some force that affects the life of everything that grows on it, and which is in turn affected by it.'

When I first came to live in Cornwall, thirty-five years ago, it was not because I had any particular desire to live in the country, but because I knew I had to escape from London. The success of my first book, *The Outsider*, left me feeling breathless and rather bewildered for it all seemed strangely meaningless to me. I soon began to find the strain of notoriety unbearable. When a friend told me he had a cottage in Cornwall which I could rent, I seized the opportunity with relief. Within a few weeks my girlfriend Joy and I had moved into the old cottage on a remote farm, several miles from the nearest village.

Then an odd thing happened. Instead of experiencing relief and relaxation, I found myself feeling curiously unsatisfied and uncomfortable. After a year of non-stop publicity I found the silence of our cottage unexpectedly unnerving. It should have been wonderful to wake up to the sound of the stream running past our window and the bleating of sheep from the opposite hillside. Yet it all seemed oddly unreal. When I walked up the farm track to collect my mail from an old shed, I was aware that the scenery was beautiful and that the air smelt of spring; yet somehow it was as if I was seeing it through thick plate glass.

So why was this reality such a disappointment? The answer dawned on me, oddly enough, as a result of reading the biography of the 'black magician' Aleister Crowley. In 1920, Crowley had established an 'abbey' near Cefalu in Italy. A film star named Jane Wolfe came to visit him there. She was a middle-aged actress whose life in the New York theatre had made her aggressive and neurotic. She met her match in Crowley, a domineering personality who would never accept defeat. Penetrating her neurotic and defensive armour became an obsession for him. Crowley informed her that she should begin her training in meditation by spending a month sitting on top of a cliff looking at the sea. When she indignantly rejected the idea, Crowley pointed out that there was a boat leaving the next day. Reluctantly, she accepted.

The first few days were just as bad as she had feared. She slept in a tent, wore only a woollen robe, and ate bread and grapes brought to her by a boy. After a few days, anger and resentment turned to boredom and a kind of sullen resignation. Then, on the nineteenth day, she plunged into a mood of 'perfect calm, deep joy, renewal of strength and courage'. Suddenly, she said, she understood what Crowley meant when he told her that she had the sun, moon, stars, sky, and universe to read and play with. The relaxation was so deep and total that she finally returned to the Abbey – at the end of the month – with reluctance.

When I came to live in Cornwall my situation was precisely like that of Jane Wolfe when she arrived in Cefalu. I was an incorrigible intellectual and self-analyst. For the first year or so I did not even go for regular walks; I worked until I was exhausted and then opened a bottle of wine.

All this began to change when we invited my parents to come and live with us. My father had always loved the country-side. His idea of heaven was to spend a long day fishing off the rocks, then go to the local pub for a few pints of beer. But he disliked drinking alone, so I began taking him to the pub most evenings. I found it unexpectedly pleasant to sit drinking with fishermen – some of whom could remember Cornwall as it was in the nineteenth century. These fishermen loved their steep cliffs and bare moorlands, and the tiny harbours surrounded by hills. For the first time in my life I began to experience some of the same contentment. In more cynical moods I suspected that it was the beer, yet as I walked back to the car through the narrow streets of Mevagissey and heard the crying of seagulls, I knew than it was something deeper than that.

In retrospect, I also see that another experience was more important than I had realized at the time. We naturally spent time driving my parents to see different parts of Cornwall – the Lizard peninsula, St Michael's Mount, the spectacular scenery of Land's End. I observed then the curious atmosphere of some of these bleak and remote places. There were moorlands with coarse, wiry grass and curious ancient megaliths that date back a thousand years before Christ, and in such places I experienced a strange sense of timelessness, as if the centuries had drifted past like clouds over a landscape. D.H. Lawrence speaks of the Cornish as 'people who believed in the darkness and magic'. Gradually I began to recognize that this was not merely Lawrence's imagination. With his deep sensitivity he had instantly 'tuned in' to something to which I was virtually tone-deaf.

One day a friend asked me to drive him to an ancient stone circle called the 'Merry Maidens', not far from Penzance. The circle consists of nineteen upright stones, each about four feet high, and is probably older than Stonehenge. No one knows why our ancestors erected these megaliths, although it seems to be generally agreed that they were the scene of pre-Christian religious ceremonies involving the sun and the moon. My friend produced a 'dowsing rod' from his pocket – two thin strips of plastic bound together at the end with string – and as he approached each stone, gripping the ends of the plastic in either hand, I saw the rod twisting upwards as if it were alive.

He showed me how to hold them and I walked towards the nearest stone. To my astonishment, the rod bent upwards as I approached it, and gradually bent downward again as I walked past. At first I assumed that I was doing it myself by altering the tension on the rod. After ten minutes I realized this could not be the correct explanation for it worked every time – and reacted even more powerfully in the centre of the circle. And after playing with this new toy for most of the afternoon I noticed something else – that I was feeling oddly tired, as if I had done a hard day's writing.

We went on to another stone circle, this one hidden in the midst of fields and surrounded by steep Cornish hedges. It is reputed to be the oldest circle in England. Here the dowsing rod responded with even more force. My friend explained that the 'power' of the 'Merry Maidens' had probably been drained by the number of tourists tramping around it, while this place was like a fully-charged battery!

Now I was taking regular afternoon walks and began to observe that I did not need a dowsing rod to experience this strange sense of power in the landscape around me. It was particularly strong at certain points along the cliffs, often looking across the bay to distant headlands. But I could also sense it if I stood still and simply allowed myself to relax into the silence. Standing there, smelling the odour of last year's leaves, I would experience an odd sense of belonging, as if I could stand there for half an hour absorbing some 'vibration' that was a part of the landscape.

Now I am aware, beyond all shadow of doubt, that the earth itself contains some force that affects the life of everything that grows on it, and which is in turn affected by them. There are times when I can relax so deeply that I can sense this force as clearly as if I were listening to music. I can understand what Wordsworth meant when, looking up at a mountain above Lake Windermere, he was overwhelmed by a sense of 'unknown modes of being'. My thought-riddled nature is still too strong to experience it as powerfully as D.H. Lawrence did, yet there are occasions when, tired from writing, I can still my senses until I become aware of the vibration and feel refreshed and relaxed.

I know that this is what most city dwellers have lost as they hurry to catch their trains and buses. Yet at least many of us are now aware that we have lost it. This took me so long to discover because I was not even aware that I was tone-deaf to these vibrations. And in recent years I have come to realize that perhaps the most astonishing thing that has happened in my lifetime is that so many who were formerly also tone-deaf have now awakened to the recognition that the earth has a voice, and that we only have to learn how to be silent to understand its message.

PART FIVE

The Spiritual Quest

Stephen Levine

WHAT WAS YOUR FACE BEFORE YOU WERE BORN?

Stephen Levine, meditation teacher and past Director of the Hanuman Foundation Dying Project. Author of *A Gradual Awakening, Who Dies?, Meetings at the Edge, Healing into Life and Death*; and co-author with Ram Dass of *Grist for the Mill*. He says: 'There is a sacred journey we were each born to undertake. It is the healing we took birth for . . . It is not to become Buddha or Jesus, rather it is to be the light to which each referred when they said "I".'

WHAT WAS YOUR FACE BEFORE YOU WERE BORN?

When the heart bursts into flame
history completely disappears
and lightning strikes the ocean
in each cell.

There, before origins,
where the double helix
is struck like a tuning fork
there is a hum
on which the universe is strung.

A SACRED JOURNEY

There is a sacred journey we were each born to undertake. It is the healing we took birth for.

We are explorers of the sacred unknown, of the truth that remains when all grasping at truth has subsided. We are technicians of the heart.

We are on a sacred pilgrimage that explores to our edge and beyond. Investigating the process and the space in which this process is floating, we are mapping the vibrating boundary between the known and the unknown. And we proceed, like Buddha or Madame Curie, past the fear at the gates into the space beyond our knowing. We take another step into unexplored territory where all growth occurs; approaching the truth and healing that arise from the heart when we go beyond the mind.

We have taken birth into this scintillating, flickering body to discover the body in the body. The speck around which the pearl is formed.

Approaching this bright spark, we enter the breath within the breath, that to which Kabir referred when he spoke of God.

And it turns out our true nature isn't even this spark that lights our body with consciousness, but the fire from which the spark was thrown. The formless 'uh' of being, no different from pure awareness.

We are born to explore our little body to find our true body. We are born to explore our little mind to find our true mind. We are born to explore our little heart to find our true heart. Our true heart, our true mind, is our Real Body.

There is a sacred exploration that awaits us all. It is to travel from here to now! It awaits in 'just this much', this very instant, this millisecond of being. It is to discover what lies within. And within what? It is not to become Buddha or Jesus, rather it is to be the light to which each referred when they said 'I'.

FIRST SNOW

For this first amazing snow
I thank all the tiny Gods
Krishna, Athena, Jesus and Buddha
that float in my Real Body.

Even in our flickering body
somewhere toward the surface
there is a glistening
like the sun
reflected in a whirlpool.
It is the cycle of birth and death
a peripheral cosmos
a universe of possibilities.

The formless protrudes
into form –
the Big Bang
or the least thought
can do it.

Einstein recommended the meditation
at the edge where nothing
expands into 'less than nothing' –
where content is invisible
and form depends on content.
Where the surface of the swirling worlds
evaporates into consciousness
there is a distant galaxy
dissolving
like these amazing snowflakes
imposturing reality –
unable to measure
the melting.

Thich Nhat Hanh

PRACTICING PEACE

Thich Nhat Hanh, Vietnamese Zen master, nominated for the 1968 Nobel Peace Prize by Martin Luther King Jr. Founder of Plum Village, France. Author of *Vietnam: Lotus in a Sea of Fire*, *The Cry of Vietnam*, *The Miracle of Mindfulness*, *The Raft is Not the Shore*, and *Being Peace*. He says: 'Please do not be frustrated. We are not trying to make peace this year, or next year. We have to make peace for many thousands of years. Therefore everything you do, and everything you do not do, should be placed in the light of mindfulness.'

In my tradition, every time we hear the bell, we go back to ourselves, breathing in and out, and enjoy our breathing and the sound of the bell. When we breathe in, we say 'Listen, listen,' and when we breathe out, we say 'This wonderful sound brings me back to my true self.' Each village temple in Vietnam has a big bell, like those in Christian churches in America and Europe. Every time the bell is heard, the whole village stops what they are doing and pauses for a moment to breathe in and out, following their breath. This is one way to practice peace. You have one moment of peace. Please stop from time to time as you read this and just enjoy your breathing. Breathing can be very enjoyable. We become more alive when we return to ourselves. The bell of mindfulness is a kind of messenger that calls us back to ourselves and to life.

In Plum Village, the community where I live in France, we

use many kinds of sounds to bring us back to peace. For example, every time the telephone rings, we all stop and breathe in and out, saying, 'Listen, listen. This wonderful sound brings me back to my true self.' We call it telephone meditation! It is very easy to practice telephone meditation. When you hear the telephone, just stay where you are. When you hear the first sound, breathe in and out consciously, and smile. When you hear the second sound, you can breathe in and out again, and enjoy the sound of the telephone. It is possible to do so. If the other person has something very important to tell you, he or she will wait for at least three rings. Your calm and your smile has become more solid during the second practice of breathing. When you hear the third sound, you can continue to practice breathing in and out, and move to the direction of the telephone. You are quite yourself. When you pick up the telephone, you are smiling, calm, and serene. That is not only for your good, but also for the one who is calling. If you are not yourself, if you are irritated or grouchy, then he or she will have to receive that.

All of us know that by practicing loving speech we can make many people happy. Sometimes we hear something so nice that we stay happy for the whole day, maybe several days. We know that we have the power of distributing happiness around us. By mindful speech, we can engender peace within ourselves and around us. Saying something mean or cruel can create suffering and despair in the mind and heart of another person. That is why practicing conscious breathing and right speech are two foundations for practicing peace.

To practice peace, everything must be done in mindfulness. We increase the quality of our work by mindfulness. Don't think that you can only meditate in the sitting position. If you are in the garden, pulling weeds and watering the vegetables, you can breathe in and out and maintain full awareness of what you are doing. When you walk into the house, you can do so in the style of walking meditation, step by step, aware of each step. Peace is every step.

In the kitchen, whenever you remember, you can pause while you are cutting carrots, or chopping bananas, and breathe in and out, and smile. You can use all kinds of sounds or other cues in order to return to yourself, to practice peace, smiling, and breathing. This is so important. You can practice meditation not only in the meditation hall, but everywhere – in the garden, in the kitchen, and so on.

When you are peaceful, when you are happy, wherever you are is the Pure Land, the Kingdom of Peace. The Kingdom of Peace is within yourself. Whenever you have peace in yourself, you are in the Pure Land. When I studied the Gospels, I noticed that Jesus told people that the Kingdom of God is here and now, not after death.

You only need to make one step in order to enter the Kingdom of God, or the Pure Land. Just one step. When you hear the bell, or when you hear a bird, or when you see a star, or the eyes of a child, you can enter into the Kingdom of Heaven right away. But you need awareness, you need awakening, you need mindfulness in order to really see the stars, to really perceive a flower, or to realize the presence of a child. This beautiful flower has been there for days, but its presence may not be real to us at all because our mind, our heart, is not there. The beautiful flower belongs to the Kingdom of God, to the Pure Land. We need only to look at it in a mindful way, with awareness, and we realize its wonderful presence. When you do see it in its beautiful splendor you are immediately in the Pure Land, in the Kingdom of Peace.

Jesus is described as the Prince of Peace. During the Last Supper he had with his students he broke the bread and he shared the bread with his students saying: 'Here is my body broken for you. Please have it.' Usually we eat our daily bread in forgetfulness, thinking of so many things at the same time. While we eat our bread, we should think only of eating our bread, but we don't do this. We are not with what we are doing in the present moment. Therefore life is not with us, and peace is not with us. 'Life be with you, peace be with you' – that is only possible when you dwell in the present moment, and realize what is going on in the present moment. That is the essence of meditation.

To practice meditation, to practice contemplation, is to be aware of what is happening in the present moment. This beautiful flower is happening in the present moment. It is a messenger sent from the Kingdom of Peace. Also the bread that we eat every day represents the whole cosmos. It is a wonderful emissary from the Kingdom. But in our daily life, we eat our bread without mindfulness. We eat our worries, our jealousy, our fear, our anger, but we do not eat our bread. So, Jesus, when offering the bread to his students, really wanted them to eat the bread. He used a very drastic image, in order to wake up his disciples. 'My friends, please really eat this bread. This bread is life. This bread is peace, it is the Kingdom of God.'

Peace is there, available to us, within ourselves and around us. The Kingdom of God, the Pure Land, is also available in the present moment, within ourselves and around us. It needs us to make one step: to go back to peace and the Kingdom of God. It takes one step in order for us to be able to protect peace, to be peace. The best way to protect peace is to be peace. If we don't know how to do that, we are letting war replace peace. War then replaces the Kingdom of God.

When I contemplate a beautiful sunset, I also become beautiful, as beautiful as the sunset. I know that because I have eyes capable of seeing the beautiful sunset, I cherish my eyes very much. Usually we take our eyes for granted. We only need to open them and we can see all kinds of colors, shapes, and forms. Not only do we have eyes, but we have ears capable of listening to many kinds of sounds. Sometimes the cry of our baby is wonderful to listen to. The sound of the rising tide, the bird, the bell, the words spoken by our beloved one are wonderful. Yet we are not happy, we are not satisfied with elements that belong to the Kingdom of God. We are looking for a kind of happiness that is not there in the present moment. We are looking for a kind of happiness that may be in the future, or that may have been lost in the past. We are not capable of coming into contact with the real Kingdom of God, of Peace, in the present moment.

The Buddha said: 'Do not regret the past. Do not dream, or be afraid of the future. The past is already gone, and the future is not yet here. The wise one dwells peacefully, and happily, in the present moment.' Jesus also wants us to go back to the present moment. He wants us to enter the Kingdom of God, the kingdom that is available in the present moment. You do not have to die in order to enter the Kingdom of God. In fact, you have to be alive in order to step into the Kingdom of God, and you do it here and now. You only have to practice the exercise that Jesus proposed – eating your bread with all your being in the present moment, in mindfulness, becoming one with the piece of bread. That piece of bread is a wonderful reality. Look deeply into the piece of bread and you can see the sunshine in it. Without the sunshine, the wheat would not be able to grow. There is also a cloud in the piece of bread. If there is no cloud, there would be no rain for the wheat to grow. There is the earth in the bread. The whole cosmos has come together in order to bring about the piece of bread. The piece of bread is the ambassador sent from the Kingdom of God. If you know how to eat your piece of bread, you are life, you are peace. You need to take only one step in order to go into the Kingdom of God. If you are able to eat your bread, then you will be able to hold your baby in such a way that you and the baby become eternal.

When you are able to taste peace, and taste the Kingdom of God, you will be able to help preserve peace. Otherwise, no matter what we do, we will not be able to work for peace, and to protect peace.

One day the Buddha was sitting in the woods with about thirty monks. Suddenly a man came by looking very unhappy. He asked the Buddha: 'Monk, did you see my cow passing by here?'

The Buddha asked: 'What cow?'

And the man said: 'I am the most unhappy person on earth. I have only twelve cows and they just ran away. All of them. I have a few fields of sesame seeds, but this year the insects ate all my crops. I think I will die.'

The Buddha said with compassion: 'No, we have not seen your cows. Maybe they went in the other direction.'

After the farmer left, the Buddha turned to his monks and said: 'You people are very lucky. You do not have any cows.'

If you have cows, inside or outside, let them go. Otherwise the Kingdom of Peace, of God, will not be available. If you practice so that you can release your cows, the easier it will be to enter into the Kingdom of God.

Mindfulness is a zone of energy that we can produce within us. Everything that goes through our mindfulness becomes beautiful. They reveal their true nature, the nature of the Kingdom of God. When we live in forgetfulness, everything passes unnoticed. But with mindfulness – a kind of light – everything reveals its depth. Producing awareness in your daily life is to make everything beautiful, within you and outside of you. Even when you have things that are not so beautiful coming from inside or coming from outside, such as anger, jealousy, fear, or war, under the light of mindfulness these things will be slowly transformed. If you have anger and you allow anger to be based in the light of your awareness, it will slowly be transformed. If you want your anger to be transformed quickly, then you have to solidify your mindfulness. You have to increase the power of your mindfulness. That is what we call concentration, looking deeply.

If you have some pain in your muscle, you know that if you can help the blood come to the painful point and circulate better, it will be able to wash away the pain in your body. Sometimes our blood does not have enough oxygen. So we increase the quality of our blood by breathing in and out deeply. Then the blood will have more power to transform the pain, to wash away your pain. But there are other ways, too. If you let the blood circulate by itself, the effect will be slow, but if you use your hands to do massage then you help the blood to come into every cell and remove the pain quickly. Massage is to do the movement again and again, several times. Mindfulness is like the blood. When blood comes to that corner of your being, mindfulness will be able to bring about the beauty of things, and also transform the pain within yourself. If your mindfulness is still not strong enough then you can increase its power by practicing concentration: breathing in and out, making your mindfulness stronger. With that mindfulness, if you continue to focus, to come again and again to the anger, or despair, or fear, then your blood will be able to massage and transform that mental formation. We call it 'looking deeply.' You send waves of contemplation into the same object. The kind of energy of looking deeply will penetrate into the painful formations and will transform them.

In Buddhist psychology our psyche is described in terms of seeds. There are seeds of peace and there are seeds of war. The seeds of peace, if you expose them in the light of mindfulness, will increase and develop. The seeds of war, if you are able to bring them into the light of mindfulness, will be transformed.

Sowing the seeds of peace and transforming the seeds of war is what we should be practicing.

During the eight months that the American soldiers were in the Persian Gulf, what was their practice? They were waiting for the order for the land offensive. They knew that they had to learn to kill if they didn't want to be killed. There were only two things: to be killed or to kill. So, every day they practiced killing, day and night. During the day they carried bayonets, and they shouted, screamed, yelled, jumped, and stabbed the bayonet into a sandbag that represented an Iraqi soldier. During the night, they continued to practice killing in their dreams. They had to learn to kill, or they could be killed. For five, six, seven, eight months, they sowed the seeds of war every day, and every night, instead of sowing the seeds of peace. Did they have an alternative?

When we talk about the casualties of war, we usually think about the number of bodies that were killed, the number of bridges destroyed. But we do not take into account the destruction and the damage inflicted on our collective psyche. Suppose I am an American soldier, and I was killed. If you are my wife or my child, and you hear the news of my death, you will cry. You will suffer a lot. But if I survive and come back to you, you will hold me in your arms and cry out of happiness. I will cry too, because I was able to survive and return to you. But I am not the same person. I am carrying with me a lot of wounds in my psyche. I have been practicing killing every day, every night. You will have to suffer. Our relationship, our life, will never be the same again. I have sown so many seeds of war and of fear in myself, I do not know how to transform them. In my daily life with you, I will say and do things that make you unhappy. The military men who return, whether from Vietnam or Iraq, suffer in this way. These are the true casualties of war. These seeds of unhappiness and suffering will be inflicted on our wives, our children, and the children of our children. Think of all the suffering of the Vietnam veterans. Their suffering has spilled over to their families, and to society.

If you want to work for peace, you have to look deeply in order to see the true casualties of a war. You need to show your people all these kinds of suffering. You need to help your people look more deeply into the matter, and not be satisfied with the superficial things, like a so-called clean and fast 'victory.' You need a filmmaker who can show all different aspects of the psyche of a soldier who has come back, an image that reveals the depth of his suffering.

Working for peace is not easy. We need time. We cannot wait until war comes to react. Sometimes we have to begin one thousand years before the war breaks out.

'What if someone came and killed my wife and my children, how could I react with nonviolence to protect my family?' I have been asked that question thousands of times. My answer is this: 'Do you have time? Do you have one second? Do you have one thousand years? If you do not have time, how can you work for peace? If you don't have one second in order to breathe and look deeply at your child, or the flower, how can you work for peace? If you don't have one thousand years, how can you prepare for peace? There are things that Jesus said nearly two thousand years ago, and only today does someone finally begin to understand. Sometimes it takes two thousand years for one seed to become a flower. You have to take the time to prepare. If you are confined in the world of no-time, you cannot do anything. Peace education is what we have to do in order to protect the Kingdom of Peace, the Kingdom of God.'

If we do not have time to do these kinds of things, how can peace be possible? How can we see things deeply? How can we prepare to avoid war? To prepare for our children to continue being, let us not live in forgetfulness, waiting until there is a war in order to react. It is too late. It is always too late.

So practice eating your bread, listening to your children, making peaceful steps, listening to the birds, and the telephone, smiling, and breathing, so that peace can be possible in ten years, in twenty years, in a thousand years. It is very important. When the time comes, because you are ready, because you are lucid, you will be able to shine, to guide your countrymen away from the path of war. But if you wait, it will always be too late. Please do not be frustrated. We are not trying to make peace this year, or next year. We have to make peace for many thousands of years. Therefore everything you do, and everything you do not do, should be placed in the light of mindfulness. Hug you child mindfully, breathing in and out deeply. Eat your breakfast in peace. Speak lovingly to your husband, make him happy in the present moment. All these kinds of practices are the practices of peace. When something happens to you, to your country, you are already peace, and you know what to do and what not to do in order not to destroy the Kingdom of God, which is inside us and around us. Peace is every step.

Father Theophane Boyd

FINDING GOD

Father Theophane Boyd,
Benedictine monk for over forty
years at St Joseph's Monastery,
Massachusetts. Author of *Tales of
the Magic Monastery*. He says: 'God
touched me the first time I went there
[to the Magic Monastery]. All night
long God beat the drum and I danced.
The next day I beat the drum and
God danced.'

When I was young I set out to find God. I had heard of
a certain monastery on the other side of the mountains. I
decided to go.

On the way I met so many people. One said: 'Wonderful –
pray for me when you get there.' Another said: 'Why don't you
stay and do God's work here?' Another said: 'The mountains
are too high, you will never make it.' Another said: 'Hogwash,
there is no such place.'

In one village the cobbler, on hearing my story, just smiled
and said: 'Well, I have found God here.' I looked around at the
shabby house and village and moved on.

But the cobbler lingered in my mind. Not that I had doubts
about the Magic Monastery, but wouldn't it be fine if I went
back and persuaded this deluded cobbler to come with me?
And so I went back, determined to listen respectfully to him

in order to win his confidence. 'Sir, I was impressed with what you said. Would you care to tell me how it goes with you?'

'It is very simple,' came the answer. 'I just live here in God. Each day I mend pairs of shoes. I do it with Him and for Him, and it is my service to other people. This is what makes me happy.'

'But I have heard of a wonderful monastery across the mountains where everything is organized around the presence of God,' I replied. 'Will you not come with me?'

'Oh no,' said the cobbler. 'Across the mountains means tomorrow. I have no time for tomorrow.'

DANCING WITH GOD

People do not believe me when I tell them I go to the Magic Monastery in order to dance. I suppose other people go there to pray, or to hear a sermon, or to repent. But I go there to dance.

God touched me the first time I went there. He made these stiff bones dance. All night long God beat the drum and I danced. The next day I beat the drum and God danced. The preachers went on preaching and the workers went on working, but God danced.

Bernard Tetsugen Glassman, Sensei

ZEN AND SOCIAL ACTION

Bernard Tetsugen Glassman, Sensei. Director of the Zen Community of New York, former Executive Director of the Zen Center of Los Angeles. Founder of the Greyston Network and President of the Greyston Family Inn which provides housing, job training, counseling, and youth activities to the homeless. He says: 'I consider the homeless state to be the nature of our existence. We have to differentiate between what is normally called homelessness and what is our basic state ... The state of residing somewhere is holding on to what we call the past or longing for what we call the future instead of just allowing the *now* to be.'

I consider the homeless state to be the nature of our existence. We have to differentiate between what is normally called homelessness and what is our basic state. As a monk I took the vow to be consciously homeless. In the Zen tradition it is a state in which we do not reside anywhere and thereby can allow the *now* to unfold. The state of residing somewhere is holding on to what we call the past or longing for what we call the future instead of just allowing the *now* to be. The Diamond Sutra, favored by the sixth patriarch in China, teaches: 'Abiding nowhere raise the mind.' Without holding on to any concept as our self we can let the full nature of the oneness of life just be – just manifest. This is the true state of homelessness in the absolute sense. When we talk about homelessness in the relative sense, which we read about in the newspapers, that's quite different.

The homelessness that exists in our society is basically due to treating people as throwaways, as garbage. A Zen master who taught in America, Nakagawa Soen Roshi, used to pick things from garbage cans and proclaim: 'This is not garbage.' Nowadays we have an ecological consciousness concerning the preservation of our biosphere, our planet; yet at the same time we are treating people as garbage, as throwaways. I'm speaking of war and homelessness. Our society has thrown away the homeless people that are housed by the government in welfare motels. We simply do not know how to value their existence or to allow them to become part of our working society. We spend money, time, and effort figuring out how to take care of these throwaways, how to keep welfare motels from being blights – as if one room, no kitchen, one mother and three, four or five children can ever be made into a non-blight. That has to end. It can only end when we stop considering people as garbage.

This is not just our culture. Throughout all generations, the basic issue that religion has dealt with has been rejection. People must first be taught how not to reject. The biggest difficulty is that we reject ourselves. How many people have the confidence and the ability to deal with themselves as complete human beings? We are constantly belittling ourselves. We reject ourselves and so we reject others. Wherever we are there are huge segments of society that we reject.

In Buddhism we create a mandala and then invite everything into its sacred enclosure. People ask: 'How can you invite everything in? You don't want the demons or the enemies.' But yes we do. We want to eliminate rejection. It's an age-old principle. If we can look at the elements that we are rejecting and bring those back in we will find that all of a sudden we are accepting ourselves. In our Zen community we have dealt with this principle from the very beginning. We have to learn how not to reject the rich, how not to reject the poor, how not to reject any element of our society. When I started to work in the field of homelessness my aspiration was to create a Board of Directors who would bring together all the factions which were fighting each other. So we brought in a Republican and a Democratic, both former mayors of Yonkers, New York. And we brought in black ministers and white ministers.

We are working with the homeless directly because this is the arena where the rejection is actually happening. It's more laboratory work than classroom work. I remember someone saying that Zen is the laboratory of life. Zen master Hakujo says: 'A day of no work is a day of no food.' It's the touchstone of whether what we are saying is real.

One of the forms of Zen koan study deals with finding Zen directly in daily life. The spinning top, moving so rapidly that you cannot see it spin – that it appears to be sitting still – is the model for our life. We deal with life itself, the hurricane of life, and remain at the center of the storm. That is the ideal of Zen. We have a famous koan: 'How do you stop the sound of a distant temple bell?' Many people conclude that the way you stop the bell is to get into a deep state of meditation. But the Zen answer is to become the bell in its full glorious ringing. Being at one with that bell there is nothing to start or to stop. Life is that way. Hakuin Zenji said that if you really want to practice Zen you have to go into the middle of Tokyo and be one with the core of what Tokyo is. Anyone can sit on a mountain. That's not what Zen practice is. All this does not negate the need for meditation but that the meditative state is to be created in the midst of activity.

I would like to create a circle of one people. It has always been a dream of mine to present the interdependence of life and the oneness of humanity in a concrete way, not just talk about it. We chose homelessness as a major way for our Zen community to become involved in terms of social action. But it will not be our only way. When we work in social action my feeling is that every aspect of life has to be there – education, livelihood, religion. The whole mandala has to be completely interwoven. We are working with the model of Five Buddha Families. The center of our mandala is the state of *shunyata* (emptiness) or the state of non-duality. In the words of the Sixth Patriarch: 'No separation between subject and object.' This is the Buddha sphere. And the four other spheres or families move around that center. We learn how to be at one with whatever we are doing. At the center of it all we are not even aware that we are doing anything. The manifestation of that central Buddha sphere is perceived as one of four surrounding spheres: livelihood, study, communication, or social action. Within the arena of livelihood we can be at one with our work – not working for something but allowing work itself to be the celebration of the oneness of life.

We are starting companies in many diverse areas and we are hiring local unemployed people. Livelihood is the Ratna or jewel sphere. I want the training within these companies to be of high quality. I want people to learn how to work in that state of consciousness where work itself is seen as a celebration of life. Social action is the Karma or action sphere. But social action has to be a celebration of oneness. Not seen as helping someone but simply as right action. As a direct manifestation of the central state of non-duality. The Vajra or diamond sphere I call study. There are many schools and institutes and many ways of study. In the Zen community we are developing a study program that is not the study of Buddhism as an abstract entity but the integration of non-duality into one's entire life. Everything we do is within the context of daily life, not an abstraction away from it. The Padma or lotus sphere I call communications. This particular Buddha Family emphasizes the role of integration. It generates the integrative force needed to keep the mandala whole. This is the sphere where energies and practices are being created which minimize the rejection-forces that are within us. We are constantly trying to separate, to create dualities, to divide the subject from the object. We are always pushing things away from ourselves. This is a necessary part of the act of creation; but the act of atonement is bringing us back to one, to non-duality. There is a constant dynamic. Creative force is necessary and at the same time we need integrative force which I call atonement or at-one-ment, turning, turning around, turning back to the source.

Every activity arises here which can bring us back to the oneness of life. In addition to our social work, we have a vision to build a cathedral of one people. We want to create the environments and the energies to bring back the sense of the oneness of life. There would be a space where talk goes on, lectures and discussions that are bringing people together, and a space of silence that is open to all the traditions, where people can share silence together.

And then I see chapels around that central space, chapels that are celebrations of the individual traditions. There should be a mosque, a zendo, a Catholic chapel, a synagogue. I feel this cathedral should be built in a low income area. The upper and the middle income groups will be able to travel to such a place and to join hands with those who live there. If you create this space in the country, or in economically exclusive areas, the poor will not come and you will create more separation. For this to be a cathedral of one people, all economic and social groups have to be able to come together. It will be a live cathedral. I'd also like to see it be a space that does not get completed. Let the vision be big enough to go on for generations.

This reflects the very process of life and death. You could say that God created man in His image to create a space to sanctify and to celebrate the oneness of life. The whole planet is nothing but that. If we look carefully we can see that everyone is just trying to recreate what is, trying to create space in the daily moment so that we can see the oneness of life. Or it is like working on a great koan. When we work on the koan what we try to do is open a space where a person can see this oneness. But you have to make a meta-leap out of the flat plane of that space or it will remain one-dimensional. In order to appreciate what the mandala of the five spheres really is you have to come out of that plane and directly perceive the oneness. If you are confined within the mandala you can't really see it. It's not enough to create the space. We also have to provide the opportunity for making that meta-leap so we can fully see, so the oneness of the space becomes fully integrated within our own lives.

Before we make such a meta-leap we look around and see various businesses, social action, and all these other activities. In our heads they are all separate processes and they are not us, they remain something other than us. Mountains are mountains. Then we become more deeply committed to our work, to our effort. We reach the place where there is no longer any separation between us and our daily life. We are just right action. We no longer think that we're doing business or social action. We wouldn't call it that any more. It's just daily life. At this stage there are no more mountains. Then comes the meta-leap and we see the whole landscape again. But we see all of it as aspects of our own life, not as separate processes or persons. We perceive all existence in an integrative way as we do when we see the blood and the limbs of our own body as being one body. We actually see the oneness. Then we can say: 'Yes. Mountains are mountains!' They are no longer separate entities. They are no longer different from us. Yet we can clearly differentiate them.

Ken Wilber

THERE ARE NO OTHERS TO SAVE

Ken Wilber, foremost authority on transpersonal psychology and East/West studies. His two dozen books include *The Spectrum of Consciousness, The Atman Project, No Boundary, Up from Eden, A Sociable God, Transformations of Consciousness,* and *Grace and Grit.* He says: ... let us hold our visions lightly. Let us not think that in changing from iron chains to gold chains we are somehow free ... But let us finally release all dreams and visions and hopes ... and realize that very divinity which is always already, without any help or hope at all, our own primordial state.'

Great sages from Eckhart and St Dionysius in the West to Shankara and Nagarjuna in the East, to Krishnamurti and Love-Ananda in the present, have unanimously told us that the very highest state, the ultimate state, the purest spiritual state, is not divine knowledge but divine ignorance (or emptiness). Knowledge – high or low, sacred or profane, exalted or debased – is simply a contraction in awareness. It separates seamless consciousness into one state which sees or knows, and one state which is seen or known. In this mutilated and fragmented state, we never have reality – we relate to the world by 'knowing' the world 'out there,' seeing the world out there, grasping the world out there, as if consciousness and the world were not one and the same event.

Thus, in lesser states, we can indeed know this or that, desire this or that, visualize this or that. But you cannot know the ultimate state simply because it is one with the knower itself, and you cannot know the knower any more than your eye can see itself. The ultimate state will not split into seer and seen, and thus although you can certainly *be* that ultimate state, you can never *know* it as an object, whether object of worship, object of science, or object of hope and vision.

This is not to say that science, hope, and vision do not have their place in relative reality for, within the dream of dualism, they are noble enough. It is to say, however, that they have absolutely nothing to do with ultimate reality and final release in being. As the old sage Lao Tzu said: 'The man of learning gains every day; the man of Tao loses every day.' Loses knowing, loses dualistic hopes and visions, loses any form of grasping or seeking, and rests instead in divine ignorance, in the cloud of unknowing, which for Lao Tzu was the Great Mystery (his term), the mystery of pure awareness which can never be known or grasped and yet contains the entire majesty before your own eyes right at this moment.

This, surely, is why the aim of all three vehicles of Buddhism (Hinayana, Mahayana, Vajrayana) is to put an end to hope and fear. It is *not* to gain knowledge, gain yet *more objects* in awareness, objects separate from subjects which then together conspire to cut asunder and tear the fabric of seamless consciousness.

But this same consciousness, upon realizing that it can never be seen as an object, is released, radically released, from the chronic headache of an eye trying to see itself. And it is precisely in that relaxation, in that uncoiling, in that release, that consciousness, resting in divine ignorance, can simply *be*, in this timeless moment, that pure divinity that our knowing and hoping and grasping had heretofore obscured.

Visions are nice in the dream world. They help turn bad dreams into pleasant dreams. But it is our visions, high or low, sacred or profane, that hold firmly the scales over our eyes and block not our knowing but our being divine. And it is visions, lovely alluring visions, that convince us that having pleasant dreams is the same as waking up.

The great saints and sages mean this absolutely, uncompromisingly, and radically. As St Augustine said, if in searching for God one *sees anything*, one is seeing *at best* angels (for they are indeed subtle or higher objects), but never, never God.

This does not mean, as I said, that holding in mind some lofty vision is of no use in this relative and dualistic world of the pleasant dream. It is just that visions, no matter how noble and wonderful, are ultimately perverted, because, ultimately they are not real.

And so let us hold our visions lightly. Let us not think that in changing from iron chains to gold chains we are somehow free. Let us not go into that dark night thinking that the pleasant dream is the coming of the light.

Let us do what we have to do in this relative world to make the dream more pleasant for all those caught in it. But let us finally release all dreams and visions and hopes and, resting in divine ignorance, realize that very divinity which is always already, without any help or hope at all, our own primordial state.

Joan Halifax

OUR THOUSAND ARMS

Joan Halifax PhD, international Buddhist teacher and cultural ecologist. Founder of the Ojai Foundation and the Upaya Foundation. Author of *Shamanic Voices, Shaman, The Wounded Healer,* and *True Nature: Views of Earth from Buddhism and Shamanism.* She says: 'Peoples of elder cultures often say that the survival of human beings depends upon being able to hear the language of the birds and beasts, the language of the river, rock and wind, being able to understand what is being said in all the tongues of plant, creature, and element; listening to the garbage as well as the rose with the same ears.'

According to Tibetan Buddhists, the Bodhisattva Avaloki-tesvara, when he/she looked out into the world and saw the immense suffering of all beings, shed tears of compassion. One of these tears was transformed into the Noble Mother Tara, the embodiment of wisdom and compassion in Tibet. Tara travelled across China, to south east Asia and Japan. She became synthesized with local protectresses, old Earth and Water goddesses, who combined with Tara to give birth to Kuan Yin, Kuan Seum, Kanzeon, Listening to the Sound of the World.

In her display as Avalokitesvara (or Kanzeon), she has six heads with which to perceive the world in all of its forms, and a thousand arms and hands to help those who are suffering. She has given herself to the world to be shaped by its needs. All her hands hold instruments of effective action. Like the mother of the world, she is outside of us but, like our own mother, she also lives inside each of us as well. In fact, she lives inside each thing. She can be found everywhere – in the falling rain which nourishes the Earth and eases the summer's heat, and in the starving child who awakens our compassion. She is the part of us that enters the body of communion without hesitation. She enters this body naturally and fearlessly.

When Ungan asked Dogo: 'How does the Bodhisattva Kanzeon use all those many hands and eyes?' Dogo replied: 'It is like someone adjusting their pillow at night.' Here compassion is a natural response to the world, not mediated by thought, or rule, or law, or vow, or intent, not regulated by religion or social duty. Buddhists say that the eyes of Mother Kanzeon see into every corner of Calcutta. The ears of Kanzeon hear all the voices of suffering, or the voices of felled cedar and mahogany, or struggling sturgeon who no longer make their way up the River Volga to spawn. The hands of Kanzeon reach out in their many shapes, sizes, and colors to help all forms of beings. They reach out from the ground of understanding and love.

This natural generosity is practiced in many forms in elder cultures. Spiritual practice among Lakota peoples, for example, is grounded in the expression 'All my relations' which proclaims that spiritual activity is not only for those immediately participating in it but for all beings everywhere. Antonio Garcia of the San Juan Pueblo explains how the spirit of generosity is at the heart of his religion: 'When I was a kid I remember everything we did was religious. My parents used to get up in the morning, they'd take sacred cornmeal, they'd blow their breath on it so the Gods would know who they were and they'd feed the gods and they'd ask for good weather, they'd ask for rain, and they'd ask for good fortune for everybody, not only people of the Pueblo, but everybody in the world. Now that is beautiful.'

In these old Earth cultures, the shaman is not only the servant of the people but is also the servant of the gods and ancestors, the creatures, plants, and elements. When the world is out of balance, whether on a large or small scale, it is the way of the shaman to redress the situation. The view of illness here, of being out of balance, focuses on the loss of the sense of connectedness, of relatedness, the experience of a kind of existential alienation. This alienation expresses itself as a divided self, a self which has forgotten the extensiveness of its being. It is the shaman's duty to help restore balance by opening and renewing the lines of communication between realms or, to put it another way, to recreate the experience of communion. Zen poet Matsuo Basho says: 'Unless we see or hear phenomena or things from within the things themselves, we shall never succeed in recording them in our hearts.'

In Buddhism, the metaphor of Indra's Net from the Avatam-saka Sutra has been used over the generations to exemplify how not one thing is separate from any other thing even though things are different from each other. At each intersection in Indra's Net there is a shining and distinct jewel. Each jewel reflects all other jewels in the Net and has no real or separate self nature. It sustains the light from all the other jewels. A single jewel and all other jewels thus exist in a pattern of presence and mutual activity.

If we consider this metaphor in terms of our own lives, we can see ourselves as both qualitatively different from and at the same time made of the same stuff as the rest of the planet. Equal and different. We are part of this Net from one perspective and from another perspective we are the Net itself, with its myriad of forms reflected in our existence. Here there can be no domination of self over other or other over self. Rather all beings, including each one of us, enemy and friend alike, exist in patterns of mutuality, interconnectedness, co-responsibility and ultimately in unity.

Poet and Zen master Thich Nhat Hanh again and again refers to this experience of the extended and non-divided self. In this poem, he makes it clear that if we look deeply, with our hearts and minds open and attentive to the world around us, we can see the roots of relatedness in each thing:

> Do not say that I'll depart tomorrow
> because even today I still arrive.
>
> Look deeply; I arrive in every second
> to be a bud on a spring branch,
> to be a tiny bird, whose wings are still fragile,

learning to sing in my new nest,
to be a caterpillar in the heart of a flower,
to be a jewel hiding itself in a stone.

I still arrive, in order to laugh and to cry,
in order to fear and to hope,
the rhythm of my heart is the birth and death
of all that are alive.

When we plant a tree, we are planting ourselves. Releasing dolphins back to the wild, we are ourselves returning home. Composting leftovers, we are being reborn as irises and apples. We can 'think like a mountain' and we can discover ourselves to be everywhere and in everything and know the activity of the world as not separate from who we are but rather of what we are.

Moving away from the anthropocentric view that holds us away from the world and discovering how we are related to and indeed embedded in all that which exists, has profound political and environmental implications. The Earth is imperilled. It is suffering. Living as part of its body, we suffer with and through it. Awakening through this suffering, we might be able to help the Earth, and ourselves heal it, and thus heal ourselves. It is our body. And its voice can be heard even in the desert silence.

We can ask ourselves, then, when will we see our True Eye? When will we discover our True Hand? Kanzeon has innumerable hands. They appear in every shape and color. She is everywhere, hearing the suffering of Earth. Kanzeon is Earth, as well, in its many forms of suffering and beauty. Her hands reach out through clearcut forests, poisoned rivers, and hungry children to awaken us. Her hands reach back to her through our compassionate response to victims of war, slaughtered rhinos, and grasslands that are now wastelands.

It seems as if we are being clearly asked to listen to the sounds of the world. The migrating birds that used to pass through in the fall and spring are fewer in number each year. I still listen for the resonant honk of the Canadian geese but they don't often pass this way any more. And where are the monarch butterflies landing these days? The bright orange clouds of monarchs that used to bring wild joy to me were smaller this year when I visited their habitat. I remember the flowering eucalyptus tree that hummed with the beating wings of these delicate creatures. In the heat of summer nights when the crickets' high-pitched song is matched by the silence of their absence in the winter, I think of the impoverishment of being born and dying in New York or Mexico City where these songs are not heard.

Sometimes it is difficult for me not to feel discouraged by the increasing noise of traffic on Highway 150 that runs beneath the ridge on which I live, or the increased presence of airplanes on Sunday that fly over to view the valley below. Recently I spent time fasting in the desert near Death Valley. Every afternoon military planes roared overhead as they trained for a war that should not happen. It is true that I can no longer deny the consequences of living in a world where the sound of machines instead of the sound of crickets is the auditory background humming behind our dreams.

Airplanes and automobiles are part of my world. I connect with the world around me through travel and through words. There is no doubt in my mind that not a little has been sacrificed that these words can be read in this form. My practice calls me not to forget or deny the outcome of the choices I have made about how I live. Looking deeply into the nature of these choices, that simply by living we take life, can open the heart of compassion as we feel the tread of our presence on the Earth. The Japanese call this 'the slender sadness, *mono non aware.*'

In the Vietnamese form of Buddhism, there are small poems of mindfulness that can be recited to remind us of exactly what we are doing at this very moment. One of these gathas is for throwing out the garbage. It goes as follows:

> In the garbage I see a rose.
> In the rose, I see the garbage.
> Everything is in transformation.
> Even permanence is impermanent.

'Garbage can smell terrible,' says Thich Nhat Hanh, 'especially rotting organic matter. But it can also become rich compost for fertilizing the garden. The fragrant rose and the stinking garbage are two sides of the same existence. Without one, the other cannot be. Everything is in transformation. The rose that wilts after six days will become a part of the garbage. After six months the garbage is transformed into a rose. When we speak of impermanence, we understand that everything is in transformation. This becomes that, and that becomes this.

'Looking deeply, we can contemplate one thing and see everything else in it. We are not disturbed by change when we see the interconnectedness and continuity of all things. It is not that the life of any individual is permanent, but that life itself continues. When we identify ourselves with life and go beyond the boundaries of a separate identity, we shall be able to see permanence in the impermanent, or the rose in the garbage.'

It is said that the last sense-faculty to cease to function upon our dying is our hearing. It is also said that things originally came into being through their vibration, through their sounding. 'In the beginning was the Word,' so the scriptures say. When a thing ceases to be, its sound disappears from the world. Kanzeon is the intimate presence within all things that responds through perceiving the sound of life-activity, no matter how small the voice, no matter how deep the suffering, how great the joy. I believe that we are being called to put our ear against the body of the Earth, to listen closely to what is really being said, and to consider the consequences of what we are hearing.

We discover that the Word, breath and wind are related through the experience of Spirit and psyche. This relationship is both linguistic as well as existential. The atmosphere circulating around and within us is so polluted that the necessity to hear into, to listen to, the Spirit of all things is becoming a necessity for our common survival. Peoples of elder cultures often say that the survival of human beings depends on being able to hear the language of the birds and beasts, the language of the river, rock and wind, being able to understand what is being said in all the tongues of plant, creature, and element; listening to the garbage as well as the rose with the same ears. Who listens in this manner is Kanzeon. It is she who 'abides in ultimate closeness' with all beings. It is she who embodies the principle of intimacy and communion within each of us.

John Harricharan

ONE DROP OF WATER

John Harricharan, teacher and former Fortune 500 Executive. Author of *When You Can Walk on Water, Take the Boat,* and *Morning Has Been All Night Coming.* He says: 'I learned at a very early age that all people are shipmates on the voyage of life, and that one cannot sink one's shipmates without sinking oneself.'

It was many years ago. The boy was not more than ten years old as he stood beside the man that early morning. They were both standing on the shore of the Atlantic looking east toward the rising sun. The chill morning air caused a slight shiver to run through the boy. The man, seeming to know without even looking, took off his jacket and dropped it over the small shoulders of his son. They walked up to the water's edge as the man spoke: 'You see that wide expanse of water? It is made of billions of gallons, and each gallon is made of tens of thousands of drops.'

The little boy seemed curious. 'And what are the drops made of?' he asked.

With a smile, the man replied: 'The drops are made of smaller and smaller drops, and each in turn is made of bits and pieces of things that make the very world we live in.'

'What am I made of, Dad?' the boy asked after a short while. 'Am I made of the same stuff as the ocean?'

The father smiled as he replied: 'Everything is made of everything else, and everything is a part of other things. As you stand here this morning, you are a part of this land, this shore, this ocean. Look at that tree, the sky. They are parts of the very me and the eternal I. There is a force that keeps us together. Some call that force God, others Allah, Jehovah, or Jove. There are a thousand names for this force, but it does not matter what it is called. It just is. As you grow older and wiser, you will find the stirring of this mighty force within you. You will know that it is always there, and that you are safe and happy within it.'

The boy, with a puzzled expression, looked at his father and asked: 'How can this force, this God, be within me and at the same time be in everything else I see?'

'Because,' the man replied, 'God is everything and everyone. God is in you and in me, in those gulls you see over there, in the sand under our feet and the lilies of the field. God is everywhere and everything, and there cannot be two of everything. God is a part of you just like the drop of water is a part of this ocean. Remember this well and you will grow up to have a sense of peace, joy, and understanding.'

Decades have passed since I stood on that shore with my father. I have since travelled to many countries, lived in various cultures, and experienced deep sorrow and great joy. I have seen the best and the worst of my fellow human beings. Yet, through it all, I could hear the voice of my father telling me: 'God is everywhere and everything, and there cannot be two of everything.'

As a Hindu boy, I grew up in a small village of Hindus, Christians, and Moslems. I learned at a very early age that all people are shipmates on the voyage of life, and that one cannot sink one's shipmates without sinking oneself. As I studied the Vedic writings and compared them with the words of the Hebrew prophets and the teachings of the New Testament Apostles, I found that the common thread that ran through everything was love. The greatest commandment ever given was 'Love your God and love one another' – all others are simply variations of that theme.

Lex Hixon

JOINT CITIZENSHIP IN PARALLEL SACRED WORLDS

Lex Hixon PhD, author of *Coming Home, The Heart of the Koran* and *Great Swan*. Initiated as Nur-al-Jerrahi in the Sufi tradition, also initiated in the Eastern Orthodox Church, the Gelugpa Order of Tibetan Buddhism, and the Ramakrishna Vivekananda Vedanta order. He says: 'If we recognize that the sacred is found in many different forms and expressions then no one can accept as valid only one sacred tradition. In so doing we immediately limit the sacred, and limitation denies the very essence of sacredness.'

Human beings require breathable atmosphere, clean water, balanced nourishment, and a just and loving community. We also require a coherent sacred world. Some neutral social existence with ethical values and religious aspirations super-imposed upon it is not adequate. We are beings designed to live in a world which is intrinsically sacred, and which is by nature infinitely meaningful in its very existence.

Hinduism, Buddhism, Taoism, Confucianism, Judaism, Christianity, Islam, and the innumerable indigenous or re-gional traditions of sacredness are not primarily social institu-tions which can be studied from the outside. A sacred tradition is an entire sacred world – boundless in scope, inexhaustible in teaching and blessing. It has no *outside*. An authentic sacred world alone can provide breathable atmosphere, clean water, balanced nourishment, and a just and loving community for the entire human being.

We cannot simply enter an impressive landscape and encounter God. We cannot merely close our eyes, look inward, and discover the True Self. We cannot analyze our limited personal and cultural experience and reach timeless Truth. We cannot run along beaches at dawn or make love with a close partner and automatically experience the supreme passion for the Sacred. We may indulge in romanticism and wish-fulfilment, even engage in moral, artistic, or religious aspiration, without actually meeting the Sacred face to face. This meeting is the ultimate encounter, and upon this encounter authentic human existence depends.

Many people repeat: 'I reject organized religion'. Perhaps we could ask them in return: 'Do you accept organized language, an organized nervous system, organized civil rights, an organized ecology?' Maybe the more appropriate word, in all of these cases, is *organic*. For a truly sacred world and all the subtle structures that sustain it is, in essence, an organic manifestation – rather than an arbitary or even oppressive form of organization.

We cannot construct a sacred world like a bridge, clock, or computer. We cannot even bring a sacred world into being through the genius of creative imagination like a play, film, or novel. A sacred world is neither an individual nor a collective work of art. It is not poetry or music. Yet all of these express sacredness, for no being or event exists outside of the Sacred.

If we recognize that the Sacred is found in many different forms and expressions then no one can realistically accept as valid only one sacred tradition. In so doing we immediately limit the Sacred, and limitation denies the very essence of sacredness. We are faced instead by a paradoxical plurality of sacred worlds – surprisingly different landscapes with equally surprising correspondences.

The cultural style of openness in contemporary Western society allows us to consider becoming Buddhist, Hindu, or Muslim, or to return anew to our religion of birth, be it Native American, Jewish, or Christian. It even allows us to stand outside sacred tradition entirely or to sample various esoteric or secular teachings. We can stroll through a cultural and counter-cultural shopping mall, rather than truly existing – with awe, and life and death commitment – within an integral environment of sacredness.

The spiritual solution is to regard the contemporary secular world itself as a call from the Sacred. Cultural and religious pluralism are actually an invitation from the Sacred to modern humanity: *Penetrate further into the unity of sacred existence*! But sacredness cannot flourish as an intellectual abstraction, a romantic nostalgia, or a socially imposed norm. It springs only from free commitment and just community.

The subtlety and complexity of the human body provides a metaphor for the functioning of sacred traditions. Scriptures, guides, moral disciplines, rites, symbols, music, dance, teaching, sacraments of communion, propitiation and initiation are like the various enzymes, designed to digest different foods. Sacredness must be properly digested and its energy distributed to the entire communal body. The principle of nourishment remains the same, but forms of nourishment and modes of assimilation differ dramatically.

We may therefore ask: 'How far does this differentiation go?' There is obvious wisdom for keeping a spiritual lineage disciplined rather than splitting and diffusing the sacred energy whenever some charismatic leader or rebellious initiate becomes inspired to do so. Can we have a global civilization if a different language is spoken in every valley? Of course, branching is healthy and fruitful for a fruit-bearing tree, but a certain amount of pruning is also necessary. For sacredness is essentially shared experience – unifying, not dividing. The sacred struggle is for unity, continuity, community, commitment, coherence. Diversity and self-expression, simply for their own sakes, are not characteristic of a sacred world, which must have the cohesive power to extend through generations and across cultural frontiers.

For contemporary planetary civilization to achieve that unity, continuity, community, commitment, and coherence which sustains the genuine experience of sacredness, we need to accept the possibility of joint citizenship in parallel sacred worlds. We can contribute concretely to the future by becoming responsible citizens, or initiates, of several sacred worlds, bearing them carefully and harmoniously within our own being.

Sacred worlds do not stop at political, ethnic, or historical frontiers but present a coherent vision and daily revelatory experience of reality as a whole. Parallel sacred worlds do not cancel or annul each other, any more than French invalidates Arabic. One sacred world is not more true than another. Each one bears the fullness of living Truth.

Can one person live authentically in several alternative universes, each with different standards for faith and action, for what is good and what is real? The answer is non-Euclidean. Parallel worlds do meet, while remaining parallel. They meet in sacredness without losing their uniqueness. This is why we speak of sacred worlds as *parallel* rather than as *divergent* or *convergent*.

In a consciously committed, initiatory sense, I am Hindu, Buddhist, Christian and Muslim. I am among the advocates of joint spiritual citizenship. I do not judge or evaluate any of these traditions in terms of the others. I simply live, worship, meditate, work, play, and commune within these sacred worlds as a fully naturalized citizen of each. To connect with the integrity and fullness of each concerns me greatly and involves serious responsibilities in five lineages: the Halveti-Jerrahi Order of Islam; the movement of Ramakrishna Paramahamsa and Sarada Devi of Bengal; the Greek-Russian-Arabic line of the Eastern Orthodox Church; the Nyingma-Kagyu-Sakya-Gelugpa line of Tibetan Buddhism; and the Soto–Rinzai fusion of Japanese Zen.

I am a formal spiritual leader in only two of these lineages, yet I carry all these active initiations inwardly and simultaneously. My principle is to keep each sacred tradition uncontaminated by either the rational, secular world or by the eclectic New Age movement, which are mirror reflections of each other. I am also careful about casually mixing or making facile equivalences between these five sacred worlds, which are each ineffable, unique, incomparable, non-interchangeable, inclusive, integral, and complete. They are not in need of any interpretation or infusion from outside, nor are they locked within themselves, always remaining fundamentally open to the Sacred. Nonetheless, it is a fact that these various currents of initiatory energy are flowing within a single person, so they cannot be hermetically sealed off from each other. There is a healing interaction similar to deep friendship between the various initiatory streams within a citizen of parallel sacred worlds. This experience far transcends ecumenical dialogue or liturgical experiment.

Sacred traditions exist not to bind or suppress but to free us, both personally and collectively, from narrow subjectivity which usually remains unconscious. However, the sense of sacredness does not imply naïvety. Even the most genuine traditions fall into delusions and partial perspectives, needing to be constantly renewed by the living Truth at their core. We do not enter a sacred world to engage in fantasy but to unveil Truth in order to facilitate the fullest future for humanity.

Due to the natural ecology of the Sacred, spiritual maturity can manifest. But our contemporary sacred space is becoming severely polluted from both ends of the spectrum – religious fundamentalism and anti-religious or merely non-religious secularism. Each of these pollutants reinforces the operation of the other. We need to take new steps together to meet this situation – cleansing, healing, reconciling, illuminating. We must become citizens of parallel sacred worlds.

Father Thomas Keating

THE SEARCH FOR THE ULTIMATE REALITY

Father Thomas Keating, Benedictine monk for over forty years. He served as Superior of St Benedict's Monastery, Colorado, and as Abbot of St Joseph's Abbey, Massachusetts. Teacher of the Christian contemplative tradition. Author of *Open Mind, Open Heart, Crisis of Faith, The Heart of the World, The Mystery of Christ,* and *Awakenings.* He says: 'All true paths tend to converge at the source like the spokes of a wheel. To come closer to the source along one path is to come closer to every other path ... If one completes the journey to one's own heart, one will find oneself in the heart of everyone else.'

Many paths lead to the Source. Depending upon our cultural or religious frame of reference, we call this Source the Absolute, Infinite God, Brahman, Great Spirit, Allah, and other names. The term *Ultimate Reality* has been chosen here to designate the transcendent Mystery to which all these words are pointing.

An unprecedented awakening to transcultural human and religious values has begun to take place throughout the world. Those who seek the Ultimate Reality as a result of this awakening relate to everything that is true and of genuine spiritual value in every religious tradition. They are united in the greatest of all adventures. They resonate to human values wherever they can be found whether in religion, nature, science, art, human friendship, or the service of others. This is not an attitude of eclecticism, a kind of homogenizing of human values; still less an abdication of one's personal convictions and experience. It is rather a centering of one's attention upon what unites rather than what divides; the developing of a hierarchy of values in which transcultural values come first, without denigrating the particular values of one's own race, culture, or religion. True unity is expressed in pluralism: unity in the experience of the fundamental values of human life; pluralism in one's particular response to these values in the concrete circumstances of life.

Those who seek the Ultimate Reality are people of faith, even if they do not belong to a particular religion. Faith is more profound and comprehensive than a belief system. Belief systems belong to the level of pluralism, faith to the level of unity. Faith is openness to the Ultimate Reality as such, before the experience of the Ultimate Reality is broken down into various belief systems. Faith is the acceptance of authentic living with all its creativity, and the acceptance of dying with all its potential for a greater fullness of life. The experience of the transcendent dimension in oneself is an expression of faith at work at the most fundamental level.

Perhaps the most precious value that the world religions have in common is their accumulated experience of the spiritual journey. Centuries of seekers have discovered and lived its conditions, temptations, development, and final integration. This wealth of personal experience bears witness to the historical grounding of our contemporary search. It is not just a passing fad. It invites the spiritual teachers of the various disciplines of the world religions to pool their common experience, resources, and insights for the benefit of seekers in every religious tradition.

Certain requirements or characteristics of the spiritual journey are present in every religious tradition. To focus on examples from the Christian tradition, the story of the Magi described in the Gospel of Matthew can be taken as a parable of the spiritual journey. The Magi are symbols of those who genuinely and painstakingly seek the truth in every generation. They found what they were seeking, probably to their great astonishment, in a manger. The Magi understood that the advent of a brilliant new star was a gracious reaching out of the Ultimate Reality, inviting them to search for its meaning and source. All true paths tend to converge at the source like the spokes of a wheel. To come closer to the source along one path is to come closer to every other path. The main thing is to choose one's path in the light of the inner and outer signals coming from the Ultimate Reality, and to persevere in that path regardless of the difficulties that arise from the length of the journey, the politics of the time, or the opposition of other people.

The Magi returned to their homeland by a route different from the one by which they came. The parable may be hinting that once the goal has been found, the route itself no longer has the same importance. In order to reach the goal, the route at a certain point has to be transcended – not necessarily by leaving it, but by the inner freedom that attaches itself to the goal rather than to the path.

Every seeker has to pass through the experience of death and resurrection, perhaps many times over. Joseph's love of Mary and his vision of life with her – and later his love of Jesus and his vision of life with him – were both visions given him directly by God and both taken away from him through circumstances over which he had no control. These two visions were the two eyes that he had to give up in order to see with God's eyes: he had to surrender these two visions and become totally blind to them in order to become one with Vision Itself.

Our contemporary world desperately needs persons of boundless generosity who dedicate themselves to great ideals; who wish to transform themselves and contribute to the transformation of the world. Commitment to a great vision is what gives ordinary daily life its direction and purpose. As one journeys across the desert, prairie, or sea – images in sacred literature of the tedium of daily life – one may come upon a place of rest: an oasis, a garden of spiritual delights, or a harbor. This can be an occasion of terrible temptation for a person with a great vision. It seems as if one has arrived at the end of the laborious journey and that one's immense efforts are at last coming to fruition. Actually, unless one hastens to push on, the place of rest becomes a place of poison. Spiritual consolation is a trap when sought for one's own satisfaction.

But how does one push on? Is it by giving up the vision? Not exactly. It is rather by being willing to do so. Renunciation is the only way to move beyond what one *thinks* is the vision and to experience what it actually *is*. The struggle to attain vision leads inevitably to disappointment or even to despair. This is because, in order to get to the place of vision, it is necessary to give up one's own ideas about how to reach it. It is like dying. The world as we know it must be broken and ourselves with it. Our idea of the spiritual journey, of service to humanity, of the church, of Jesus Christ – even our idea of God – must be *shattered*. The crux of the human predicament is not the personal wrongdoing for which we are responsible. It is rather our misguided *condition*, all that which causes us to reflect about our vision rather than to live it. There is another story that speaks to the hearts of those engaged in the spiritual journey. The raising of Lazarus from the dead described in the Gospel of John is a parable of the human condition. Lazarus was a special friend of Jesus. But when he fell seriously ill, Jesus did not come to heal him.

What is the nature of this mysterious illness that comes upon friends of Jesus and which he refuses to heal? It is the recognition of one's false self and the sense of spiritual poverty that results from this awareness. The false self might be described as the constellation of all the self-serving habits that have been woven into our personality from the time we were conceived. It includes the emotional damage that has come from our upbringing and environment; all the harm that other people have done to us, knowingly or unknowingly, at an age when we could not defend ourselves; and all the methods we acquired, many of them now unconscious, to ward off the pain of unbearable situations. The story of Lazarus is a kind of psychodrama; it is the acting out of Jesus' teaching that one has to lose one's life in order to save it: to lose one's false self in order to find one's true Self. The healing of the division in oneself can only come about if one identifies with the illness of Lazarus. Jesus did not heal this illness because the death of the false self is the necessary condition for inner resurrection.

At a certain point in the spiritual journey one's unconscious motivation begins to surface and the truth about oneself, whatever that may be, has to be faced. It may become impossible to believe in one's own basic goodness because there is no direct experience of it. A feeling of dread can arise as one questions what to do with this pervasive sense of loss, even to the extent of the absence of meaning in one's life. And there is the further temptation to think that no outside power can help.

According to the story, Lazarus died and was laid in the tomb, a striking image of the psychological state of one who feels alienated from the Ultimate Reality. It is at this point in the spiritual journey that one encounters head-on the anguish of contemporary society.

Abandoned to what seem to be uncontrollable forces of political and social change, our contemporary world groans under a pervasive sense of fear and despair. This is accompanied by the loss of value in life itself. At the very least, there is loneliness, confusion, powerlessness, frustration. If people are to find the Ultimate Reality, they have to search for It in a society in which, to all appearances, it has been almost totally forgotten.

The symbol of Lazarus challenges those on the spiritual journey to go the whole way in letting go of the false self with its illusions and hang-ups. Although Lazarus was not aware of it, Jesus had come to the place where he was laid and was about to call him from the tomb. The inner resurrection of one's true Self moves the whole human family in the direction of transformation. In this perspective, the spiritual journey leads to the very reverse of selfishness. It is the journey to selflessness.

What needs to be emphasized by those in search of the Ultimate Reality is the contemplative dimension of life. By the contemplative dimension I mean the growth of faith to the point where one's actions are motivated by an abiding sense of the presence of the Ultimate Reality underlying and accompanying all reality, like a fourth dimension of ordinary sense perception. To open oneself to this awareness, one may need a discipline that engages all the faculties and a structure appropriate to one's life circumstances. The contemplative dimension offers an insight into the gift of being human and enables one to believe in one's own basic goodness. It also perceives the basic goodness of everyone else. It enables one to accept physical death as a step in one's evolution toward the fullness of life. And finally, it perceives the presence of the Ultimate Reality at the heart of all reality; it no longer gets stuck on the meaning of symbols, but goes through symbols to the reality that they signify.

Our world is at a crisis point because so many structures that supported human and religious values have been trampled. To find a way to discover the Ultimate Reality at the center of so-called 'secular' occupations and situations is essential because for most people today it is the only milieu that they know. Humanity as a whole needs a breakthrough into the contemplative dimension of life. Here the human family is already one. If one completes the journey to one's own heart, one will find oneself in the heart of everyone else.

Sri Swami Satchidananda

THE KEY TO PEACE

Sri Swami Satchidananda, international inspired teacher of spirituality and yoga, founder of the Integral Yoga Institutes and Satchidananda Ashram, also of the Lotus Temple in Virginia. Author of many books on yoga, including *The Living Gita* and *The Golden Present.* He says: 'Let us remember that the way ahead is the way of the heart ... When you shine with that light, you also bring light to all around you.'

Who is the most selfish person? The one who is the most selfless! It sounds like a contradiction: if you really want to get ahead in the world – to be 'somebody' – the way is to not think of yourself at all. Why? Because by being selfless, you will always retain your happiness. A selfish person can never be happy. Know that. So to be happier, be more selfless. To be the *most* happy, be the *most* selfless.

If you want to summarize the essence of all religious teachings in just one word, that word would be 'selflessness'. Be dedicated. The tree sacrifices its flower to produce a fruit; the candle burns itself away to give us light. There is selflessness everywhere, all around us.

Look at the apple tree. It gives *thousands* of fruits. If you ask a tree: 'How many fruits did you give this season?' it will say: 'Oh, several thousand.'

'Did people come and beg for them?'

'Oh, no, I don't wait for that. I just give.'

'Without their even asking?'

'Yes. That's my nature. I find it a joy to give that way.'

'Suppose nobody comes to take them?'

'That's their business. My job is just to give. I don't want to eat my own fruit, so I just drop it.'

'But your apples are so delicious. Don't you even want to *try* one – just to taste it?'

If you have the ears to hear, you will hear the tree laughing at you. 'Do you think I'm a human being, eating my own fruit? Only the human beings run after their fruit, and that is why they are in misery.'

What's more, the tree not only gives its fruit to those who praise it, but even to those who stone it. Throw a stone at an apple tree and you will get even more fruit. Throw a stone at a person and you know what you'll get! Who is greater, then, the apple tree or the human? When I walk around and see the apple trees, I feel very humble.

So the lesson is not to expect anything. If you make an appointment for some result, you must be ready to face *dis*-appointment. Ask for nothing for yourself; just serve. That way you will retain your peace always, because peace is always in you. Peace is not something that comes from outside. As long as you don't disturb it by your expectations and anxieties, it will be there.

The best way not to disturb your peace is not to expect anything in return for your actions. Just give what you can. Don't even bother to find out whether a person appreciates or benefits from your service. Your business is giving, that's all.

That is renunciation, or dedication. When you renounce the attachment and expectation of the fruits of your actions, you retain your peace. God commanded Adam not to eat the fruit, but it is not just that once upon a time in the Garden of Eden an apple was forbidden to that one person. No, we are all Adams and we are all planting trees. Every action is a tree and every action bears its fruit. We are asked not to eat that fruit, but instead to offer it to humanity.

The *Bhagavad Gita* asks: 'How can someone be happy if he or she has not found peace? *Ashaantasya kutah sukham?*' And it gives the answer: 'The dedicated ever enjoy supreme peace. *Tyaagat shaantir anantaram.*' How can there be happiness without peace? And what is the way to that peace? Dedication, sacrifice. Our entire life, the very act of living, must be for the sake of others. Eat for the sake of others, breathe for the sake of others. Then it is guaranteed that nothing in the world can disturb your peace.

In some way or other, we must all become selfless. That doesn't mean you must become a monk or nun, to be a renunciate. Sacrifice is what we are learning even in family life. Once you have a partner, you have to sacrifice at least fifty per cent to that partner, is it not so? Otherwise you cannot make a good home together. Then you both must sacrifice for the sake of the little ones. So our own lives teach us how to sacrifice.

You will find that the more you take care of the world, the more the world will take care of you. Who are the people who are most respected, most adored, in all the world? The saintly people. The selfless ones. The ones who have sacrificed their selfishness for the sake of humanity are the ones we worship and adore. We want to follow them. We want to be like them. A selfish person is never followed or respected like that. He may be saluted as long as he is in power, and even that is probably more out of fear than gratitude. But the selfless person is loved and respected and cared for by the whole world, wherever he or she goes.

I often suggest this to anyone interested in trying an experiment: for just one week, try to be completely selfless. Perform *every* action as a service. Say to yourself: 'For one whole week, let me be selfless. Let me always give, give, give, and love, love, love.' If you really don't get any benefit – if you don't enjoy that week at all – okay, go back to your old ways. But if you get even a taste of the joy that comes from giving for the sake of giving, you will want to taste that joy again and again. You will be looking for opportunities to taste it more and more. I guarantee it.

That is what is meant by Yoga. People often think Yoga means standing on the head, doing some physical postures, doing special breathing techniques, meditating. But in simple words, Yoga means keeping the mind clear and calm to reflect the peace and joy that are in you as your true Self. Whatever helps you to do that can be called Yoga. In other words, any action that will not disturb your peace of mind is a Yogic action.

We need the right food, the right drink, the right air, the right habits, to maintain our physical ease. In the same way, to maintain mental ease we need right thinking. Anxiety, fear, worry, disappointment, hatred, jealousy – all these things disturb the mind. But there is just one cause behind all these disturbances: selfishness.

Take fear for example. Of what are we afraid? Of losing something. If you have a lot of money in the safe, you will be getting up in the middle of the night to see whether the safe is still locked or not. You will be afraid of losing the money. But if you feel: 'The money is with me now, and as long as it is there, I may use it,' then you won't have any fear of losing it. If, by chance, it is taken away, you won't be disturbed.

The cause of fear is attachment. If you are selfless, if you are not attached to anything, you never need to be afraid. This same principle applies to all of our mental disturbances. If we are not selfish, we will not be anxious about anything. There will be no need to worry, or to hate anyone, or to be jealous or angry or disappointed. That is why all the religious scriptures say: 'Don't possess anything. Lead a detached life.'

Say: 'All is Thine, I am Thine,' instead of 'Everything should be *mine.*' If you walk through a *mine* field, your peace is constantly in danger of being disturbed! All your *mines* will be waiting to explode! So if you really want to be safe, change all your *mines* to *Thines.*

'But,' you may ask, 'if I am not to be attached to anything or anyone, why should I do anything? What's the use of having or doing anything at all?' Here we need to understand that things are given to us for us to use, not for us to possess.

When I give a talk, I come in and someone offers me a nice seat and a microphone. That person might even say: 'Is "your" seat comfortable?' or 'Let's test "your" microphone.' I can certainly say the chair and the microphone are mine for the evening. But when I finish the talk, can I take the chair and microphone and go? No. They are only mine as long as I am using them. When a secretary is hired, the supervisor will say: 'Here is your desk and typewriter.' But later on when the supervisor comes and fires the secretary, can the secretary take the typewriter and walk out? No.

In the same way, we are all hired in this world to do certain jobs. In this big office, God, or the Cosmic Force, is the manager. He gives us typewriters, cars, houses, husbands, wives, children, friends, experiences – all according to His purpose. But when the time comes for us to be 'fired,' when the Divine Proprietor feels we have finished our jobs, we have to leave everything and go.

Has anyone ever taken his or her own car to the cremation ground? You can't take *anything* with you. You came alone and you go alone. In between, you may be given many things. When it is time for them – or you – to go, just let them go. Then your mind will never be disturbed.

For example, if I were to go to speak somewhere with the desire or expectation of starting a Yoga center in that place, then I would not be there just to serve everyone. Instead, my purpose would be to catch some 'fish.' Even while I was talking, I would be anxiously watching the faces: which fish is the right one to get caught in my net? I would be trying to do two things at once. My service would not be complete or perfect then. My mind would be divided. I would be anxious: 'Who is smiling at me? Who is appreciating me?' That anxiety would disturb my mind.

Suppose after the talk, I found that nobody had gotten into my net. I would be disappointed. See? All these emotions would be there if I came with a personal motive. Instead, I am just there. I share what little I know. If it suits you, take it. If not, drop it and go. I neither gain nor lose anything that way; therefore, I retain my peace and joy. I am there just to serve. If we perform all our actions in this way – purely as a service – without looking for the fruits or the results of the actions, the mind will be clean and clear, peaceful and joyful.

In all of the scriptures, the essence of spiritual practice is this: selfless service. Lord Krishna says: 'Whatever you do, whatever you eat, whatever you offer in sacrifice, whatever you give, whatever austerity you practice, do it as an offering to Me.' Lord Jesus says: 'Inasmuch as ye have done it unto one of the least of these, ye have done it unto me.' We are always doing something, so to make your *doing* a service means your spiritual practice becomes continuous. You don't need a special place or a special time. You don't need quiet. You don't even need a schedule for Karma Yoga*. From morning until evening you are doing some action, so everything can be Karma Yoga. You are a Yogi throughout your day, throughout your life.

Everything should be based on selflessness. 'Why should I meditate? What is the purpose? So I can clean the mind, calm the mind, strengthen the mind. Why? To serve well.' Then even your meditation – your work, your worship, your walking, your talking, your eating, your sleeping – it all becomes selfless service.

This attitude will easily come by itself when you enjoy your service. If you don't enjoy it, everything will weigh heavily on your shoulders. 'Oh, I *have* to do it . . . can't they find someone else for this? Am I the *only* person who is available?' If it becomes a burden to you, it's not selfless service anymore. There's nothing spiritual in it then. If you call it a spiritual practice or service or Karma Yoga, it should bring you the maximum joy. If it doesn't, it's not service, but labor.

These days we see business, business, business everywhere. The whole world is engaged in some kind of business or other. Karma means labor and labor means doing something to get something in return. That's why it's laborious! If you call something labor, it shows that you feel it's difficult or painful.

Labor is when you expect something in return. That is why there are so many labor mediation boards. The boss expects more work from you, and you expect more money from the boss. There is a continuous tug of war between employer and employee. To undo these entanglements, you need labor mediators. But have you ever heard of a 'service mediator'? No. No one goes to court in the name of service.

Even in the name of marriage, we see this. The husband says: 'Honey, I love you.' Then he looks at her face and waits.

---

*Karma Yoga means yoga in action, or working for the joy of working without seeking reward. Karma itself means action, or the result of cause and effect.

Why? To hear her say: 'Oh, Honey, I love you too!' If she doesn't say anything, what will he do? He'll go find a lawyer! Can we call it love then? No. That's business. In true selfless love, you just love. Loving makes you happy, that's all.

Real love and service are one-way traffic: you just give for the joy of giving. When there's no expectation whatsoever, there's never any trouble – neither for you nor for the one who receives your service. When you have done a service for someone and have really done it in a selfless way, he or she won't even feel an obligation. That is the best possible service. When you give a gift, don't make the recipient obliged to you. You wanted to give, you gave, and you have the joy that comes from giving. The minute you look for something in return, you lose that joy. Your peace of mind is lost. Don't even look for a smile or a 'thank you.' Then nothing can disturb your joy.

We don't even spare God these 'business gifts.' Sometimes people light a beautiful candle in church and say: 'Excuse me, God, don't just look at that. Listen to me. I have to run to the office soon. You can appreciate that later, but for now, listen. This is what I want from You . . .' We do business even in the name of God.

And God is a fair business-person. As you give, so will you receive. If you give Him ten per cent, you will get ten per cent of God's gifts. But suppose you give Him a hundred per cent; what will you get? A hundred per cent of God. Your hundred per cent is worth very little. Maybe you offer Him your 150 pounds of flesh and bone, a few ideas, some feelings, your big ego, this and that. But He doesn't care about all that; He's only concerned with the percentage. Are you giving completely? Are you surrendering totally?

When you give a hundred per cent, God says: 'This person has given me all. What am I to do? I have no choice: I must give him all of *Me* in return!' When you give yourself to Him completely, He gives Himself to you completely. So even though your Karma Yoga is a business deal too, it's a very good deal!

A great, great saint of South India named Maanikkava-chakar used to write beautiful poems. '*Maanika*' means 'gem', '*vachaka*' means 'speech'. His words were like gems. In one of his poems he says: 'Lord, you are not a very good business-man. If You keep this up, I don't even know how long you will be able to stay in business! You gave Yourself to me in exchange for this frail little body and mind. In You, I have the whole universe. By getting You, I got everything; by getting me, You got nothing. I seem to be much more clever than you!'

That is the trick of Karma Yoga. When you do everything for the sake of doing – for the joy of doing – as a dedicated act for the benefit of humanity, and not just for your benefit, you retain your joy. Don't think that you *get* joy by doing something. The joy is in you always. But by loving and giving and keeping your heart pure, you become more and more aware of that joy, until you live always and completely in that Kingdom within.

We should live to sacrifice. If we don't, we will have a debit account with all those things in nature that are sacrificing themselves for our sakes. God, or Nature, has given us food, water, sun, rain – our very breath; knowingly or unknowingly, we are using all those things constantly. How can we return the gift? By living lives that are a joyous sacrifice.

Try to return more than you receive. If someone gives you a cup of water, wait for an opportunity to return a cup of milk. If you return a cup of water, you are doing business. If you do not return anything, you are a thief. When you get something from whatever source – whether from a person or from the atmosphere – you have to return something. If you return an amount equal to what you received, you are a fair business-person. If you give more, you are a holy person, a Karma Yogi. You should know whether you are a thief or a Yogi.

For the sake of your own peace and joy, give more than you are given. Karma Yoga is called selfless action. But as I said in the beginning, a selfless action is the most selfish action. Selfless people are the most selfish people. Why? They want to be selfless so they won't lose their peace and joy. Isn't that selfish?

Let us remember that the way ahead is the way of the heart. Let us live a life of sacrifice and retain that image of God's peace and joy within us. When you shine with that light, you will also bring light to all around you. May the God who is Truth, Peace, Love, and Joy, who is within us and everywhere, bless us to come together and live together with this understanding, and to make this world a beautiful heaven. Let this be our constant wish and prayer.

OM Shanthi, Shanthi, Shanthi. OM Peace, Peace, Peace.

Sir George Trevelyan

THE RISING TIDE OF LOVE

Sir George Trevelyan MA, international teacher and lecturer, founder of the Wrekin Trust, recipient of the Right Livelihood Award. Author of many books on the spirituality and healing of humankind and the universe. He says: 'The power of light cannot be defeated by the darkness. Much outward catastrophe is possible in the coming changes, but behind it is the glory of the living Christ in power and majesty, flooding light and love into the darkened world.'

'Holism!' I looked it up in the Oxford Dictionary and read:

A tendency within nature for separate parts to come together to form ever greater wholes.

And my whole being rose in protest! This is wrong! This is wholly inadequate. I recalled the great old song:

> I'll sing you One, O
> Green grow the rushes, O
> What is your One O?
> *One is one and all alone*
> *and evermore shall be so*

True holism is the creative mind of God in manifestation. Oh the wonder, once you see it! From the Great Source was poured out thought, the archetypal *ideas* of all things, ideas so alive that they are the beings of things not yet in visible form but always integrated in a living wholeness of relationship, proliferating, complexifying, but at every stage always a oneness. In the beginning was the idea.

Then follows the wondrous process of translating the ideas into visible manifestation and form. Read Genesis Chapter 2, verses 4 and 5:

> The Lord God made the Earth and the Heavens, and every plant of the field *before it was in the earth* and every herb of the field *before it grew*. For the Lord God had not caused it to rain upon the earth.

There we have it – first the archetypal idea of each species, an infinite complexity of spiritual entities or beings, all facets of the one whole in the mind of God, and all inevitably interrelated in dynamic harmony. Then the ideas are 'realized', made real, upon Earth. The vast and intricate pattern is always a mobile living oneness of interconnection. And now for us comes the great truth. In the human being is created a living point of thinking and perceiving, a being who can in thinking apprehend the archetypal idea hidden within each natural form.

See this wondrous aspect of true holism. In Man (male/female) is a being integrally part of the whole, but a point that can become conscious and reflect the living whole (and reflect upon it!). In humanity, planet Earth is becoming conscious.

But Earth itself is a thought of God. It is a design created of intent as a setting for a supreme experiment – that on it the tenth hierarchy, the human being, 'a little lower than the angels, but crowned with glory and honour', shall evolve to consciousness and, in freedom, develop character and ego, so that ultimately he/she may come back to God of free choice and so become a co-creator. Vistas of exploration open to the fulfilled human being!

In some sense we have surely entered the 'end-days'. We live in the age of the Earth changes of which much has been written and foreseen, both by scientists and mystics. The old Earth is changing. We human beings were given the noble task of stewardship of the planet:

Be fruitful, multiply and replenish the Earth and have dominion over every living thing that moveth upon the earth.

And what have we done with our stewardship? We have exploited nature for gain, profit, and power. We have made a god of money and profit.

And now we are having to pay for this blasphemy. For Earth is a living being, an integrated oneness, with its own intelligence. It was the scientist James Lovelock who first came up with the 'Gaia Hypothesis', reviving the Greek name of the goddess of the Earth, recognizing that the Earth is a living, integrated totality and that Nature has an uncanny intelligence which enables her ultimately and always to defeat any attack or drain on her life forces.

So in our New Age vision we come to the realization that Holism implies the totality of God's creative thought outpoured from the Source into infinite complexity of creation and design, yet always and at every point integrated into a living, pulsating, ever-evolving Whole.

And the human mind – 'a pulse of the eternal mind, no less' – is seen as a divine organ within the totality of things which can think God's thoughts again and unravel the infinite complexity of Earth and Nature.

> All are but parts of one stupendous whole
> Whose body Nature is, and God the soul.

So wrote Alexander Pope. We are apprehending a truth so much grander than the nineteenth-century rational material-ism. But knowledge may be likened to a wall built in tiers, resting upon each other. Thinking is a constantly evolving structure and the crowning tier of the wall of human thought could not be without the underpinning of the earlier thought structures.

Now in our time a step is being taken into a spiritual world view. To grasp this is perhaps vital to our very survival as a race. For Gaia is upset and, as we have said, knows how always to win in any conflict and to defeat any threat to her essential life energy.

Let me here stress that this is no dogma for which belief is demanded. The so-called 'New Age vision' is in no sense a proselytizing religious movement. We are invited and challenged to think and to stretch imagination to grasp the evolving whole of which we are each integrally part. We are called on to think ideas. We must recognize that the human being is given the divine faculty of apprehending and grasping an idea for its very beauty – a priceless gift, could we but learn to use it. Quite clearly we can and do rise to certain ideas with excitement. 'Yes, yes how lovely! That must be true!' And then cold rational intellect comes in to say: 'No, no you can't prove that. It is only an idea!' But the apprehending of ideas is a divine faculty in mankind. What gives meaning to life and humanity is that we are given the latent faculty of thinking God's thoughts again. So let us look at the true holistic movement as a vision of the spiritual nature of humanity and the universe and the integration of planet Earth with this divine whole.

To begin with, you can watch your own faculty of apprehending an idea. You need not 'believe' it, but you can 'think' it. Then live and act with it *as if it were true* and you will find it proves itself to your conscious experience and you can receive it with certainty. This is a lovely process to apply to living, an adventure in creative exploration.

Thus, let us think and explore: Earth is a living creature of infinite complexity, and the human being is an aspect of its consciousness, now in process of awakening into realization of this marvellous Whole of which we are integrally part.

Earth is a divine and purposive design for this great experiment of creating a setting in which humanity can undergo long training and experience, so that ultimately each one of us can return to God in freedom as a co-creator.

It is a majestic conception. Earth may be seen as a school for souls preparing themselves to qualify for entering the university – universus, the universe. There is no possible end to the potential glory of the exploration once the self-qualification of the individual is achieved. Conceive Earth as a planet of free will, created deliberately as a school. The goal is to become ultimately and in freedom a co-creator with God.

Now we must look at another primal idea. You are not asked to believe, you are invited to *think* the idea and to follow where it leads – if you want to. If it is true, it will bring conviction, since these ideas are alive. One may explore an idea by deliberately living it and acting as if it were true, while reserving judgement. Certainty will come, as one lives with the idea.

Here is an affirmation we can work with: The being in you which can say 'I am' and can look out of your eyes and can think and love, is a spiritual entity, a droplet of God. It is alive in the endless ocean of life. Life can't possibly die. That would be a contradiction in terms.

This deathless immortal droplet is housed in a wonderfully designed mobile temple of a body, as an instrument which enables the immortal being to sojourn on the material physical plane of Earth. As soon as solid matter is created, Time must come to birth and one thing must begin to happen after another. But the divine droplet belongs in essence to the timeless world of spirit. It is a tiny bit of God undergoing training through the school of souls. No one could think they could take the final examination for entry into the university by dropping into the third form for one term. We have to experience every form and grade and so we have all passed through history.

Thus we see the logic of the belief that we, as immortal souls, have each of us to take on embodiment again and again so as to experience the evolving consciousness that is history, and ultimately qualify, after long training, to achieve our true humanity – a condition that can only be achieved after much experience, suffering, and endeavour. So we arrive at the concept of reincarnation, repeated earth lives in this school of Earth through which (given freedom of choice) we blunder and strive and make devastating mistakes which call for our return to set right the harm done.

Ultimately the soul awakens to the true purpose of life on Earth and says, like the prodigal son: 'I will go back to my father.' When that soul has cleansed itself of negative emotion and has truly allowed the inflow of love to take it over, then ultimately the need to return to Earth will be superseded, and we shall join the realm of perfected human beings, serving God in creative action. Then, from the spiritual realms we shall be able to help struggling humanity.

We need now to have the courage to conceive that beyond the darkness of our time will come a breakthrough to the realm of light. The planet is in a process of change and metamorphosis. In the changes, many will of course 'lose their bodies'. That only means that the immortal self is freed from its bond with the physical vibration and will lift on to the ethereal planes of being. It is of vital importance for each of us to grasp the unreality of death. There may of course be suffering in getting out of the body, but the supreme truth is that we, the true and timeless Self, are released to lift into the ethereal space of the 'higher worlds'. The great untruth is that we 'sleep' in the grave, or 'rest' under the sod! Death is the process of immortal soul and spirit lifting out of embodiment. But what we find after the release will depend on what we can conceive and understand. We can take no luggage through the gates of death other than our spiritual thinking. If our concepts are wholly materialistic, we shall find ourselves, like enough, in a gloomy setting, our minds turning back to the plane we have left.

We must recognize that this is the Age of the Second Coming. We speak of Christ, the Lord of Love. There has been much confusion through too close an identification of the Christ with Jesus of Nazareth. The picture is clarified through the development of spiritual knowledge. Jesus is seen to be the prepared vehicle for receiving the descent of the Christ, who can be understood as the heart principle of God, the perfect source of love. God made man in His own image, a being of thought (the head system); love and feeling (the heart system); and creative will (the metabolic or limb system). Christ may be seen as the love principle in the heart of God the Creator. At the beginning of the Piscean Age, two thousand years ago, God in Christ descended and lived as man in the human body of Jesus. Then he overcame death and lives now as the redeemer of any who turn to Him in love and for His love.

In our epoch at the opening of the Aquarian Age this exalted being, the love source of the heart of God, descends again to Earth, not to take on embodiment as was done two thousand years ago, but now to flood into any soul who of free choice can create a soul-space worthy to receive the flooding of (sheer) divine love. Thus we may see that the real phenomenon of primal importance in our age is not the warfare, strife, violence, cruelty, and darkness, but a veritable *rising tide of love* released from the Heaven source into the benighted world. That this is actually happening now is direct experience for any who can open mind and heart to this concept and inwardly watch what is taking place in our lives.

The power of light cannot be defeated by the darkness. Much outward catastrophe is possible in the coming changes, but behind it is the glory of the living Christ in power and majesty, flooding light and love into the darkened world.

This is the great hope of our age and we are all involved.

The Christ in Man is risen and stands glorified as love on Earth!

Anne Waldman

PRATITYA
SAMUTPADA

Anne Waldman, poet. Author of thirteen books of poetry, esteemed reader-performer and teacher, twice winner Heavyweight Champion Poet. Co-founder and director of the Jack Kerouac School of Disembodied Poetics, Naropa Institute, Colorado. She says: 'If you do this to that, this happens, Or that to that, that happens.'

Do you know this term, my friend?
The co-arising and interconnectedness of things?
If you do this to that, this happens,
Or that to that, that happens
Or this to this to that to this to that to that
   to this to this to that to that, this happens

The sun shines
The dreamer lies down in a suit of clothes
The rain falls on her book
The book gets wet
The seasons come around again
The weapon she dreamed of, turns back
   on her in the hands of the person
   she never considered in her plot
   to save the world

Ah, web-life! I bow to the book
I bow to the mind behind it, and
    the tender grass and the mind behind that
    and all the while thinking:
this to that to this to that to that to this to that
to that to this to this to this to that to this to that

By this merit, may all obtain omniscience

THE NUN ABUTSU

Sea wind is chilly on me
Snow rides down
Each night I look up
that moon is smaller
I'm waning too
as I travel
Not sadness brought me
to words, but How
everything resembles
something else
is a constant joy
Enormous waves rise
like magnificent flowers
The road East
is a song.

Appendix

WHAT YOU CAN DO TO PROMOTE CHANGE

**Networking Information –
Making the Way Ahead a Living Reality**

THE WAY AHEAD is a reminder to us all that each one of us *is* the way ahead, that we can do something to help and that we can do it now. So how can we go further with the information, ideas and visions generated in this book? Here are some ideas:

Contact and help groups or organizations already established that are working with these ideals, such as:

Oxfam America, 115 Broadway #506, Boston, MA 02116 USA. Tel: 617-482-1211

Eddie and Debbie Shapiro, c/o Element Books Ltd, Longmead, Shaftesbury, Dorset SP7 8PL, England.
or
Element, Inc. 42 Broadway, Rockport MA 01966, USA.

Friends of the Earth, 26–28 Underwood Street, London N1 7JQ, England.

Campaign for the Earth, 2120 13th Street, Boulder CO 80302 USA. Tel: 303-444-3800

The Rainforest Information Center, Box 368, Lismore, NSW 2480, Australia

Center for Attitudinal Healing, 21 Main Street, Tiburon, CA 94920 USA. Tel: 415-435-5022

Zen Community of New York, 5 Ashburton Place, Yonkers NY 10701 USA.

There are many more than this and we suggest looking in a local newspaper for information, or on a library noticeboard or other similar public information places.

Alternatively we can start our own group or organization. Some of the things that we can do individually or as a group are:

1) Sponsor speakers to come to our area (such as the people in this book).
2) Organize forums or panel discussions with local experts on different topics to do with the awareness of ourselves and our planet.
3) Organize public recycling and product awareness (such as those products that are biodegradable and those that are not).
4) Write to local politicians urging them to implement environmental and recycling programs, and to investigate industries that are not environmentally safe.
5) Campaign for peaceful ends to aggressive situations and promote non-violence.
6) Develop our own peace of mind and compassion through daily spiritual practice.
7) Campaign that the money being used for armaments be used for feeding, housing and educating those in need.
8) Network with other groups and organizations so that information can be shared and made available to all.
9) Make a commitment each day to the upliftment of ourselves and the world.

Credits

We wish to thank the following:

Jeremy P. Tarcher Inc. for an extract from *The Aquarian Conspiracy* by Marilyn Ferguson; Parrallex Press for extracts from *World as Lover, World as Self* by Joanna Macy; The Poetry Project Symposium for the Allen Ginsberg lecture at the Poetry for the Next Society held on 5 May 1989; New Realities magazine for the article *Changing our Attitudes about AIDS* by Gerald G. Jampolski and Diane V. Cirincione; Harper San Francisco for an extract from *Drumming at the Edge of Magic* by Mickey Hart; Faber and Faber for an extract from *Living in Truth* by Václav Havel; Doubleday for extracts from *Guided Meditations, Explorations and Healings* by Stephen Levine; Harper San Francisco for an extract from *True Nature: Views of Earth from Buddhism and Shamanism* by Joan Halifax; Parragon House, New York, for an extract by Father Thomas Keating from *Inter-Religious Dialogues* edited by M. Darrol Bryant and Frank Flynn.

Photo Credits

Francesco Scavullo for the photo of Yoko Ono
Eric Neurath for the photos of Bernie and Bobbie Siegel and
Pat A. Paulson
Alex Lawson Thomas for the photo of Eddie and Debbie
Shapiro
Robert Frank for the photo of Allen Ginsberg
William Abranowitz for the photo of Stephen Levine
Jeff Bowen for the photo of Anne Bancroft
Cotell for the photo of Jeremy Rifkin
Bill Scott for the photo of Mickey Hart

Rex Features for the photos of HRH Prince Philip,
    Paul and Linda McCartney and Colin Wilson
John Cheesman for the photo of Serge Beddington-Behrens
John Werner for the photo of Babatunde Olatunji
David Geffen recording studios for the photo of Kitaro